THE GREAT SLUMP

GORONWY REES

THE GREAT SLUMP

CAPITALISM IN CRISIS

1929-1933

HARPER & ROW, PUBLISHERS
NEW YORK, EVANSTON, SAN FRANCISCO, LONDON

FIRST U.S. EDITION

LIBRARY OF CONGRESS CATALOG CARD NUMBER: 72-138759

CONTENTS

LIST OF ILLUSTRATIONS

CHAPTER ONE

On the Eve

By Christmas 1928, when the warning shadows of the greatest economic depression in history began to fall on the western world, a little more than a decade had passed since the end of the First World War. The cost of that war to the belligerents, in life, in suffering, in material resources, had been so great that there were moments when it seemed as if they might never recover from it. Indeed, in one sense they never did, because the war destroyed for ever the social, political and economic structure of pre-war Europe and an entire world of intellectual and economic values. The lights had really gone out all over Europe and it was to be many years before they were relit. It is understandable that Karl Kraus, in Vienna, should have given to his epic drama on the fall of the Austro-Hungarian empire, one of the greatest literary works to come out of the war, the title of *Die Letzten Tage der Menschheit*: The Last Days of Mankind.

The years which immediately followed the war seemed to justify the gloomiest forebodings of the disaster which must come out of so terrible an experience. Thrones, empires, dynasties had fallen, and the vacuum they had left behind was invaded by new and revolutionary forces dedicated to the total and violent over-throw of established institutions; it seemed as if they might complete what the war had begun. One great nation, Russia, had opted out of the capitalist system altogether, and having suffered all the horrors of civil war and foreign intervention marched against the West until the Red Army was defeated at the gates of Warsaw. The dictatorship of the proletariat was proclaimed in Munich and in Budapest and was bloodily suppressed. Undeclared war raged in Silesia, in East Prussia and on the Baltic and bred in the com-batants a violent and nihilistic form of nationalism which was full of menace for the future; in the ranks of the German Freikorps marched murderers and assassins who would later form the cadres of the National Socialist Brown Shirts. Germany, having established a moderate socialist republic on the ruins of the Hohenzollern empire, was threatened by communist insurrection and right-wing *coups d'état*, of which one brought a momentary notoriety to an obscure agitator named Adolf Hitler.* There was hardly a country in Central Europe which had not been exposed to the menace of political violence and social disintegration.

Such threats were made all the more formidable by economic and financial collapse, and this weakening of the economic structure affected the victors as well as the vanquished among the war-time belligerents. In Germany, inflation was as great a disaster as the war itself and in a few short months completed the ruin of the German middle class. In France, the collapse of the currency reduced the franc to hardly more than one-tenth of its pre-war value. For a time indeed inflation threatened even the United States and in 1920 there was financial panic in New York. But in addition to these domestic crises, the war had destroyed the delicate balance of the complicated financial system, dominated by the City of London, on which before the war the international trade of the entire world depended. During the war, every major country had abandoned the gold standard which regulated the system of international exchanges, and until it was re-established, or some alternative mechanism was provided, international trade threatened to decline to the level of primitive barter. In no sphere was the disintegration of the pre-war structure more apparent than in that of banking and finance, and bankers might well have felt that W. B. Yeats's premonition of the Second Coming, written in 1917, had been literally fulfilled:

> Things fall apart; the centre cannot hold;
> Mere anarchy is loosed upon the world.

Surveying the world in 1922, John Maynard Keynes said much the same thing, reduced to terms of pounds, francs and marks.

---

* The Munich *Putsch* of November 1923, led by Adolf Hitler and General Erich Ludendorff, against the government of Bavaria.

The inflation of the currency system of Europe has proceeded to extraordinary lengths. The various belligerent governments, unable, or too timid or short-sighted to secure from loans or taxation the resources they required, have printed for the balance. In Russia and Austria-Hungary this process has reached a point where for the purpose of foreign exchange the currency is practically valueless. The Polish mark can be bought for about three cents and the Austrian crown for less than two cents, but they cannot be sold at all ... the currency of Italy has fallen to a little more than half its nominal value in spite of its still being subject to some degree of regulation; French currency maintains an uncertain market; and even sterling is seriously diminished in present value and impaired in its future prospects.

Keynes went on to say: 'We are faced in Europe with a spectacle of an extraordinary weakness on the part of that great capitalist class, which has emerged from the industrial triumph of the nineteenth century, and seemed a very few years ago our all-powerful master.'

In the same year that Keynes wrote, the 'extraordinary weakness of the great capitalist class' found a classic expression in T.S. Eliot's poem, *The Waste Land*. Eliot had himself been a bank employee for a time, and a specialist in the international exchanges; his poem, which is a threnody for the death of a civilization, is haunted by direct and indirect allusions to the decay of the City of London which had been its financial centre:

> Unreal City
> Under the brown fog of a winter noon ...

and to other cities which had suffered the same fate in the past,

> Falling towers
> Jerusalem   Athens   Alexandria
> Vienna   London
> Unreal.

In a note to the poem Eliot quotes from Hermann Hesse's *Blick ins Chaos*, A Look into Chaos: 'Already half Europe, or at least the Eastern half of Europe, is on the way to chaos, walks drunkenly in holy madness towards the abyss and sings as it goes, sings in drunkenness and rhapsody as Dmitri Karamazov sang. The bourgeois laughs painfully at such songs, the saint and the prophet listens to them with tears.'

[3]

It is unlikely that Montague Norman, sitting in the Bank of England, or Governor Benjamin Strong, of the New York Federal Reserve Bank, listened to the warnings of Yeats, or Eliot or Hermann Hesse. But they had their own visions of chaos derived from the ravages inflicted on the financial and economic system by the war. It was entirely natural they should assume that the primary responsibility for averting any further decline into chaos lay with persons like themselves and other dominant representatives of Keynes's 'Great Capitalist Class', in Paris, in Berlin, in Zürich, for it was taken for granted that the direction and control of economic and financial affairs, in so far as they were necessary at all, was the concern, not of governments, but of businessmen and those whom they appointed to serve their interests. It was equally natural that they should have looked back with nostalgia to the security, prosperity and freedom which the 'Great Capitalist Class' had enjoyed before the war and should have seen it as their primary task to restore the conditions under which the pre-war world had functioned so successfully. Reconstruction, Recovery, Peace, says E.H. Carr, were the key words of the twenties, just as, according to A. J. P. Taylor, Planning was the key word of the thirties. The shift of emphasis reveals a gulf dividing two distinct historical eras which was formed by the great economic depression of 1929–33.

What was surprising, given the effect of the war and its immediate aftermath, is how near those who were responsible for directing the financial and economic affairs of the western world came to success in their efforts to re-establish the pre-war structure. Even by 1925, the year in which Britain returned to the gold standard, the worst social and political convulsions of the post-war years were over and there was a reasonable hope that the world was on the way to recovering its economic and political stability. As a measure of the progress that had been made one might contrast Keynes's gloomy survey of the situation in 1922 with the opening passage of his *The Economic Consequences of Mr Churchill*, written in 1925.

World trade and home consumption are both moderately good – running on an even keel, midway between slump and boom. The United States has had a year of abundant prosperity; India and the Dominions are doing fairly well; in France and Italy unemployment is negligible; and in Germany, during the last six months, the numbers receiving the dole have decreased rapidly by more than half, to 4·5 per cent as opposed to our 10 per cent. The aggregate of world production is probably greater than at any time since 1914.

'Midway between slump and boom,' wrote Keynes of the economic situation as a whole; in the next four years the midway point was left behind and the western world enjoyed an economic boom whose possibilities seemed so limitless that many economists came to the conclusion that the alternation of boom and slump which had been a characteristic feature of the capitalist economy could never recur again.

To a large extent the boom was due to a stabilization of political conditions and the restoration of business confidence which followed; businessmen felt that they could plan ahead, and undertake programmes of expansion with some assurance that they would not be interfered with by violent political changes. The post-war ferment seemed to be over, the threat of revolution, either from the left or the right had abated, and stable governments had been established in all the major European countries.

Nothing contributed more to the relaxation of political tension than the *détente* brought about between the two major Continental powers, France and Germany, by Aristide Briand and Gustav Stresemann. These two architects of European peace made a strange pair. Briand was a radical, a man of the left, immensely eloquent and apt to think that words were deeds, but he had behind him his countrymen's profound longing for peace and security, and their growing conviction that they could not be obtained by force. Victory over Germany had not secured them for France. The Treaty of Versailles had cheated her of the left bank of the Rhine, which military realists like Foch had believed to be her only sure defence against Germany. The attempt to exact reparations from Germany by force had proved an expensive failure. Under Briand, the French were prepared to make the experiment as to whether friendship with Germany might not bring better results than their traditional enmity.

Stresemann, the son of a small Berlin brewer, began his political career as a nationalist of the extreme right, where he found himself among upper-class associates who despised him for his bourgeois origins but valued him for his political abilities and his immense capacity for hard work. He looked, and sometimes behaved, like one of the caricatures of post-war German capitalists depicted by George Grosz in *Ecco Homo* in 1923. But he developed from a nationalist reactionary into a German, and a European, statesman whose patriotism took the form of leading his countrymen along the path of 'fulfilment', that is, of accepting the harsh terms of the Treaty of Versailles in return for concessions which would allow Germany to recover her proper place among the nations of Europe.

The triumph of Stresemann and Briand was the Treaty of Locarno, signed in 1925, whereby Germany, Belgium, France, Great Britain and Italy mutually guaranteed the peace of Western Europe and thereby set at rest the fears and animosities which were both a cause and an effect of the Great War. The hopes based upon Locarno were immense, and the sense of confidence and security engendered by it largely contributed to the economic recovery of Europe. Nothing could better exemplify these feelings than the negotiations between Briand and the American Secretary for State, Frank Kellogg, which led, four years later, to the Kellogg Pact disclaiming war as an instrument of national policy and ratified by sixty-four nations, including Japan.

Today, the Kellogg Pact seems a cynical example of that mixture of hypocrisy and empty idealism which in America Mencken regarded as typical of *Homo Boobiens*. At the time, it was regarded by millions of people throughout the world as the expression of a rational hope for the future, firmly based upon the immense improvement that had already taken place in international relations. As A.J.P. Taylor has said, there was never a time in history when an outbreak of war seemed less likely than in 1929, or when men could more reasonably look forward to the establishment of universal and permanent peace.

It seems ironic today that, after Locarno, Briand and Stresemann were looked on as men of the future, whose practical idealism had shown nations the way to rid themselves of their fears and anxieties. In fact, their work was short-lived and was essentially an expression of the mood of euphoria that swept the western world when the immediate difficulties of the post-war period were over. Neither survived the depression. Stresemann died in 1928, having almost literally given his life to the policy of fulfilment, and at the moment of his greatest triumph, the removal of French occupation troops from the Rhineland five years before the date specified by the Treaty of Versailles; he was, however, at the moment of his death already faced by violent and mounting opposition from the German right-wing parties. Briand died in 1932, and his funeral cortège passed through the streets of Paris at the moment when one of the greatest swindlers in history, Ivar Kreuger, was putting a bullet through his heart. Either event might have been taken as symbolic of the immense changes that had taken place since 1929.

Relaxation of international tension after 1925 had been accompanied by a stabilization in internal conditions in all the major countries. In Britain, the General Strike of 1926 left bitter memories among the working class, but by 1929 the Conservative Party under Baldwin felt sufficiently assured of the future to tolerate a minority socialist government under Ramsay MacDonald, on the principle that it was only fair to give the other fellow a chance. In Germany, the revolutionary wave had died down after Heinz Neumann's abortive communist insurrection in 1924; Adolf Hitler was in prison, writing *Mein Kampf*. In 1928, the moderate socialist Hermann Müller formed a Coalition government supported by the Social Democrats and the Catholic Centre Party. In France, the franc was stabilized by Poincaré in 1926 and in the coalition governments of the next five years Briand held a dominating position as Foreign Minister. And in the United States, the indefinite continuation of republican prosperity seemed assured by the victory of Herbert Hoover in the presidential election of 1928.

The restoration of political stability from 1925 onwards was accompanied by a spectacular economic recovery. By 1926 every major country except France had returned to the gold standard, and in that year France introduced a new monetary law which was followed by a return to gold in 1927. For the statesmen, bankers and financiers of the western world the return to gold was in itself a major triumph in the struggle to restore the economic system which had been the foundation of pre-war prosperity. To them it signified a return to sound currencies, to the re-establishment of the international exchanges on which the world's trade depended, and to the operation of an international financial system whose rules were well understood and consecrated by a hundred years of experience. It was a part of the natural order of the world, of which the war

THE GREAT SLUMP

and its immediate aftermath had been a brief and deplorable interruption.

For the gold standard had been the in-built regulator of a system, delicate, flexible and worldwide, which had brought about a rapid development in the economies of the most advanced industrial countries, a vast increase in world trade, and a huge investment of capital in the underdeveloped countries of the world. The beauty of the system was that, if any sector of the world economy threatened to get out of step with the rest, the gold standard operated to bring the system as a whole into equilibrium again. Over-rapid expansion by any country provoked an expansion of credit and a rise in its internal price level relative to other countries; a rise in the internal price level provoked an outflow of gold which brought about a restriction of credit and forced prices down until they were once again in harmony with the rest of the world. Under-expansion provoked equal and opposite reactions; in a flagging economy prices tended to fall and provoked an inward movement of gold which formed the basis for an expansion of credit sufficient to raise internal prices until equilibrium had been restored.*

It was of course understood, by those who operated the system, that it was not entirely perfect or automatic. Perfection would have required that every factor in the economic system should have had the same mobility, the same flexible response, as gold, and most of all it would have required absolute freedom of trade. Unfortunately, there were things like tariffs and Trade Unions which introduced elements of rigidity into the system, and interfered with the free movement of goods in international markets and the free sale and purchase of labour as if it were a commodity like any other. But these, after all, were only minor blemishes. It was the task of statesmanship to reduce their influence as much as possible; it was part of the skill and expertise of the banker and financier to keep the system going in spite of the obstructions that interfered with its perfect functioning.

The working of the gold standard also had an in-built defect in

* Ideally, the mechanism of the gold standard ensured that an inflow of gold provoked an expansion of credit followed by a rise in the internal price level. This in turn had the reverse effect of provoking an increase in imports and an outflow of gold, restriction of credit and a fall in the price level.

[8]

that it produced recurrent cycles of boom and slump which involved both much human suffering, particularly in the shape of mass unemployment, and a less than optimum use of available economic resources. It was, however, inevitable, and was the necessary cost of the benefits conferred by the system. A standard, and excellent, textbook, Garvard and Hanssen's *Principles of Economics*, which was widely used in American universities throughout the thirties, and even many years later, showed that unemployment rose to 21 per cent of the labour force in 1921, fell to 9 per cent in 1929 and rose to slightly under 25 per cent in 1932 and 1933. But this was a necessary part of progress; it was due to 'shifts in demands and in technique'; 'so long as we have a dynamic society with continual change and progress, a considerable amount of unemployment will necessarily prevail.'

To the banker or financier it was no part of his business to alleviate such consequences of the system which he helped to manage; indeed, the more harshly he operated, the more quickly and efficiently he restored the system to equilibrium. In thinking this, he was not being heartless or prejudiced, nor was he merely judging by the results of past experience; he had the support of every reputable economist in the world, and the principles he practised in his business were the same principles which were taught in the economic departments of every university of Europe and the United States. To the banker, the financial system which he helped to operate was like some marvellous game which brought its own rewards and punishments so long as the rules were observed. Partly he was himself a player in the game, partly he was a referee; and partly he was a member of the committee of management which helped to administer the game. In each of these capacities, his main interest was to ensure that so far as possible the rules should not be broken.

He had all the greater confidence in the rules because, up to 1914, they appeared to have worked so well. Up to that date, and since the passage of the Bank Charter Act of 1844, the Bank of England as central banker to the City of London consistently followed a policy of cheap money which made it possible to provide the credit required to finance the expansion of the world's trade. For long periods the bank rate, which was the rate at which the Bank rediscounted commercial bills, stood at 2½ per cent and never rose above $3\frac{1}{2}$ per cent, except in moments of crisis, even at the cost of reducing the Bank's reserves below what was then held to be the safety limit.

It was of a return to such conditions that bankers dreamed as the great nations of the world stabilized their currencies, returned to the gold standard and re-established international exchanges. And they could well feel encouraged in their optimism because the return to the gold standard did in fact coincide with a large increase in production, in world trade and in general prosperity. Of the period after 1925, Professor (later Lord) Robbins wrote in his book *The Great Depression*:

There followed a period of good trade – a period, indeed, which . . . can be seen to have been, for some parts of the world, one of the biggest booms in economic history. Trade revived, incomes rose. Production went ahead by leaps and bounds. International lending was resumed on a scale surpassing even pre-war dimensions. The stock exchanges of the more prosperous centres displayed such strength that speculation for a rise seemed a more certain path to a secure income than all the devices of ancient prudence. It was a period in which the financial ministers of the world, looking forward to years of increasing revenue, felt no hesitation in incurring fresh obligations on the side of revenue. Men of the type of the late Ivar Kreuger moved rapidly from one capital city to another, arranging without fuss or inconveniencing anybody, what were described as 'good constructive loans' – the acolytes of the 'new economics'. It was in these days that it was said that the trade cycle had become extinct.

Nowhere was the transformation which took place after 1925 more apparent than in Germany. After the political convulsions of its early years, the Weimar Republic seemed to have achieved stability, and to have established a liberal, constitutional and democratic regime which recommended itself to its western neighbours; internal security was guaranteed by an unwritten compact between successive governments and the Reichswehr, and financial soundness by the return to the gold standard. Such conditions made Germany, which suffered from a chronic shortage of capital, an attractive field for investment, and from 1925 onwards a flood of foreign money poured into Germany, particularly from America. The foreign investor, attracted by high rates of interest, was not particularly concerned whether his funds were used to finance productive industry or municipal swimming baths, sports stadiums, schools or theatres. Despite her heavy reparations payments, Germany became a net importer of capital, on a scale which allowed her to finance both industrial expansion and social amenities.

Yet in spite of the great political and economic progress that was made between 1925 and 1929, there were also serious elements of instability in the situation. The relaxation of political tension in Europe, both domestically and internationally, was more apparent than real. It depended essentially on the continuance of economic prosperity, and, if that should fail, there were political forces waiting to seize the opportunities that would be offered. The terrible legacy of violence inherited from the war had not really been overcome; violence had become endemic in the political life of Europe, and it lurked beneath the surface until its hour should come round again. In particular, in Germany, the extremism of the campaign waged by Hugenberg and the nationalist right against Stresemann in 1928 was a bad augury for the future; all the more so because it allowed Hitler for the first time to emerge from provincial obscurity and, as an ally of Hugenberg, to become a national political figure.

But if political stability was precarious, so also was economic prosperity. Though governments and central banks might welcome the return to the gold standard, and all that it symbolized, it proved difficult if not impossible to work satisfactorily in the condition of the post-war world. The pre-war financial system had been essentially a unitary system centred on London, to which all other financial centres were subsidiary. The Bank of England had acted as the world's central bank, and since its policy had been conducive to the expansion of the world's industry and trade, its direction had on the whole been beneficial.

After the war, when the United States emerged as the strongest industrial and financial country in the world, and Wall Street as the strongest financial centre, there was no longer any unitary financial world system. The United States had been the first major country to return to gold, in 1919, and for a time it had conducted its financial policy virtually in isolation from the rest of the world. London, however, still remained a great, if no longer the predominant financial centre, and for a considerable period London and New York operated mutually contradictory credit policies.

London pursued a restrictive policy in the interest of re-establishing the gold standard at a parity as near as possible to its pre-war level and, later, of maintaining it in the face of continuous pressure on sterling. New York, led by Benjamin Strong, of the New York Federal Reserve Bank, pursued a policy of easy credit in the interest of American industry. It was at least partly a result of these contradictory policies that for America the twenties were a period of unprecedented industrial expansion, while British industry was stagnant and failed to share in the economic recovery of the rest of the western world. It is ironical that when New York and London concerted their policies, the consequences gave rise to criticism. In the spring of 1928 the New York Federal Reserve Bank reduced its rediscount rate in an endeavour to help Britain out of her financial difficulties. The Governor was thought to have been over-persuaded by Montague Norman and was later blamed for having given an additional, and decisive, spur to the extravagant boom on the New York stock market.

A further strain on the gold standard was that Britain and France had chosen parities which were out of balance with each other. The pound was overvalued; it was this which provoked Keynes to his brilliant philippic against *The Economic Consequences of Mr Churchill*, and the results which he foresaw, of credit restriction, rising unemployment and the continued weakness of sterling did not fail to show themselves.

France, on the other hand, undervalued the franc by about 10 per cent in relation to its internal purchasing power, and by so doing initiated a period of great prosperity for herself which continued until 1932 and spared her the worst results of the depression. But it also led to a large-scale inflow of gold into France, which imposed an added strain on the operation of the gold standard and was an important contributing factor to the financial disaster of 1929. Between 1928 and 1930, the gold reserves of the Bank of France rose from nearly 29,000 million francs to nearly 56,000 million francs and enabled France to follow a policy of cheap money at a time when both New York and London were restricting credit.

The relation between the return to the gold standard and the depression of 1929–33 is still a matter of acute controversy; what can be said with certainty is that, between 1925 and 1929, the gold standard worked only imperfectly and in a world which was moving steadily away from the conditions under which it had functioned before the war. For one of the permanent effects of the war had been to stimulate economic as well as political nationalism, and in a world of economic nationalism the gold standard functioned only with continually increasing difficulty and the strain of maintaining it exaggerated rather than diminished other difficulties. It could be said that the statesmen, financiers and bankers who had expected so much from the restoration of the gold standard fully understood neither the conditions required for its successful functioning nor how far or how fast the world was departing from them.

But there were other factors as well as financial ones which contributed to the onset of the depression. The economic recovery of 1925 to 1929 was essentially the result of an industrial and manufacturing boom, and was not accompanied by any recovery in agriculture.

Throughout the world the decline of agriculture in relation to industry was producing that paradox of poverty in the midst of plenty which was one of the most striking features of the depression. The relative decline of agriculture created a disequilibrium both between the industrial and the rural areas of the world, and between the industrial and rural areas within the most developed countries, and this contributed a marked element of instability to the economic system as a whole.

Lastly, there was one particular problem which, as time went by, became increasingly intractable. The war had left behind a vast burden of debts between various governments, in the form both of obligations incurred by the western allies in their efforts to finance the war, and of reparations payments imposed on Germany. The two forms of obligations were inextricably connected; and they could have been discharged, if at all, only if the creditor countries had been willing to accept payment in goods and services which would have been in direct competition with their own domestic industries; on the other hand, the creditor countries, like every other country, were increasingly inclined to forms of economic nationalism designed to protect their own industries and promote their own exports.

So long as recovery lasted, and trade and production increased, the burden of debt, and the obstacles it placed in the way of a resumption of genuinely free international exchanges, was relatively tolerable. It had been recognized, as early as 1925, that Germany would be unable to pay reparations on a scale designed to 'squeeze her until the pips squeaked', and they had been successively scaled down, first by the Dawes Plan and later by the Young Plan. Even so, the whole structure of inter-governmental debt, which ultimately depended on Germany's capacity and willingness to pay reparations, was only maintained by a resumption of foreign lending on a large scale, primarily by the United States, but also by Britain which invested heavily in Germany after 1925, despite her own languishing production and the weakness of sterling. Here again, however, post-war practice was significantly different from what it had been pre-war. Before the war, international lending had been primarily on a long-term basis; post-war British and American loans to Germany were short-term and could only be repaid by a continuous injection of new capital. Moreover, the problem of German reparations had not merely a financial, but a highly inflammable political content, and even by 1928 Hugenberg's campaign against the Young Plan was a signal for the revival of German nationalism and racialism in their most extreme form.

Thus a cautious observer of the economic and political situation might by 1928 have seen, among many signs of prosperity and recovery, others also which gave grounds for apprehension. Such a one was Barney Baruch, who, starting as an office boy, had been a highly successful speculator on Wall Street before becoming a friend and adviser to three presidents. 'By 1928 I had begun to liquidate my stock holdings and put my money into bonds and cash reserves. I am very old-fashioned in this respect. I like to have some cash around, particularly in hard times. I also bought gold, which at that time was the last repository of man's monetary faith.'

There were others who, like Baruch, believed by 1928 that the end of the great period of economic prosperity which the world had enjoyed since 1925 was already in sight, and, like him, put their money in safe places. But they were certainly, as Baruch said, very old-fashioned, and they were exceptional; not only among people of his own kind, with a direct pecuniary interest in the state of the economy, but among those who might have been expected to have been less immediately affected by the prospects of personal loss or gain: economists, university teachers, academic students of finance and industry, the theoretical spokesmen of Keynes's 'great capitalist class'. By 1928 nearly all shared the almost universal belief that, great as was the measure of prosperity which the world had achieved since 1925, it was as nothing compared with what was to come. The irony of the situation was that their own conviction helped to make it so and that for another year at least they proved to be right. The prelude to the great depression was one of the dizziest flights into economic fantasy the world has ever seen.

CHAPTER TWO

The Great Bull Market

The great American Stock Exchange boom of 1928 to 1929 is one of the most extraordinary episodes in history, and as such is as much worth the attention of the mass psychologist as of the historian or economist. It had, of course, its roots in economic and financial factors, but it reached heights of speculation which were so entirely out of proportion to any expectations which could be rationally calculated that one is forced to believe that there were also different kinds of causes at work. Barney Baruch described it as 'a classic example of the madness of crowds', and compared it not merely with such examples of financial insanity as the Mississippi Bubble or the South Sea Bubble, but with such mass movements as tribal eruptions from Central Asia or the Crusades, or with exhibitions of mass hysteria like medieval dancing madness or the witch hunt. He recommended the economist in search of an explanation to a study of Charles Mackay's book *Extraordinary Popular Illusions and the Madness of Crowds*, as more relevant and illuminating than any figures, graphs or statistics could be.

The irrational element, the mysterious infectiousness of the speculative mania, is all the more significant because only three years earlier, in the Florida Land boom of 1926, the United States had experienced, though on a smaller scale, another outburst of gambling madness which might have served as a classic warning of what may happen when speculation ceases to bear any relation to reality. There were many good reasons for the rise in population and land values which took place in Florida after 1920, among which one might include climate, the mobility conferred by the motor-car and the general prosperity conferred by America's industrial growth. Inflated by extravagant and bizarre promotional campaigns, which included lectures on the Florida climate by

William Jennings Bryan sitting under a sun umbrella on a raft in a lagoon, such reasons persuaded thousands of Americans to invest their money in desolate swamps and miasmic marshes in the belief that overnight they would become flourishing cities and glamorous pleasure resorts. In the service of such campaigns, in 1925 the *Miami Herald* carried a larger volume of advertising than any paper had ever previously carried anywhere in the world and the exuberant claims made by estate agents (of whom there were twenty-five thousand in Miami alone) seemed to be justified by the profits that were to be made. In 1918 a strip of land at Palm Beach was valued at 240,000 dollars. In 1923 it was sold for over 800,000 dollars. In 1924 it was broken up into building plots and sold for 1,500,000 dollars. In 1925, its value was estimated at 4,000,000 dollars. But by 1925, the speculator was no longer buying actual plots of land, even if they were only mangrove swamps. He was buying options to buy plots, for which he was only required to deposit a small proportion of the purchase price, and he was no longer hoping to enjoy Florida's sunny climate and warm seas, but merely to get rid of his options in the morning at a large profit.

The boom lasted until 1926, when it began to show signs of collapse; the collapse was completed by two hurricanes which struck Miami in September of that year, and reduced much of the new developments along the Gold Coast to rubble; a five-masted steel schooner was deposited in the middle of the fabulous City of Coral Gables which had claimed to be 'America's Most Beautiful Suburb'. The hurricanes marked, in the most dramatic way, the end of the boom and the equally spectacular slump which followed; bank clearings from Miami, which had risen to over 1,000,000,000 dollars in 1925, had by 1929 fallen to 142,316,000 dollars, at a time when the rest of the United States was enjoying unprecedented prosperity. There were thirty-one bank failures in Florida in 1928 and fifty-seven in 1929.

The Florida Land boom displayed in miniature so many of the features which were later reproduced on a much larger scale on Wall Street in 1929 that it is curious that its lessons went unnoticed by the greater part of the nation. 'What will happen when they stop bidding?' said a friend to Baruch as they drove through Florida when the boom was at its most frenzied. Very few people asked themselves this question three years later, and if they did it was to receive the answer, backed by the most respectable authority, that there was no reason in the world why the bidding should ever have to stop. The same combination of greed, gullibility, and a kind of irrational conviction that at last a reign of limitless prosperity had dawned, which showed itself in Florida, repeated itself in 1929, but this time on a nationwide scale; the shock of the depression which followed was all the greater because of the frenzy which had preceded it.

Yet just as in Florida there had been a solid foundation, in the facts of geography and climate, for the expectations which led to the land boom, so the Great Bull Market had its roots in the unprecedented capacity for growth revealed by American industry in the twenties. By 1922, the United States had recovered from the severe trade depression which followed the extravagant inflation of the immediate post-war period, and thereafter business activity followed a steadily rising curve. America seemed to have overcome the cycle of boom and slump which had hitherto been characteristic of a capitalist economy; while prices and wages remained remarkably stable, productivity increased, largely as a result of rapid technological progress, scientific management, and the organization of industry into increasingly larger units. There were slight recessions in 1924 and in 1927, but otherwise the trend of business activity was steadily upwards and there seemed to be no reason why the rise should ever come to an end. As a result of her industrial efficiency, American costs were significantly lower than those of other countries and business profits rose sharply. The national income, which had been 33,200 million dollars in 1914, had risen to 79,200 million dollars by 1925.

Thereafter the increase continued. Between 1925 and 1929 the number of manufacturing establishments in the United States rose from 183,900 to 206,702 and the value of their product from 60 billion dollars to 68 billion dollars. At no time in human history had wealth increased so rapidly, or on so vast a scale, and at no time had man seemed to have come so near to solving the fundamental problems of production.

It is not surprising that this great increase in wealth, continued unbroken over so many years, should have engendered in Americans a sense of boundless optimism and an unlimited confidence in the future. These showed themselves in a general belief that, for

America and for Americans, nothing was impossible; and in particular they showed themselves in a steady and later a spectacular
rise in stock exchange values. No doubt this rise reflected rational
calculations of the earning capacity of American industry; but they
also reflected men's expectations of the future, and as business
activity and business profits continued to increase those expectations became increasingly exaggerated and extravagant, until at
length men set literally no limit to their hopes.

The rise in stock exchange prices at first closely followed the
curve of industrial production. The price of securities began to rise
in 1924; in that year the *New York Times* average of share prices
rose from 106 in May to 134 in December. In 1925 the rise continued, and by 31 December the average had reached 181. During
1926, prices suffered a slight decline and by the end of the year
were roughly where they were at the beginning; but in 1927 the
rise was resumed and by the end of the year the average reached
245, an increase of 74 points on the year. In the three years 1924
to 1927 share prices had on the average increased by nearly $2\frac{1}{2}$ times.

It is difficult to say when precisely the Great Bull Market got out
of hand. To most people the rise in share prices seemed merely to
reflect the increasing efficiency, productivity and profitability of
American industry. Yet as early as 1926, Baruch was writing to
Mark Sullivan: 'Now let me make a prediction to you. Business has
already reached its zenith and what we see in motors, steel and
railroad statements is evidence of what has gone by and not of what
is before us.' A year later he wrote to Winston Churchill: 'Business
conditions in this country are not as good as the newspapers make
them appear.' But Baruch adds in his autobiography: 'There was
not much of an audience for those of us who felt uneasy about the
state of our economy. To most people, from financier to labourer, it
seemed as though prosperity would never stop, that everyone
would go on making, and spending, more and more money.' Soon,
he was to find himself receiving stock market tips from the old
beggar who patrolled the street outside his office, and from his
cook, who had a brokerage account.

Despite Baruch's gloomy predictions, business activity continued to increase. The Federal Reserve index of industrial
production, which had stayed at 100 between 1923 and 1925 rose to
110 by July 1928 and to 126 in June 1929. Share prices, however,

rose at a rate which overshadowed anything that had gone before. In March 1928, the *New York Times* average of industrial share prices rose by 25 points, in a great surge of buying which was partly stimulated by an optimistic forecast of automobile sales in the forthcoming year by John J. Raskob, a director of General Motors, and Al Smith's choice as chairman of the Democratic National Committee. General Motors, indeed, made a generous contribution to the Great Bull Market, not only because rising automobile sales were taken as a guarantee that the boom would continue, but because it also supplied some of the market's greatest speculators, among them Raskob himself, William Crapo Durant, who had originally organized the company and had been thrown out by Raskob and the du Ponts, and the seven Fisher Brothers, who speculated in the Stock Exchange with the huge fortune they had made by the sale of the Fisher bodyplant.

In the summer of 1928 there was a break in the market. In the first three weeks of June almost all the gains of March were lost. A New York newspaper announced the end of the Bull Market; in September, it was predicted that there would be a catastrophic slump if Al Smith won the presidential election. This was probably the last moment at which the market could have been successfully brought under control. It was, however, only a case of *reculer pour mieux sauter* and thereafter, for a year, the market took off into the blue and left reality far behind. On 6 November Hoover was triumphantly elected, and a great wave of buying carried leading shares five to fifteen points higher; 16 and 20 November saw further frenzied buying and by the end of the year the *Times* average had risen to 351, a gain of 55 points during the year. Some of the gains registered by favoured shares far exceeded the average: Du Ponts rose from 310 to 525, Montgomery Ward from 117 to 440, Wright Aeronautic from 69 to 290, Radio Corporation of America from 85 to 420. The last two shares show to what an extent speculation was predicated upon the future. Neither had even an average record of earnings. Radio Corporation had never paid a dividend. But both were new scientific industries which belonged to the brave new world of unlimited hope and possibility.

The speculators on Wall Street were not the only ones who registered their unbounded hope and confidence in America's dazzling future. In December the retiring President, Calvin

Coolidge, declared in his last State of the Union message to Congress:

No Congress of the United States ever assembled, on surveying the state of the union, has met with a more pleasing prospect than that which appears at the present time. In the domestic field there is tranquillity and contentment . . . and the highest record of years of prosperity. In the foreign field there is peace, the good will which comes from mutual understanding.

Today it seems a quaint New England comment on what was happening on Wall Street that 'the main source of these unexampled blessings lies in the integrity and character of the American people'.

Integrity and character revealed themselves in the new year in renewed speculation. In January, the *Times* average rose by 30 points. In March there was a bad break in the market and at one moment the average was down by as much as 15 points. But the market recovered for new flights, which carried it to hitherto unprecedented heights. In June the *Times* index rose by 52 points; in July by another 25 and in August by another 33, a total gain of 110 points in three months, as against 85 in the whole of 1928, which was itself one of the most remarkable years in financial history. But August also saw the end of the boom. 'On September 3rd,' says Professor Galbraith, 'by common consent, the Great Bull Market of the 1920s came to an end.'

The nature and extent of the speculative mania which ceased in America in 1928–9 cannot be understood simply in terms of the almost daily rise in share prices; what was equally significant was the increase in the extent of the market. There had been a time when, in 1925 and 1926, men of vision had predicted that the day would come when five million shares would change hands on the New York Stock Exchange, but even in the optimistic America of the twenties this had been regarded as a wild, if well intentioned, exaggeration. By 1928, the prediction had been realized. On 12 March, 3,875,910 shares were traded, an all-time record; on 27 March, 4,790,270; finally, in the wave of selling that struck the market on 12 June, the magic figure was passed and 5,052,790 shares changed hands. It was the volume of trading, as much as the fall in prices, on that day which led a few people to believe that the Bull Market had come to an end.

Thereafter, the apparently impossible became a commonplace. By November, five-million share days were regular occurrences; on 23 November, seven million shares were traded, and this was on a rising and not a falling market. On the terrible day of Thursday, 24 October 1929, nearly thirteen million shares changed hands.

The passion for speculation affected all classes. The change in figures of share prices on the ticker tape, relayed to brokers' offices throughout the United States, displaced even the World Series as an object of popular interest. And as in every form of popular sport, the great majority of those who watched, or betted on the result, were profoundly ignorant of the game that was being played; they operated on a system of tips, rumours, hints, superstitions which had no more relation to the real value of the shares they dealt in than a roulette player's hunch to the laws of chance. One object of superstition was the intentions, or the supposed intentions, of the large-scale speculators, like Raskob, or Charles Mitchell of the National Bank, whose operations were on such a scale that they could determine the movement of the market or of the particular stock which they were about to 'fix' or to 'take in hand'. When, at the end of 1928, Mitchell became a director of the New York Federal Reserve Bank, it was taken as a sign that the authorities would cease to exercise any restraining influence on the boom, and that the Bull Market would continue. And in this case popular belief was right; and indeed by that time Mitchell's own personal fortunes and those of the National Bank were dependent on the continuance of the boom.

Yet the small investor, or gambler, following a tip in the hope of a quick profit, was hardly to be blamed for his ignorance, because every day he was assured by the most eminent authorities, from the President of the United States downwards, that in speculating on a continued rise in share prices he was following the path of ordinary wisdom; to be 'a bear on America' (so demonstrating scepticism about America's wonderful future) was an affront to common sense and decency. It is not so much the folly of the ordinary man who played the market during the stock exchange boom as the folly of those to whom he looked for advice and guidance which is most striking. In some cases of course this was more, or worse, than folly. Many of those who offered advice, nearly always in the direction of increasing already exaggerated expectations, were personally interested in the continuation of the Bull Market; but since in most cases they followed their own advice, they could hardly be accused of deliberate deceit. They were for the most part self-deceived rather than deceiving. And by the end even those who had doubts, and acted on their doubts, hesitated to utter them in public, out of fear of the appalling financial consequences which might follow if confidence in the market were undermined. Ultimately it is difficult to avoid the conclusion that those who were responsible for directing the financial affairs of the United States during the Great Bull Market either did not understand the system that they were supposed to be controlling, or, if they did, were powerless to control it. At least one, but perhaps the most important, of the factors leading to the financial disaster which followed the Bull Market was a profound failure of understanding on the part of those whose responsibility was the greatest; and this failure of understanding in the face of a boom was to be repeated when the boom turned into a depression.

The Bull Market, however, was not simply a matter of how people thought and felt about America's economic prospects in 1928-9, or how they behaved and invested their money as a result. If they were to achieve the full consequences of their speculative impulses, the technical means for doing so had to be available. Professor Galbraith has pointed out that people do not speculate merely because they have the necessary funds; they must have the wish and the will to speculate if the funds are to be actively employed. It is equally true, however, that even when the wish and the will are present, they will be ineffective unless the means are provided by which they can be translated into the terms of the stock market. One of the fascinating features of the Bull Market was the degree to which Americans were willing not merely to speculate but to gamble; another is the unexampled ingenuity with which the market responded to the demand which this created.

A large part of the speculative activity of the twenties was financed out of business profits, which rose rapidly and consistently up to about the middle of 1929. Nevertheless, business profits alone would not have been sufficient to finance the market. Nor was it financed out of the savings of small investors. Indeed, though the gambling mania that seized on the country was a phenomenon which has often been described and which no contemporary chronicler fails to mention as a distinctive feature of the times, the numbers actually involved in stock market operations seem to have been relatively small. A Senate committee which later investigated speculation in securities reported that 29 exchanges throughout the United States had a total of 1,548,707 customers; of these, 1,371,920 were customers of the New York Stock Exchange. It would appear therefore that rather less than 1½ million, out of a total population of about 120 million and of between 29–30 million families, conducted any form of operation on the stock market, and of these more than half were engaged in normal investment. 'The striking thing about the Stock Market speculation of 1929,' says Professor Galbraith, 'was not the massiveness of the participation. Rather, it was the way in which it became part of the culture.'

One of the most characteristic features of the Bull Market was the extent to which the mechanism of the stock exchange made it possible to finance it through the medium of brokers' loans to their clients. The practice of the New York Stock Exchange, unlike the London Stock Exchange, was to require a settlement at the close of every day. Brokers were usually in the position of lending their clients the means to effect such a settlement; as R. G. Hawtrey says, they lent the money if they were bulls buying for a rise and they lent them shares if they were bears selling for a fall. In normal times this was simply a matter of convenience, but during 1928–9 the enormous rise in brokers' loans was one of the best indications of the growth of speculation. In some cases, banks also lent directly to their customers for speculative purposes, and some of the largest operators, like Charles Mitchell, or Albert H. Wiggin, of the Chase National Bank, had access to the funds of their own banks; but by far the greater proportion of loans for speculative purposes were made through banks to brokers and by brokers in turn to their customers.

In January 1926 statistics of brokers' loans compiled by the New York banks showed a total of 2,126,000,000 dollars, which was in itself a very large increase on two or three years earlier. During 1926 and 1927 they rose to 3½ billion dollars, by 1 June 1928 to 4 billion dollars, by November to 5 billion and by the end of the year to 6 billion. By October 1929, immediately before the crash, the total had risen to nearly 7 billion dollars. This immense increase, however, in the funds made available for speculation was only partly the result of loans made directly by the banks to brokers. Of the total of 6,800,000,000, in October 1929, only 2,900,000,000 dollars was lent directly by the banks. The additional funds came in the main from industrial or commercial concerns, which, as banks became increasingly reluctant to increase their loans to brokers, found it profitable to lend their surplus resources at the high rate of interest prevailing for this type of loan, which by the end of 1929 had risen to 12 per cent. Such rates were attractive not only to Americans; foreign investors also felt the charm of making short-term loans at 12 per cent, well secured by collateral, which could be called in at any moment, and a flood of foreign money poured into New York. And despite their uneasiness, the rise in the volume of loans made by the banks shows that they also found it hard to resist the temptation of borrowing from the Federal Reserve Bank at 5 per cent in order to lend brokers at 10–12 per cent.

Thus brokers, corporations, private investors, foreign lenders, banks, the Federal Reserve system itself, combined to maintain the flow of money into the stock market. The volume of speculation supported by such funds was increased by the latitude allowed for buying securities on margin. The speculator who borrowed from his broker to buy stock was required to pay only 40–50 per cent in cash, the securities themselves serving as collateral for the balance. Since in his, and the broker's opinion, the market was certain to rise, this was a beautiful device for increasing the speculator's profit, which involved no element of risk whatever; only in the improbable event of the stock failing to increase or maintain its value would the speculator be called on to make up the loss in cash. So long as the market continued to rise, buying on margin was a foolproof method of maximizing speculative profits, and it is estimated that by 1929 some 600,000 people had availed themselves of the opportunities it offered. It is not true, however, that all speculative buying was on margin, and many conservative-minded investors, who could afford it, paid the full price of their securities in cash.

But the Bull Market of 1928–9 did not only require a generous and steady flow of funds into the market; the funds also required an outlet, in the shape of securities which could be readily bought and sold if the speculative fever was to be satisfied, and by that time a shortage of such securities had begun to be felt. Here again the market showed itself fertile and ingenious in satisfying the needs of its clients. In the normal course of events, the progress and prosperity of American industry, which had provided the initial basis of the boom, was in itself sufficient to promote a steady stream of new capital issues, and between 1926 and 1928 the annual total of new American capital issues increased from six to ten billion dollars. Between 1928 and 1929 it increased by over two billion dollars, but in this case only a small proportion of the increase was represented by a genuine investment of new capital in industry. Nearly three-quarters of it was accounted for by the creation of investment trusts, which in most cases were simply a means of providing the hungry market with new securities as an object of speculation.

Investment trusts had originated in Britain where, under conservative and prudent management, they had served a useful purpose in diversifying investments. They were a comparatively new form of security in the United States; in 1927, there were only some 160 investment trusts in existence, and another 140 were formed during that year. But the development of the Bull Market, and the insatiable demand for common stocks which it created, brought the investment trust into its own. In 1928, nearly 190 were formed; and in 1929, when for the first time investment trusts were allowed to be quoted on the New York Stock Exchange, 265 were formed which sold about three billion dollars' worth of securities to the public, as compared with four hundred million dollars in 1927. This represented about a third of all the new issues coming on to the market during the year.

Investment trusts, as they were organized in 1929, were one of the most characteristic features of the Bull Market, in that they exemplified the complete divorce that had taken place by that time between the speculative boom and the industrial prosperity which had initially provoked it. They were also characteristic in that, though their stock represented purely speculative values, they were formed by the most respectable financial organizations, including the House of Morgan, which thereby endowed them with a prestige which helped to increase the already eager demand of the investing public. Their stock was usually bought at a large premium over the

[26]

price at which they were offered. To their promoters they brought very large returns, in the shape both of commissions and management fees, and on the profits realized by the initial sale of stock to the public. When Morgans launched the United Corporation Investment Trust in January 1929, Morgan partners and their friends were allotted shares at $75; four days after trading in them began, they were being eagerly bought at $99.

The trusts sought and received the advice of the most distinguished economists of the day: Professor Irving Fisher of Yale, Professor Kamerer of Princeton, Professor Davis of Stanford, were glad to serve on their boards, and share in their profits, and the public were readily convinced that, in investing in their securities, they were buying the services of the most efficient business management and the best financial knowledge then available. This, together with the purely speculative appeal of the trusts, helps to explain the paradox that the stock of the trusts was worth more than all the securities they owned, which were their only asset.

The financial expertise of the trusts, however, was chiefly shown in the ingenuity with which they manipulated the device known as 'leverage', by which the rise in value of the securities they owned accrued entirely to the holders of their common stock, as opposed to their bonds or preference shares; it could be applied in such a way that the common stock of a trust conferred control of a whole series of subsidiary trusts which it had itself in turn created, and in the almost mystical financial jargon of the day, their value often depended on the 'high' or 'low' degree of 'leverage' which they were believed to possess. By 1929, the common stock of American Founders Group, an investment trust which began business in 1922 with a capital of $500, controlled resources worth more than five billion.

The classical case of the investment trust, which seems to exhibit all the elements of unreality, of unlimited optimism and wild fantasy of the Bull Market in its final stages, was Goldman, Sachs and Company. In December 1928, it promoted Goldman, Sachs Trading Corporation, with an initial capital of one million $100 shares, of which 90 per cent was sold to the public at 104. In February 1929, Goldman, Sachs merged with another investment trust, and four days after the merger its stock stood at $225·5, largely as a result of heavy trading in its own shares by the company.

[27]

In July, the company, together with Harrison Williams, an expert in the art of leverage, promoted Shenandoah Corporation, with 5,000,000 shares of common stock, issued at $17·50, which reached 36 on the day of issue. In August, Shenandoah sponsored Blue Ridge Corporation, with a capital of $142,000,000, and 7,250,000 shares of common stock, of which Shenandoah subscribed 6,250,000. On 20 August, Goldman, Sachs announced the acquisition of Pacific American Association, an investment company which owned a number of smaller trusts and American Trust Company, a large commercial bank with several branches in California; the purchase was financed by the issue of another $71,400,000 of common stock, which was exchanged for the stock of American Company, a holding company which owned American Trust.

In rather less than a month, Goldman, Sachs had issued rather more than $250,000,000 of securities to the public; in that month nine other investment trusts had been formed, with the same object of supplying the demand for new securities. This was very nearly, though not quite, the end. In September, another $600,000,000 of investment trust stock was issued, and at last even the Bull Market could take no more. After this short and glorious bonanza, the investment trusts (or rather, those who had bought their stock) were some of the worst victims of the crash which followed; testifying before the Senate three years later, Mr Sachs stated that the stock of Goldman, Sachs Trading Corporation, originally sold to the public at 104, then stood at 'approximately' $1\frac{3}{4}$.

The final irony of these transactions, however, was that, like many other trust companies, Goldman, Sachs employed the huge resources they created both in investing heavily in their own companies and in supporting the price of their stock. So long as the boom continued, and the public preserved its passion to buy, this was highly profitable business. When the crash came, and the public developed a panic to sell, at almost any price, it proved disastrous and provoked a chain reaction to which the magic of 'leverage' worked in reverse. As Professor Galbraith remarks: 'the autumn of 1929 was, perhaps, the first occasion on which men succeeded on a large scale in swindling themselves.' In the end, companies like Goldman, Sachs revealed a kind of financial gullibility which even surpassed that of their customers.

The brief history of Goldman, Sachs epitomizes the totally unreal nature of much of the speculation that took place in America at the height of the Bull Market. But perhaps Americans should not be blamed too much either for gullibility or cupidity, for when they could foreigners also rushed in to take their share of the fortunes to be made on Wall Street, among them a small syndicate formed by some of the Fellows of All Souls College, Oxford, to invest their savings in the Bull Market. But outside America, the speculative boom had the added effect of drying up the supply of funds available for investment abroad, especially in Germany, and from 1928 onwards the short-term loans by American banks, finance houses and private investors which had financed German recovery, and on which its continuance depended, began to dwindle away. Until then, foreign loans had made it possible for America to finance her own favourable balance of trade, the repayment of debts owed to her and economic recovery in Europe, and failure to renew them threatened the entire financial structure which had been built up during the war. The United States became an importer of gold, and this coincided with a flow of gold into France after the stabilization of the franc; from 1928 onwards the United States and France together absorbed the whole of the world's available gold supplies. At a time when all the major countries had, by strenuous exertions, returned to gold, this placed an intolerable strain both on their domestic economies and on their international balance of payments.

But if Americans would not lend directly to foreign governments or municipalities, there were others who were eager to fill the gap, and in particular the great Swedish financier, Ivar Kreuger, the wonder and admiration of the entire financial world. Kreuger had created a great financial empire by the simple process of refusing to reveal to anyone the secrets of his operation, combined with an almost magical gift of persuading everyone that whatever he chose to tell them was true. He was able to compete with the American stock markets' demand for funds because of the high rates of interest he offered on the loans he raised, because his own stocks became a favourite object of speculation, and because of his impeccable reputation for shrewdness and integrity, backed by the supposedly vast resources of his two main companies, Swedish Match and Kreuger and Toll. Kreuger's word was so much beyond reproach that no one cared to inquire into the reality which lay behind it, which was an incredibly complicated network of deceit, fraud, and speculation on a grand scale, all of which he carried in his head so that he was never at a loss for an answer on any question of detail. The profoundly respectable and well established banking firm of Lee, Higginson and Co., which underwrote most of his most important issues in America, and was represented on the boards of many of his companies, were so much beneath the spell of his dominating personality that they never asked for an audit of his accounts and never troubled to attend a board meeting.

Kreuger's power was so great that he became one of the decisive figures in the world of international finance, dealing as an individual on terms of equality with governments and central banks. His really large issues in America began in 1927, when he offered for sale fifty million dollars' worth of debentures in Kreuger and Toll, which were heavily oversubscribed; the proceeds were used to assist the French government in stabilizing the franc, an operation which earned him the enmity of the House of Morgan, to whom the French government repaid the balance of a highly profitable loan. In 1928 and 1929 Kreuger issued another thirty-four millions of debentures. But however much Kreuger borrowed, Americans were always eager to lend more. By the beginning of 1929 the common stock of Kreuger and Toll stood at 730 per cent of par and its debentures at 863 per cent. One of his colleagues one day heard him murmur as he looked at the stock market figures: 'They're mad; they're mad.'

With the money he raised in America, Kreuger financed loans to European and other countries in return for match monopolies; by 1929 they amounted to 185 million dollars. Some saw in his operations the mark of a man of genius, immensely shrewd and immensely imaginative, who performed an invaluable service to a Europe starved of capital. Others saw reasons for criticism. The New York *Journal of Commerce* was reminded of 'the great merchant trading companies of the Middle Ages and of early modern times which, in addition to their regular operations, financed wars and overthrew dynasties'; it complained that something was wrong 'when a private company is able to approach the world's markets more successfully than states which are presumably stable and are in possession of sources of monopolistic income which might be pledged directly for loans instead of being farmed out to private capitalists'. But no one doubted Kreuger's honesty.

To the needy governments of Central Europe Kreuger appeared as a fairy godmother; if he had not existed, he would have had to be invented. He himself took a cynical pleasure in the gullibility of the American investors and the United States became his favourite source of raising new capital. 'I've built my enterprises on the safest ground that can be found,' he said; 'the foolishness of people.' Yet even he became alarmed by the fantastic optimism on which the Bull Market was based. 'It is risky,' he said in 1929, 'to introduce securities on Wall Street, because once New York operators start working on paper their quotations lose all relationship to real value.'

Kreuger's own stock fell well within this category, and there is a certain irony in such a comment, coming from him; he himself exploited to the full the unbounded enthusiasm with which his successive issues were received in the United States. But there were others who saw the American gift for discounting a future of unlimited prosperity, not as an opportunity but as a cause for alarm, and who tried, though without any success, to restrain it.

The most important of these, in 1929, was the new president of the United States, Herbert Hoover. His victory in the election of 1928 had inspired a remarkable wave of buying, the 'Hoover boom', and during November the market reached heights that had never previously been exceeded. Of all this Mr Hoover thoroughly disapproved; he considered speculation a curse that was worse than murder; since 1925 he had watched its growth with increasing alarm and as Secretary of Commerce he had done what he could to restrain it.

Mr Hoover was in some ways the most tragic president who ever entered the White House. There have been few, if any, men who were ever better equipped for the tasks of the presidency. He had none of the failings of his predecessors, neither the good-natured corruption of Harding, nor Coolidge's almost frivolous assurance that in America all was for the best in the best of all possible worlds. His character was above reproach; he had been an admirable Secretary of Commerce; he possessed remarkable gifts as an administrator and an executive. His landslide victory in November was evidence of how much he commanded the confidence of his countrymen. No one ever entered the White House with better prospects of becoming not merely a good but a great president; to no one could one better apply Tacitus' epigram about Galba: *omnium consensu capax imperii nisi imperasset.*

But he became president at a moment when America was about to enter a great crisis, and to face problems of a kind she had never had to face before. In meeting this crisis, Hoover revealed unexpected and fatal defects, which made his presidency a tragic anti-climax to his brilliantly successful career. Immensely able, honest, intelligent, he was inhibited from taking effective action by an intellectual outlook which took it for granted that government intervention in business affairs was to be deplored and a profound conviction that the orthodoxies of *laissez-faire* provided the only solution for economic problems. In this, of course, he was typical of the overwhelming majority of his fellow countrymen; but it made him incapable of leading them in their hour of need. Within four years of his electoral triumph, the great engineer who would apply to the presidency all the arts of scientific management had become a laughing stock, leaving as his memorial the thousands of nomadic slums, bitterly christened 'Hoovervilles', in which the unemployed camped on the outskirts of every American city.

Despite his uneasiness at the development of the Bull Market, Mr Hoover did little to restrain it after his November victory. Neither the outgoing president, Mr Coolidge, nor Mr Andrew Mellon, the millionaire Philadelphia banker who had served as Secretary of the Treasury under two presidents and was held in almost religious awe as a fount of financial wisdom, shared Mr Hoover's alarm, and so far as they could encourage the boom they did so. In this they were representative of the financial establishment as a whole; and in view of the prevailing temper it is doubtful if Mr Hoover could have taken any effective measures even had he wished to. For in fact the government of the United States did not regard itself as responsible for directing the business affairs of the nation; by common consent, in which it concurred, its function was limited to holding the ring so as to give the greatest possible scope and freedom to the wisdom and initiative of businessmen. It took the depression itself to modify this attitude, which was fundamental to the ideology of capitalism as it had developed in the United States.

So far as financial control of the economy belonged to any single institution it rested not with the government of the United States, but with the Federal Reserve Board, which was itself carefully protected against interference by the government. In theory, the Board exercised its control by directing the credit policy of its member banks, and, through them, the banking system as a whole. In practice, the Board, which throughout the twenties was composed of men of singularly mediocre abilities, did little to exercise this function, and the determining influence on banking and credit policy fell to the most powerful of its member banks, the Federal Reserve Bank of New York.

For the greater part of the twenties, until October 1928, the Governor of the Bank was Benjamin Strong, the most influential central banker the United States had known since the days of Nicholas Biddle. In the history of the Great Bull Market he occupies a dominating and highly controversial place. By some, the policy of easy credit and cheap money rates which he consistently pursued is regarded as responsible for provoking an inflation which laid the basis for the unrestrained speculation of the Bull Market; by others, Strong is credited, because of that policy, with having made possible the unprecedented expansion of American industry during the twenties. Strong, says A.G.Hawtrey in *The Art of Central Banking*, could have killed the speculative boom at any moment, but only at the cost of killing America's industrial growth, and he contrasts America's prosperity with the stagnation, during the same period, of industry in Britain, where from 1925 onwards the Bank of England had followed a policy of severe credit restriction.

During the twenties the Federal Reserve system, in which the New York Reserve Bank played the predominant role, had two instruments of credit control at its disposal. The first was the rediscount rate, at which member commercial banks borrowed from Reserve Banks in their area, and could be encouraged or discouraged by lowering or raising the rate. The second was open market sales or purchases of government securities or commercial bills; sales automatically reduced the cash resources available to commercial banks, while purchase automatically increased them. In 1924, after a credit contraction whose effects had been more severe than had been expected, the New York Federal Reserve Bank initiated a policy of credit expansion, both by open market operations and by reducing the rediscount rate from $4\frac{1}{2}$ per cent to 3 per cent. This policy was continued in 1925 and 1926, during which the rediscount rate fluctuated between $3\frac{1}{2}$ and 4 per cent, though its general effect was to some extent counteracted by the policy of severe credit restriction pursued at the same time by the Bank of England, where bank rate stood at 5 per cent throughout most of the period.

By 1927, Britain was suffering one of the exchange crises which have been a permanent part of its history since the return to the gold standard in 1925. In that year, a formidable delegation descended upon the shores of the United States. It consisted of Montague Norman, Governor of the Bank of England; Hjalmar Schacht, Governor of the Reichsbank, and Charles Rist, Deputy-Governor of the Bank of France, and together they represented all the ancient financial wisdom and prestige of Europe. Their object was to persuade the Federal Reserve authorities to relieve the pressure on their currencies by intensifying the policy of cheap money so as to increase American domestic prices and reduce interest rates.

It is a significant reflection of the financial arrangement of the western world at that period that this appeal, which virtually affected the economies of four great nations, should have been made, not as between governments, but as between the vitally independent individual controllers of their central banks, and there was no one who thought it anything but proper. Governor Strong responded to the appeal, all the more readily, perhaps, because there was evidence of a business recession in the United States, with a gesture of international cooperation which, in the eyes of many, made him guilty of betraying the interests of the United States. The rediscount rate of the New York Federal Reserve Bank was not reduced to below $3\frac{1}{2}$ per cent but, even more important, the Federal Reserve Board engaged in open market purchases of government securities and of acceptances in what has been described as 'the greatest and boldest operation ever undertaken by the Federal Reserve system'. These measures were so successful in achieving their object that the market was flooded with money and in the twelve months ending July 1928 the United States lost over $500,000,000 of gold, which was absorbed by Europe.

But they also released funds which became available to the stock market, and for some 1927 marks the fatal moment which led

[34]

inevitably to the crash of 1929. 'From that date,' says Professor (now Lord) Robbins, 'the situation got completely out of control.' Governor Strong was believed to have fallen a victim to the charms and snares of wily European bankers; in his memoirs, President Hoover described him as 'a mental annexe of Europe'. A dissenting member of the Federal Reserve Board later described the operations undertaken in 1927 as 'one of the most costly errors committed by it or any other banking system in the last 75 years'.

It is ironical that Strong should have incurred these charges as the result of one of the few attempts by America and Europe to concert their central banking policies. But even domestically, Strong's policy was appropriate to the continued growth of American industry, which by 1927 had fallen slightly from the peak it had reached in 1926. It was not easy credit which caused the stock exchange inflation but the unbounded and irrational expectations aroused as American production resumed its upward movement.

During the winter of 1927-8, the market was comparatively quiet, but in March there came one of the violent upward movements which became one of its characteristic features until the final crash. The rediscount rate had been raised from 3½ to 4 per cent in February; in May it was raised to 4½ per cent and in July to 5 per cent, the highest at which it had stood since 1921. At the same time, large-scale open market sales reduced the Federal Reserve holding of government securities from $600 million to $219 million between February and May. Severe as they were, these measures were ineffective in restraining the rising tide of the market; moreover, the market's failure to respond to them showed that the two traditional instruments for controlling credit had lost their power. Differences of one or even two per cent in the rediscount rate made little difference, so far as speculation was concerned, as the call money rate for brokers' loans rose to 10 per cent or even, as in May, to 20 per cent; and open market sales had so reduced the Federal Reserve holdings of government securities that no attempt was made to repeat the operation.

From the summer of 1928, it could truly be said that there was no longer any effective control of the Bull Market, and that from now on the crash of 1929 became inevitable. In October, Benjamin Strong died and was succeeded as Governor of the Federal Reserve

Bank of New York by George L. Harrison; a more significant change was the appointment as a Class A Director of the Bank of Charles E. Mitchell, one of the most devoted and reckless adherents of the Bull Market. From now on the Federal Reserve Board restricted its efforts to restrain the market to verbal warnings and admonitions, but relapsed into silence as soon as they showed signs of having an effect; like many others, they were alarmed that if they were taken seriously they might provoke a calamitous collapse in share values and be held responsible for the result.

The market was by now highly unstable and ready to respond to any rumour. On 2 February 1929 the Federal Reserve Board issued a letter to its member banks, instructing them that federal reserve loans should not be employed for speculation. This was followed on 7 February by a warning to the public against the dangers of speculation, but in terms so guarded and qualified that anyone might be forgiven for thinking that they did not apply to him; on the same day, in Britain, the bank rate was raised to $5\frac{1}{2}$ per cent, in an effort to prevent the flow of funds to America. This sequence of events was enough to provoke a serious break in the market. In March, the Federal Reserve Board held a weekend meeting, on the 25th and 26th, but made no announcement about its deliberations; an even more serious break followed, in which over eight million shares changed hands. The rate for call money rose to 20 per cent. The alarm caused by the Board's silence was promptly and effectively counteracted by Charles E. Mitchell, who on behalf of the two banks of which he was chairman announced that they were prepared immediately, as a mark of their confidence in a situation that was fundamentally sound, to put $25,000,000 into the call money market. Mitchell's intervention achieved its purpose. But for a moment uneasiness had been widespread. There is a legend that the great speculator, William Crapo Durant, visited President Hoover in the White House at dead of night to warn him of the catastrophe that would ensue unless confidence in the market was restored. The story is not authenticated; but given the atmosphere and circumstances of the time, there is nothing inherently improbable in it.

This was probably the last moment at which a concerted and responsible attempt could have been made to bring the market under control. No doubt the consequences would have been serious, because by then some form of collapse was inevitable; but they would have been less disastrous than what actually occurred. During the summer all restraint vanished, though the administration and the Federal Reserve Board continued to make ineffective gestures that expressed their alarm. In August, the rediscount rate was raised to $5\frac{1}{2}$ per cent. President Hoover tried to allay his anxiety by despatching a Los Angeles banker to Wall Street to discuss the market; his emissary was able to assure him that it was sound. He also summoned Richard Whitney, Vice-President of the New York Stock Exchange, who understood as little as anyone what was going on around him, and asked that steps should be taken to curb the market. This was like calling on devils to exorcize themselves; nor was it strictly a part of the president's duty, as direct responsibility for controlling the New York Stock Exchange belonged to the Governor of New York, Franklin D. Roosevelt, who however made no attempt to do so. By then, indeed, there was nothing that could be done, except to watch as the market, during the summer and autumn of 1929, took off on its final, unbelievable flight into the blue.

CHAPTER THREE

The Crash

In the summer of 1929, while the Great Bull Market was making its last convulsive advances, there were already some indications that the long period of economic prosperity which had originally inspired it was beginning to come to an end. In Europe, moreover, there were also signs that the period of political stability, which had been the condition of her economic recovery, was also drawing to a close; even so, there were few observers at the time who foresaw the terrible consequences which were to follow. In spite of the shadows which were already apparent, the summer of 1929 was the last time in which the capitalist world as a whole might reasonably look forward to the future without forebodings of war, revolution or economic collapse; it was the last time, perhaps, in which men and women in the western world could still hold to that belief in the inevitability of progress, and the rationality of the social and political order, to which most of them had subscribed since the eighteenth century.

In this sense, the summer of 1929 may be regarded as marking the end of an era, in a way in which even the summer of 1914 had not. The war indeed had dealt a disastrous, perhaps an irreparable, blow to the fabric of western civilization and had released uncontrollable forces of violence and destruction. But when it was over it was still possible for people to believe that, with goodwill and mutual understanding, between nations and individuals, the damage could be repaired. One of the most widely read books of 1929 was Robert Graves's autobiography, *Goodbye to All That*. It was a marvellously vivid and lucid account of how one man had survived the appalling holocaust of 1914–18. It could be read without pain, and with a measure of hope, because it seemed, as its title indicated, a record of events which were already far off and long ago; it was still possible to believe that the experiences which

Graves described were wholly exceptional, and that the world might still return, and to a large extent already had, to the condition for which President Harding had invented the word 'normalcy', that is to say a state of affairs such as had obtained before the war ever happened.

Behind such hopes, beliefs, illusions, there lay the objective fact that, just as American men, money and supplies had saved the western allies from defeat in 1918, so the unprecedented growth and expansion of American industry in the twenties provided an example of the unparalleled possibilities that still lay open to the western world; at the same time, epoch-making discoveries in the physical sciences showed that these possibilities were literally inexhaustible. Against such a background, even the extraordinary events that were taking place on Wall Street seemed of minor significance; in 1929 it seemed of more importance, as a sign of renewed international confidence and the restoration of good relations between nations, that the United States should have granted diplomatic recognition to the Soviet Union, and that agreement was reached to summon the World Disarmament Conference for 1932.

Yet already the stage was being set for events which would overshadow all such hopes and make them seem irrelevant. In Britain, in particular, one problem had made itself felt which was to become the almost obsessive, and intractable, preoccupation of governments for the next four years, defeating all attempts at a solution and provoking disastrous political consequences: the problem of unemployment. In April a general election had returned the Labour Party to power as the largest of the three political parties, but without a majority in the House of Commons, and a minority government had been formed under Ramsay MacDonald. Politically, the Labour Government was in no position to master, or survive, a crisis; intellectually and emotionally it was committed to a form of old-fashioned, doctrinaire socialism which had no relevance to Britain's economic and industrial problems. Indeed, in the election, the only relevant answer to these problems had been provided by the Liberals under Lloyd George, who made his last serious attempt to return to power on a programme of deficit government financing and large-scale public works.* The programme was

* *We Can Conquer Unemployment* advocated large public investment in roads, housing, etc., even though this would create a budget deficit.

elaborated in the Liberal manifesto, *We Can Conquer Unemployment*, written by John Maynard Keynes, Hubert Henderson, and Seebohm Rowntree. It contained many of the ideas which were later to be applied by Roosevelt and the New Deal and today are taken for granted by all capitalist governments. But at the time they were novel and even revolutionary, and Keynes himself had not yet worked out the implications of the economic theory on which they were based; certainly they had little or no appeal for his countrymen, and all the less when propagated in the service of Lloyd George, for whom, despite his immense gifts, the electorate had come to feel an invincible mistrust.

Yet *We Can Conquer Unemployment* was an attempt to provide a radical solution for a problem which had become endemic in the British economy and was soon to threaten the structure of the entire capitalist world. It was also a declaration that the problem could only be solved by direct and large-scale government intervention and as such was a challenge to all the financial and economic orthodoxies of the day. It is perhaps therefore not surprising that it should not have recommended itself to the British electorate which, though willing to tolerate a minority socialist government, remained at heart profoundly conservative.

It is, however, equally not surprising that the measures suggested in *We Can Conquer Unemployment*, which had to wait so long before they gained general acceptance, should have first become an active electoral and political issue in Britain. For Britain had benefited less than any other major country from the economic boom of 1925–9, and during the twenties had entered a period of industrial stagnation combined with a high level of unemployment which was to continue until the beginning of the Second World War. If Britain suffered less than other industrialized countries from the shock of the world economic depression, it was because depression was already a permanent feature of her economy. Throughout the twenties, unemployment never significantly fell below the rate of ten per cent and by September 1929 stood at 1,203,000. It was concentrated in the heavy industries, iron and steel, mining, shipbuilding, and in the textile industry, which were the basis of Britain's export trade and were vital to her balance of payments. It was the export industries, and the regions in which they were concentrated, the North of England, Scotland and South Wales, that exposed Britain to the shock of the depression, and it was characteristic of the historical development of her economy that when the shock of the depression struck her it should take the form of a crisis in her balance of payments. For that reason she was already, in 1929, peculiarly susceptible to the repercussions of a decline in international trade. But precisely because of Britain's failure to share in the benefits of the post-war economic boom, her economic and political situation was inherently less unstable than that of other advanced industrial countries, particularly the United States and Germany, and the shock of the depression was therefore the less severe.

Yet Britain was one of the first countries to experience one of those financial scandals which, like the rumblings of an approaching storm, accompanied the coming of the depression. By the summer of 1929 Stock Exchange dealings in London had assumed, in less spectacular ways perhaps, some of the essentially speculative and even fraudulent forms which they were exhibiting on Wall Street; in particular, in September 1929, there came the sensational collapse of Clarence Hatry, who had built an industrial and financial empire on assorted enterprises which ranged from penny-in-the-slot machines to investment trusts and high finance. Like Kreuger, Hatry was credited by many with financial genius, but in the end he was reduced, again like Kreuger, to the simple expedient of forging share certificates in order to maintain his empire. His collapse caused widespread personal distress in Britain, and many who had thought themselves rich suddenly found themselves poor. But it also had repercussions abroad, because of the shock it administered to confidence and because it cut off some of the funds available for speculation on the American market. It has even been thought to have been one of the immediate causes of the Wall Street crash, but this is to exaggerate its importance. By September 1929, speculation on Wall Street had reached a point at which a crash was inevitable, with or without Hatry, and could not be averted much longer. Hatry was sent to prison; after his release, the legend of his financial genius was still strong enough to find him backers who set him up in business again, but by then the magic had deserted him.

If conditions in Britain were relatively stable, because she had never really shared in the boom, in Germany by the autumn of 1929 events were already beginning to expose the precarious nature of her economic recovery; and, even more, the violence of the political forces which had been held in check so long as recovery lasted. Indeed, what was characteristic and significant about developments in Germany was that, even before the boom ended, the forces of nationalism, racism and reaction had already assumed a revolutionary form which showed that it was already prepared to reject absolutely the whole of the Weimar 'system'.

This was remarkable because 1929 was, on the surface at least, a year of political triumph for Germany, in which she secured, greatly to her own advantage, the settlement of the two most important problems created by the Treaty of Versailles; the problem of reparations and the problem of the Rhineland. Both were the subject of discussion at an international conference which opened at The Hague in August. By the end of the month the British, French and Belgian governments informed the German delegation, headed by Stresemann, that they were willing to complete the evacuation of the Rhineland by 30 June 1930, or five years earlier than the date prescribed in the treaty; the conference also accepted the Young Plan for settling Germany's reparations payments, which had been proposed by the American banker, Owen D. Young, chairman of the committee of experts appointed to study the reparations problem. The plan provided for the payment of reparations by Germany over a period of sixty years, rising from 1,700 million marks to 2,400 million by 1965, and thereafter progressively diminishing; it also provided for the establishment of a bank of international settlements as a means of carrying out the difficult and complicated financial operations involved in the plan.

The Young Plan and the evacuation of the Rhineland represented the culmination of Stresemann's policy of fulfilment; they were intimately connected because the withdrawal of the Allied occupation forces was conditional on Germany's acceptance of the Young Plan. They were the work of that 'spirit of dreams' which was so characteristic and so ephemeral an achievement of the twenties; its magic was so strong that, in return for German acceptance of the plan, the Allies surrendered every form of sanction and control, military, financial and economic, which had previously been imposed on Germany, which thus resumed complete sovereignty over the conduct of her own affairs. But the 'spirit of dreams' was apt to look somewhat different from the other side of the Rhine; at The

Hague Stresemann finally achieved the aim described by his official biographers: 'First get rid of the last foreign soldier, abolish the Commissions in the Reichsbahn, the Reichsbank, and all the rest of them, then carry on the fight for national aims in foreign politics.'

Stresemann did not live long to enjoy his triumph, and his death, in October 1929, was as much the end of an era as the Wall Street crash was. Moreover, in the eyes of many Germans it was not even a triumph, but a betrayal, and it inaugurated a period of growing political instability in Germany, which coincided with the economic depression; in particular, acceptance of the Young Plan provoked, despite the advantages it brought to Germany, a violent agitation in which the nationalist leader Hugenberg joined with Hitler in enlisting the most extreme racialist and reactionary forces in opposition to the plan. The campaign culminated in a popular referendum in December, in which nearly nine million votes were cast against the plan. They were not sufficient to defeat it. President Hindenburg, in agreement with the socialist Chancellor, Hermann Müller, authorized the government to accept the plan, but only on condition that three hundred million gold marks of the loan provided for under the plan should be used to give long-term credits to the Prussian landowners. It was Hindenburg's *quid pro quo* for his estate of Neudeck, which had recently been presented to him by the Prussian landowners, as a sign of their appreciation of his services to the nation.

The agitation against the plan was less significant for any direct results it achieved than as a revelation of the recklessness, violence and corruption of the extreme nationalist forces in Germany. It marked a turning point in German history and the beginning of the end of the Weimar Republic; in particular, it gave Hitler, as a result of his alliance with Hugenberg, a share in the huge propaganda resources – newspapers, press agencies, the UFA film company, controlled by Hugenberg, and almost overnight turned him into what he had never hitherto been, a national political figure, with the aura of respectability which his association with the German nationalists conferred upon him. Up to that time, Hitler had been generally regarded as a failure, an obscure Bavarian politician whose only claim to fame was his part in the Munich *putsch* of 1923; in fact, by 1929, he had already succeeded in reuniting the racist groups who provided the revolutionary dynamism of

[43]

the National Socialist Party, had subjected them to his own absolute personal authority, and had established contacts with German heavy industry which was a first step to the conquest of power. The National Socialist Party already had 176,000 members, and, in the brown-shirted Storm Troops, an organized para-military force. The existence of such a party, dominated by the demonic will of Hitler, at a moment when Germany was about to be struck by the full effects of economic depression and mass unemployment was, in the autumn of 1929, the most sinister portent in Europe.

From 1925 up to the end of 1929, unemployment in Germany had fluctuated around one million; that is to say, about the same number as in Britain, but given Germany's higher industrial population, and the effects of war and inflation, this represented a significantly higher degree of economic recovery. But German recovery depended essentially on the renewal of the large foreign loans, mostly short-term, and particularly from the United States and Britain, which made up for her chronic shortage of capital. According to Dr Schacht, President of the Reichsbank, 'during the period 1924–1930, the immense sum of £2,000,000,000 (reckoning the British £ at 12½ Reichsmarks) was advanced to Germany by foreign creditors.' By 1929, however, this huge flow of capital was beginning to dry up, and during the year Germany negotiated only two minor loans, one of 210,000,000 marks in the United States, and one of 500,000,000 marks floated in Sweden by Ivar Kreuger, but these were hardly sufficient for her needs. It is significant that even in August 1929, immediately after the Young Plan had been approved by The Hague conference, Stresemann was already envisaging the possibility of a moratorium on Germany's foreign debts, including the reparations payments provided for in the plan.

Like Germany, the diminutive Austria which had emerged from the war was dependent on foreign loans to maintain her political and economic stability. As in Germany also, such loans were made available through the banking system, which was greatly overdeveloped for post-war Austria's needs; Vienna, reduced to the status of a provincial capital, had a banking structure adapted to the finance of a great multi-racial empire. It was perhaps natural, therefore, that one of the first signs of the increasing strain upon the financial system of Europe should have shown itself in Vienna;

in October 1929 the Boden Credit-Anstalt, a large industrial and agricultural bank, was only saved from bankruptcy by absorption, at great loss to its shareholders, into the Credit-Anstalt, a banking house owned by the Austrian Rothschilds. But in fact the Credit-Anstalt was itself already under severe financial strain. The absorption of the Boden Credit-Anstalt, together with two other banks, further weakened its position; when the full force of the economic depression broke, it collapsed beneath the strain, with consequences which paralysed the banking system throughout Europe.

But though in Europe, in the autumn of 1929, there were ominous signs of instability, the origins of the catastrophic depression which was to follow were to be found elsewhere. Indeed, the difficulties which were beginning to accumulate in Europe were primarily a reflection of conditions in the United States, and it was developments in the United States which brought to an end the economic boom of the twenties. The boom had been an American boom, and the depression was an American depression; but its effects upon the essentially unstable political and economic structure of Europe were disastrous.

In fact, the boom had already come to an end as the stock market in the United States climbed to its last dizzy heights in the summer and autumn of 1929. Indeed, production in many countries had begun to decline before 1929 and world commodity prices had begun to fall in the second half of 1928. In July, in the United States, there were signs of a business recession as a result of the Federal Reserve Board's policy of credit contraction; one of the difficulties of the situation was that the Federal Reserve Board could not have reversed its policy without giving an added stimulus to the wild speculation that was taking place in the stock market. In June, the index of manufacturing production rose to 127, the highest point it had ever reached, and thereafter began to fall; by October it was down to 119. In the summer the production of motor cars rose to 5,358,000, the highest ever; it would take nearly twenty-five years before it was exceeded. Automobile production was regarded as one of the best indications of business prosperity, and the optimistic forecasts, which were not to be fulfilled, of the automobile manufacturers, including Ford and General Motors, was one of the factors which helped to sustain the expectations of manufacturers.

But despite the evidence of a decline in business activity, the market continued to rise throughout the summer and into the autumn. This was not in itself unreasonable; the decline was after all a moderate one, and the boom had gone on for so long that, for a generation which had learned to believe that in the long run the stock market always rose and never fell, it was very natural to assume that the business recession was only temporary and, as in 1927, would be quickly reversed. By September the index of industrial share prices stood at 216; in the five years since 1924 it had more than trebled, while in roughly the same period, between 1923 and 1929, industrial profits had risen by 156 per cent.

In the course of September, the market continued to rise, and by the end of the month the index of industrial shares, at 218, had gained another two points. But the rise had been irregular, and there were bad days as well as good; on both, dealings were heavy and on the New York Stock Exchange four to five million shares changed hands every day. Brokers' loans increased by 675 million dollars, by far the largest increase that had ever occurred in any single month, and the best indication that the fever of speculation was still rising. By now the market was attracting the money of everyone who had available resources, both in the United States and abroad.

Looking back with the benefit of hindsight at those closing days of September, it is almost impossible not to feel a sense of excitement and apprehension, as in the closing moments of some great tragedy; for so many years the market had sustained so many hopes and so many dreams, had created fortunes that had grown unbelievably out of nothing, had given millions of Americans the sense that a future of limitless and dazzling possibilities extended before them. And now all this was over, or nearly over, for at last the Great Bull Market was finally coming to its close.

Some time towards the beginning of October, large numbers of people must have come to a decision, individually and collectively, that the moment had come when it was best to take one's profits and get out. What motives determined their decision it is impossible to say, or whether it was taken by instinct or after mature deliberation; they may have behaved as irrationally as, on the whole, they had behaved throughout the speculative boom. Some may have been influenced by the Hatry crash in Britain, some by the recession in business activity, some, it is thought, by the refusal of the Massachusetts Department of Public Utilities to allow Boston Edison to split its stock four to one* and by its comment that, at the market value of the stock, 'no one, in our judgement . . . would find it to his advantage to buy it'; to how many other stocks did the same judgement apply? Or it may have been due to some general sense that, at long last, speculation really had outrun all rational, or even irrational, expectations. As Professor Galbraith says: 'What first stirred these doubts we do not know'; what was important was that the doubts had arisen and that innumerable investors, large and small, had decided that the time had come to call it a day.

It is not likely, however, that any of them envisaged how catastrophic the effect of their combined decisions was going to be, particularly when the high priests of the market continued to exude an unchanging confidence. In the middle of October Charles E. Mitchell announced that 'the industrial condition of the United States is absolutely sound', and Professor Irving Fisher stated that share prices seemed to have 'reached a permanent high plateau; I expect to see the stock market a good deal higher than it is today within a few months.'

Despite such predictions, the market took a sudden move downwards. During the half-day session of Saturday, 19 October, nearly 3½ million shares changed hands and the *Times* industrial index was down twelve points; it was significant that brokers sent out large numbers of margin calls, asking for cash to cover their customers' losses. Yet there appeared to be no particular reason for the break in the market, and on the following day, Sunday, the press was full of reassurances that the fall would be quickly reversed. Many people, however, refused to be reassured; on Monday, 21 October, six million shares changed hands, though the losses were less than on the previous Saturday. The very large volume of trading, on a falling market, had one effect which some people found peculiarly disturbing. The ticker tape failed to keep up with the market and at

* The issue of new shares in the proportion of four new shares for every one already issued. Splitting of stock was a common practice during the Bull Market.

the close was over an hour and a half behind. On a rising market such an occurrence was inconvenient but not alarming. It simply meant postponing the pleasure of knowing what one's profit had been; it was slightly unnerving that on a falling market one might be ruined without even knowing it.

Once again the bulls, commercial and academic, went to work. Charles E. Mitchell reiterated his faith in the market, and Professor Irving Fisher repeated the many reasons for confidence; he attached particular importance to the tonic effect of prohibition on the productivity of the American worker. Other market experts, however, concluded that the time had come to sell stocks and buy gold, and they appeared to have carried conviction with many investors; on Wednesday, 23 October, there was heavy selling, particularly at the close, and margin calls by brokers were higher than had ever been known.

Thursday, 24 October, opened with the announcement of a new issue of Kreuger and Toll certificates, at $23, but that day most people were more anxious to sell than to buy. During the morning there was an avalanche of selling, which developed into uncontrollable panic; 12,894,650 shares changed hands, and some stocks became virtually unsaleable at any price. Throughout the country the ticker tape fell hopelessly behind the market; losses, heavy as they were, were exaggerated and multiplied by rumour, so as to create an atmosphere which was something between terror and stupefaction. A curious clamour, as from some vast beehive, arose from the Exchange in New York, and crowds, aware that something strange and terrible was happening within, gathered round it and around the branch offices of brokerage houses throughout the country. Special police were despatched to keep order in Wall Street. By midday stocks were selling for nothing, the exchanges were closed in Buffalo and Chicago; eleven well-known speculators had committed suicide. At 12.30 the visitors' gallery of the New York Stock Exchange was cleared; among the spectators of the frenzied scenes on the floor was Mr Winston Churchill.

For a few hours on that day a mood of fear and consternation reigned in all the financial centres of the United States, in the stock exchanges, in brokerage houses, as if, suddenly and unbelievably, a bottomless pit had opened before men's eyes. Most men simply could not understand, or believe, what was happening to them;

[48]

their faces, said an observer, showed 'not so much suffering as a sort of horrified incredulity'.

In New York at least action was quickly taken to bring the panic under control. At 12 o'clock a meeting took place at the offices of J.P.Morgan and Co. at 23 Wall Street, which was attended by Thomas W. Lamont, senior partner of Morgan's, Albert H. Wiggin, chairman of the Chase National Bank, Charles E. Mitchell, chairman of the Board of the National City Bank, William C. Potter, President of the Guaranty Trust Company, and Sewell Prosser, Chairman of the Bankers' Trust Company. Merely the news of the meeting was enough to alleviate the panic. To the speculator it meant that the most powerful financiers in the United States, controlling between them almost unlimited resources, had decided to 'organize support' for the market and for the moment this was sufficient to restore his nerve. The belief that, in the last resort, 'organized support' of a falling market would always be available was a popular and widespread one, and was based on assumptions in which cynicism and piety were curiously mixed. It was thought that the bankers, as trustees of the financial soundness of the United States, would never permit a collapse in share values, and that they were themselves too heavily involved to be able to afford one. It was also thought that their funds were amply adequate to arrest any decline, however steep, and that the investment trusts in particular had ample cash available which they would be only too glad to employ in picking up bargains which would inevitably recover their value.

On this occasion, popular belief was justified. The meeting at Morgan's quickly resolved to support the market and formed a pool to be devoted to this purpose. The size of the pool has never been revealed, and estimates of it have varied from $240 million down to $30 million. But the size of the pool was not important; what was important was the news that the high priests of finance, with all their mysterious prestige and authority, their expertise and their untold wealth, intended to intervene on the scene of panic. Lamont announced to the press that 'there had been a little distress selling on the Stock Exchange', and that this had been due to 'a technical condition of the market' and indicated that the bankers had decided to take matters in hand. This was enough; panic selling ceased and prices began to rise. Visible and dramatic

[49]

evidence of the bankers' decision was provided at 1.30, when Richard Whitney, acting president of the Stock Exchange, a floor trader for Morgan and brother of a Morgan partner, appeared on the floor and, moving from stand to stand, placed orders for fifteen or twenty well-known stocks in blocks of ten thousand shares. Action had been added to words and the market responded; though selling orders continued to pour in from all over the country, prices so far recovered that, by the close of the day's trading, the *Times* industrial index was only twelve points down; some stocks, like U.S. Steel, which had been an object of Whitney's operations, and J.I.Case, a favourite speculative share, even made small gains during the day.

Yet in spite of the market's recovery, thousands of 'investors' or speculators were ruined or sold out in the course of the day. Initially, the catastrophic fall in prices had been concentrated, after a quiet opening, into the morning hours on the New York Stock Exchange: by 11.30, with Whitney's operations on behalf of the bankers' pool, it was over in New York. But the fall was so precipitous that once again the ticker tape fell behind the market and did not catch up with it until eight minutes past seven that night; throughout the United States men watched the almost incredible figures flickering across the board knowing that, calamitous as they were, they might not as yet have spelled out the worst. Fear and uncertainty were magnified by rumour; by 11.30 utter panic had set in. In Buffalo and Cleveland the stock exchanges were closed.

Panic drove many investors to sell; others were sold out by their brokers when they failed to respond to margin calls, and such forced sales contributed to increase the panic. Selling orders continued to pour in throughout the day, despite the bankers' intervention. The technical means of communication were inadequate to deal with a panic of such proportions, and this in itself contributed to the ruin of many investors. On the other hand, those who were able to follow the operations of the pool were in a position to end the day with a profit. U.S. Steel, the stock chosen by Whitney as the starting point of his operations, opened in the morning at $205\frac{1}{2}$, fell to $193\frac{1}{2}$ by the time Whitney began to buy, and ended the day with a gain of two points.

It is probable that the greatest losses during Black Thursday were incurred by small investors, handicapped both by inadequate resources to cover their margin losses, and by inadequate means of keeping in touch with the dramatically changing course of events in the market. Financial experts, indeed, took an almost moral pleasure in this 'shaking out' of the small investor and confidently predicted that this would provoke a renewal of the boom on a purer, saner, sounder basis. Evidence for this view was found in the effect of the bankers' intervention; on Black Thursday, they had shown both their strength and their wisdom and for the moment their reputation for both appeared to be vindicated. But not for long. When, in the following week, the market suffered even heavier blows, and when, this time, there was no organized support from the bankers, it began to be rumoured that they had not only profited by Black Thursday but had actually provoked it by a gigantic bear operation against market values.

Black Thursday saw the ruin of many paper millionaires, the destruction of many hopes, the dissipation of many dreams. But among the greatest losers were also, in the long run, the bankers; it saw the beginning of the decline in their reputation for wisdom and integrity and of the fall of the banker from his position as one of the mythical American heroes.

For many investors, Black Thursday was a personal intimation that for them the American Dream was over. They were the first victims of the disaster which would spread to the whole nation. But the general reaction was that, the worst having happened, it was now over; the morning of Black Thursday was so bad that it could not possibly happen again. And now once again the chorus of reassurances broke out, that the market was 'fundamentally sound', was 'laying the foundation for the constructive advance which we believe will characterize 1930', that the trouble of Black Thursday was 'purely technical', that 'there is nothing in the business situation to justify any nervousness'. Again the market seemed to correspond; on the two days following Black Thursday, trading was heavy but prices were steady, with a small gain on Friday and a small loss on Saturday, which meant that though many wanted to sell there were also others who were willing to buy. President Hoover announced that 'the fundamental business of the country, that is, production and distribution of commodities, is on a sound and prosperous basis', but he would not go any further and refused a request by the bankers' consortium that he should give some

THE GREAT SLUMP

direct encouragement to the share market. From Poughkeepsie, Governor Roosevelt denounced the 'fever of speculation' that had led to Black Thursday.

Whom did people believe? The weekend of 26–7 October provides fascinating, but baffling, evidence for anyone interested in mass movements of public opinion. To judge by the public evidence available, nearly everyone was agreed that the severe 'shakeout of the lunatic fringe' which the market had suffered in the past week was a good thing (except perhaps for the lunatics); that now the market, confident in the support of the bankers, would stage a recovery and go on to new triumphs; that stocks being at the moment relatively cheap would invite eager and heavy buying when the market opened on Monday. Brokerage houses reported an immense volume of buying orders waiting to be executed. No doubt much of this optimism was wish-fulfilment and much of the comment was inspired; the bankers, flushed by the success of their saving operation on Thursday, were busy organizing vocal support which would prevent their having to repeat it on Monday. Yet the point is that these were the voices which the speculator and investor had listened to for years and whose advice he had consistently taken; why should he reject it now?

In fact he did. Over the weekend investors and speculators throughout the country reached, by methods and for reasons we have no means of ascertaining, a common decision which contradicted all the advice offered to him by sources which he normally respected, and this decision found a spectacular expression on Monday. No doubt during those two days the investor engaged in all the normal activities, pleasures and amusements of an American during the last weekend of the Jazz Age. Like everyone else he drank his bootleg liquor, listened to the radio, read bestsellers like *All Quiet on the Western Front*, and took his family out for a picnic in one of the three and a half million new cars that were on the road; but, against all the advice of those who had any business to know, he also decided that tomorrow was the time to get out.

He was lucky if he did so without disaster. When the market opened on Monday, 28 October, there was an immense and irresistible rush to sell. The volume of trading, though not as large as on Black Thursday, was still enormous; $9\frac{1}{4}$ million shares. But the loss in share values was even greater; Steel down $17\frac{1}{2}$ points, General

[52]

Electric 47½, Westinghouse 34½, and the *Times* industrial index by
49. The prices at which Richard Whitney had rallied the market on
Thursday were quickly left far behind, and in contrast with
Thursday there was no recovery as the long day wore on; in the
last hour three million shares changed hands at prices which were
falling so rapidly that in some stocks 'air spots' developed; that is to
say, they were offered for sale but no bids were available at any price.

Monday differed from Thursday in other respects also. There
had been bad days on the New York Stock Exchange before, but
they had nearly always ended with a recovery. In the two days
following Black Thursday, many investors had been tempted back
into the market in order to buy at what appeared to be bargain
prices, while the bankers' pool had disposed of many of Thursday's
purchases at a profit. Monday's collapse, following on Thursday's,
seemed to indicate that something abnormal and unprecedented
was happening, so that past experience no longer offered any guide
and no one could say what the morning would bring. The abyss
that had opened for a few hours on Thursday, before it was closed
by the bankers' pool, now gaped open again and it was not clear
how, this time, it was to be closed.

For on Monday it became clear that the bankers would not, or
could not, repeat their rescue operation; far from rescuing others,
some of them were by now in need of rescue themselves. There
were, it is true, rumours that 'organized support' was again on its
way. When, at ten minutes past one, Charles E. Mitchell was seen
entering Morgan's offices, there was a momentary rally and Steel
recovered from 194 to 198. The effect would have been different if
it had been known that, far from organizing general support for the
market, Mitchell was almost certainly seeking a personal loan from
Morgan's in order to extricate himself from his difficulties, which
had become pressing.

The bankers did indeed meet at Morgan's, from 4.30 to 6.30, but
only to announce afterwards that they were not committed to supporting any particular level of share prices but only to maintaining
an orderly market. In fact, their brokers were not able to do more
than stop up the 'air holes' which were appearing in some stocks.
Even so, there were still optimists who retained some faith in the
power of the banks, who spoke hopefully of the organized support
that would appear in the morning.

That night, the market resembled some battlefield on which the staff of a defeated army tries desperately and hopelessly to reorganize its demoralized forces. The weekend had hardly allowed the brokers time to clear up the unfinished business left behind by the huge volume of trading on Thursday; now, writes F.L.Allen:

once more the ticker fell ridiculously far behind, the lights in the brokers' offices and the banks burned till dawn, and the telegraph offices distributed thousands of margin calls and demands for more collateral to back up loans at the banks. Bankers, brokers, clerks, messengers were almost at the end of their strength; for days and nights they had been driving themselves to keep pace with the most terrific volume of business that had ever descended on them. It did not seem as if they could keep it up much longer.

Worst of all, no one could say what the morning would bring.

The question was soon answered, in a manner which exceeded the blackest expectations. Tuesday, 29 October, was even worse than Monday; it was, says Professor Galbraith, 'the most devastating day in the history of the New York stock market and it may have been the most devastating day in the history of markets'. Nothing like it had ever been seen before and possibly never will be seen again. As soon as the exchange opened, it was inundated with orders to sell. Three million shares were sold in the first half-hour; by two o'clock, eight million; by the close, 16,410,030. It was catastrophic; moreover the fall in share values was almost as great as the day before and the *Times* industrial index fell by 43 points, equal to all the gains that had been made in the whole of the preceding year. Huge blocks of shares were thrown upon the market to sell for whatever they might fetch and even so there were no bidders; the air holes which had worried the bankers became great vents and fissures impossible to repair. A single example illustrates what happened to many stocks. In the course of the Bull Market, the stock of the White Sewing Machine Company had stood as high as 48. On Monday, 28 October, it fell to $11\frac{1}{8}$. On the Tuesday, someone – it is said, a clever messenger boy – put in an order to buy at 1, and there being no other bidders bought the stock for a dollar a share.

Selling orders came in such huge volume that it was impossible to handle them; some were simply overlooked or forgotten, and found unexecuted at the end of the terrible day. By midday the market was so utterly demoralized that the governing committee of the Stock Exchange, meeting by stealth so as not to provoke rumours, considered whether to close the exchange, but decided against it. So the selling continued; Blue Ridge which had been launched so successfully at 24 in September, and had fallen to 12 on 24 October, finished on this day at 3. And now there was not even the hope of support from the bankers' consortium; rather, the horrid rumour began to circulate that they were selling short; at the end of the day Lamont had to deny that the bankers had been conducting a bear raid on the market. The 29th October may be thought of as the day when the bankers of the United States first lost that mysterious aura of power, prestige and integrity which had previously clothed them and which they, or at least some of them, had grossly exploited in giving their blessing to the Bull Market.

Yet in fact the New York bankers, if they could not stem the panic, did their best to mitigate some of its worst consequences. Between 26 and 29 October brokers' loans to clients had fallen by over a billion dollars as marginal accounts were liquidated. In spite of this, in the course of the 29th corporations and large institutions which had been glad to lend their money in the market at up to 12 per cent called in over two billions as the news from New York came in, leaving the banks through whom the money had been lent with no alternative between taking over the loans themselves, or ruining their clients. Many of the banks accepted the risk and increased their own loans by a billion; otherwise, a financial panic would have been added to the stock exchange panic. There is a story of one banker who authorized loan after loan until a white-faced subordinate informed him that the bank was insolvent; 'I dare say,' he said, and continued to lend. There were in fact no important stock exchange failures as a result of the crash, though one firm declared itself bankrupt as a result of a clerical error by an employee who had collapsed under the strain. Indeed, such errors became distressingly common as a result of the unmanageable volume of business and the strain of nights and days of continuous work.

Yet at the end of the worst day that the New York Stock Exchange, or possibly any stock exchange, had ever known the market rallied. Steel, bought by Whitney the previous Thursday at

205, had fallen to 167 in the course of Tuesday, 29 October, but rose to 174 at the close. Westinghouse opened at 131, dropped to 100, and closed at 126. When the governing committee of the exchange met in the evening, this late rally decided them to open again the next morning, even though there was a strong feeling that it might be better to close, not least because everyone concerned in its operations was physically exhausted and in need of sleep. On the morning of the 30th it seemed, miraculously, as if the decision was justified. U.S. Steel and American Can had declared additional dividends. Mr Hoover's Assistant Secretary of Commerce repeated the president's magic incantation that the business of the country was fundamentally sound. John J. Raskob announced that he and his friends were buying, since stocks were now at bargain prices. Most effective of all, perhaps, one of the genuine patriarchs of aggressive capitalism, John D. Rockefeller, declared, in almost Old Testament terms, 'Believing that the fundamental conditions of the country are sound and that there is nothing in the business situation to warrant the destruction of values that has taken place on the exchanges during the past week, my son and I have for some days been purchasing sound common stocks.' If they had, nobody had noticed; but whether or not as the result of such pronouncements, Tuesday's late night rally continued, and this flicker of renewed confidence allowed Richard Whitney to announce that the exchange would not open until midday on Thursday, and would be closed on Friday and Saturday.

His announcement was greeted with cheers. It came as a relief to overstrained nerves, and there was no renewal of the panic which had struck the market. During Thursday's short session, trading was active and busy; seven million shares changed hands and the *Times* industrial index gained 21 points. There were other reasons for encouragement. The rediscount rate was reduced from 6 to 5 per cent. The Federal Reserve Bank undertook active open market operations. Margin requirements were cut to 25 per cent. Brokers' loans, the best thermometer of the intensity of speculative fever, had fallen by over a billion dollars in the past week.

Relaxation of credit provoked the hope that, after its terrible experience, the market might resume its upward movement, but purged, purified and restored to sanity, with its 'lunatic fringe' shaken off, and stocks selling, as *Barron's* said, 'ex-hopes and

[56]

romance'. While the exchange remained closed, business news was good. The automobile industry declared its confidence in the future, and Ford announced a general cut in prices as 'the best contribution that could be made to assure a continuation of good business'. The one item of bad news was the failure of Foshay of Minneapolis, a twenty million dollar company owning utilities in twelve states and four countries. It might be said that Foshays in Minneapolis and the Boden Creditanstalt in Vienna were the first, almost premature victims of the depression.

But despite the generally encouraging atmosphere, at the week-end the investor, speculator, gambler in the market, again took the decision to sell; no one quite knows why. On Monday, 2 November, the market took another great dip downwards. Six million shares were traded and the *Times* industrial index lost 21 points. On Tuesday, the exchange was happily closed for the elections, in which Jimmy Walker, the Democratic mayor of New York, and himself one of the characteristic figures of the age of the Great Bull Market, triumphantly defeated his Republican opponent, the 'Little Flower', Fiorella La Guardia. On Wednesday, as on the following two days, the exchange was only open for three hours, and there was another steep fall; six million shares were traded, and the *Times* index fell another 37 points.

There was now a sickening feeling that it was impossible to know how long the fall would continue or where it would end. November brought no relief, and on the 11th, 12th and 13th there was a further heavy decline, in which the *Times* industrial index fell by another 50 points. And by now there was no good news from anywhere to lighten the darkness of the stock exchange. Steel production was down, car loading figures were down, and the stock exchange collapse seemed to have infected commodity markets; cotton fell heavily, and there was panic selling in the wheat market. Even so, there were still some bankers who felt they had the power to halt the collapse. Barney Baruch, happy at having sold everything by the end of September, was approached by Thomas Lamont with an invitation to join a pool which the House of Morgan was forming to stabilize the market. He declined. 'The day was past when the House of Morgan could rally Wall Street in such a crisis.'

On 13 November the market reached what, for the moment,

seemed to be the bottom. Since September average share values had declined by nearly a third, representing a loss, on paper, of twenty-six billion dollars. The following table shows the losses incurred by some leading stocks between 3 September, when the market was at its highest, and 13 November.

Stocks	3 September	13 November
American Can	181⅞	86
American Telephone & Telegraph	304	197¼
Anaconda Copper	131½	70
General Electric	396¼	168⅛
General Motors	72½	36
Montgomery Ward	137⅞	49¼
New York Central	256⅜	160
Radio	101	28
United Carbide and Carbon	137⅞	59
United States Steel	261¾	150
Westinghouse E. & M.	289⅞	102⅝
Woolworth	100⅜	52¼
Electric Bond & Share	186¾	50¼

In the same period, the *Times* average for fifty leading stocks had fallen from 311·90 to 164·43, and its industrial index from 469 to 220·95. The Great Bull Market was, at last, stone dead, and no efforts could revivify the corpse. All that remained to do was to count the cost.

It was, however, not only the Bull Market that was dead, though at first people were slow to realize it. Barney Baruch, for all his shrewdness, confesses: 'I never imagined, in these last months of 1929, that the collapse of stock prices was the prelude to the great depression. Anyone who knew the potentialities of the American economic system, as I had come to know them, could not help but believe that the market break would just as inevitably be followed by an even greater prosperity.' The present writer, in 1929 an undergraduate at Oxford, enjoying the last golden glow of the twenties and fascinated by the sensational press accounts of the scenes of ruin and desolation on Wall Street, questioned his economics tutor about the significance of the Wall Street crash. He was assured that it was a purely stock exchange phenomenon, with no wider significance, and with no relevance to the fundamental economic forces making for continued prosperity and progress. On the whole, there were few reputable economists who would have disagreed with such a judgement at that date.

Of course there were some, not economists, who would have taken a less cheerful view, and for whom the Wall Street crash meant the end not only of all their hopes but of life itself. There was the commission agent who, on Thursday, 24 October, was fished out of the Hudson River with $9·40 in small change in his pockets, together with some margin calls.* There were the two speculators who, sharing a joint account, also shared their death by jumping hand in hand from a window in the Ritz. More typical, perhaps, if less spectacular, was the acquaintance of Baruch's, head of a distinguished firm of brokers in government bonds, well known for his large charities, whom he was used to see, in shining top hat and morning coat, walking up the steps of Morgan's, with whom he did a large business. After the crash, he came to Baruch to borrow a few hundred dollars, and later to borrow successively smaller amounts, always professing that life still held a future for him; 'By this time there was not the slightest resemblance between the broken man in my office and the banker in shining top hat who had once given large sums of money to charity.'

Such personal tragedies, and sudden transformations from wealth to poverty, were numerous. In the early stages of the crash it was primarily the small investor and speculator, with no other resources than the stock he had bought on margin, who was cleaned out; hence the initial expectation that the banks, finance houses and investment trusts, with large untapped resources, would sooner or later come to the support of the market. But in the second week of the collapse, the huge blocks of stock that were offered for sale showed that large speculators and institutional investors had also lost confidence or were being forced to sell; on the terrible day of 29 October, Albert H. Wiggin of the Chase National Bank, was several millions short of his liabilities. And the supposedly vast cash resources of the investment trusts proved quite inadequate at

* As shares fell in value, brokers called on clients to make good in cash the losses incurred on stocks bought on margin. In most cases, by definition the cash was not available.

providing support for the market; indeed, they were not even sufficient for the task of supporting their own stock, to which they were largely applied. For as the market fell, the peculiar structure of the trusts, and the principle of 'high leverage' which had been considered the golden key to fortune, worked relentlessly in reverse. 'Leverage' had concentrated all the profits of the boom on the common stock of the trusts, as opposed to their bonds and preferred stock; the losses also were concentrated on the common stock, which became in some cases literally worthless.

Moreover, the investments held by the trusts as cover for their own securities were very largely in the form of each other's common stock; they formed a closed circle in which each invested in the others, and as the market fell, this close interlocking operated like a machine marvellously designed for self-destruction. Far from being able to use their cash resources, which were largely lent on the call market, for general support of the market, they had to call them in and apply them in a vain effort to support their own stock. Moreover, as their own stock became worthless, they ceased to have any value as collateral against margin calls, and thus pressure was increased to sell sound securities, like Steel, or General Motors. The investment trusts, the last and brightest creation of the Bull Market, were also among the first and most spectacular victims of its collapse, and in their ruin contributed significantly to the general disorganization of the market.

There were also other victims of the crash, whose losses could not be estimated in purely financial terms. Chief among them, perhaps, should be counted the bankers, who almost overnight lost their reputation, not merely for prudence and sagacity, but even for honesty; a popular music-hall joke of the depression was: 'Don't tell my mother I'm a banker, she thinks I play the piano in a brothel.' Nothing could better illustrate this fall in popular esteem than the change from the hope and confidence with which the market, on 24 October, greeted the news that the bankers were coming to its support, to the ugly rumours which swept the exchange in the first week of November that the bankers were selling short in a deliberately executed bear raid on the market.

Later investigations were to show that this loss of reputation was not, in particular cases, unjustified. When, in March 1933, Charles E. Mitchell was arrested for evasion of income tax, it was shown that in 1929 he had speculated heavily in the stock of his own bank, the National City Bank, and, in the week of 28 October, had arranged to borrow twelve million dollars from J.P.Morgan in order to support its shares on the falling market. He had, incidentally, in order to avoid tax and establish a tax loss, sold to his wife the stock which had been pledged to Morgan's as collateral for his loan. Albert H. Wiggin, of the Chase National Bank, had used a private company of his own, Sherman Corporation, in order to operate a huge pool in the common stock of Sinclair Consolidated Oil Company, together with Harry F. Sinclair and Alfred W. Cutten, both notorious speculators; as head of Chase National, he had lent another of his companies, Murlyn Corporation, $6,558,430, in order to finance a brilliant bear *coup* against the bank's common stock; it yielded a profit of $4,008,538.

With two of America's greatest banking institutions in the hands of men like Mitchell and Wiggin, it is not surprising that bankers as a class should have fallen into contempt; when their practices came under investigation, and they themselves were called in to explain and justify them, it was not so much the deviousness of their conduct that was startling, as a kind of naïve and innocent unawareness that there was anything reprehensible in it, as if they did not quite understand what they were doing. Wiggin defended the making of a loan by a bank to its own officers in order to gamble in its own shares, on the grounds that it gave them a personal interest in the bank's fortunes; in his own case this had expressed itself in selling its stock short.

In this attitude, in which irresponsibility and a kind of moral anarchism and obliviousness to the social consequences of their actions were all combined, the bankers were neither better nor worse than most of their fellow countrymen; they were more like juvenile delinquents than criminals, and sometimes, as in the case of the investment trusts, their intricate and elaborate financial manœuvres seemed no more than devices for swindling themselves. In a sense, the fall of the bankers, in the public eye, from an irreproachable and immaculate respectability to a position in which they could be denounced as the money changers who must be swept out of the temple was symbolic of a change that had taken place throughout American society during the post-war economic boom. Their behaviour was symptomatic of an attempt to exploit and enjoy the vast wealth and power commanded by the United States on principles derived from the primitive individualism of a frontier society. For the Great Bull Market, and the subsequent crash were not matters which affected only those who were directly engaged in speculation; they had become, in Professor Galbraith's words, central to the whole American culture, and displayed its characteristics in their most extreme form. One of the most difficult lessons which the United States had to learn in the dreary years which lay ahead was how to acquire new patterns of behaviour and new ways of thought which were better adapted to the affairs of what had become the most powerful state in the world.

In a short, nostalgic essay, *Memories of the Jazz Age*, Scott Fitzgerald noted how the kind of innocence, the dreams of infinite possibilities, which he associated with the early twenties, degenerated in himself and his contemporaries, as the Bull Market developed, into something sinister and evil; how the sudden access of wealth and power also brought a feeling of release from all restraint, as if money dispensed one from the normal obligations of social life; how this expressed itself in a growth of violence, so that sudden death, murder, suicide, beatings-up became a frequent occurrence even in the circle of his friends; how the years of the Bull Market were also the years of the rise and rule of the gangster, and the bootleg liquor on which he flourished, so that great cities like Chicago, the heart of a huge industrial empire, could become his undisputed private domain. 1929, which saw the end of the Bull Market, also saw the arrest and conviction of Al Capone for evasion of income tax, and when he emerged from prison a year later it was to find a world in which everything had changed, including the economic basis of gangsterism.

CHAPTER FOUR

Whistling in
the Dark

Even today, with all the advantages of hindsight and increased knowledge, we do not understand to what extent the Wall Street crash was responsible for the great economic depression which followed it. But there seems little doubt that it intensified tendencies which were already at work, and by putting an end, for the time being, to Stock Exchange profits it contributed to that contraction of effective demand which was one of the most striking features of the depression.* Professor Galbraith has pointed out that the loss of speculative profits had a peculiarly widespread effect because of the unequal distribution of incomes in the United States. In 1929 the rich, that is to say, five per cent of the population, received approximately one-third of all personal incomes, and the economy was heavily dependent on their expenditure, both on personal consumption and on investment. It was this class which was most heavily hit by the crash and their reaction to it had a correspondingly heavy effect, and reverberated throughout the economy.

To this must be added the psychological, one might almost say the symbolic effect of the crash. The Great Bull Market reflected a general condition of economic euphoria, which affected even those who were not personally interested in the Stock Exchange. It seems probable for instance that many businessmen had greatly increased their inventories in expectation of a continued expansion of the economy. The catastrophic collapse of the stock market was a shattering blow to such hopes, and since businessmen act on expectations rather than verifiable facts, the sudden deflation of

* Loss of profits reduced expenditures both on personal consumption and on investments.

[63]

the American Dream had an effect on even the hardest-headed of them.

Even so, men did not draw from the crash the right conclusions, which might have helped to prevent some of the worst features of the depression. For the crash pointed to certain weaknesses in the economic structure of the United States, which were even more sharply exposed in the years to come. There were, for instance, the dangers implicit in a banking system composed of separate and independent local units, each too weak to withstand financial pressure on its own, and yet each fatally communicating its weakness to its neighbours. The banking system of the United States was a relic of pioneering days; its instability increased as one approached the limits of the old frontier. It is significant that, with one small exception, there were no failures of the brokerage houses which were at the very centre of the hurricane on Wall Street; on the other hand, there were over 350 bank failures, while the behaviour of two of America's greatest banks, the Chase and the National City, amounted to criminal folly. Unfortunately, nothing was done to correct these weaknesses until they revealed themselves on an even greater scale during the national banking crisis of 1932–3.

There were also the dangers entailed by the development of holding companies, like the investment trusts, standing at the apex of an infinitely complicated pyramid of subsidiaries and specifically designed to milk them of their profits. The failure of the investment trusts was one of the most spectacular features of the crash; but the pattern of their failure was to be repeated later in an even more spectacular form by the giant holding companies organized in the field of public utilities by speculators like Samuel Insull or Howard C. Hopson. Hopson's own comment on Black Thursday, that it was 'undoubtedly beneficial to the business interests of the country to have the gambling type of speculator eliminated', has the Podsnap touch which characterized so many pronouncements by the financial establishment after that dreadful day.

But these were shadows whose warnings were not heeded. At the end of 1929 there were few to take them to heart and very few indeed among those with the power to influence events; hope, not warnings, was what was desired. This was forthcoming; indeed, reassurance came even before the market finally hit bottom. 'There are present today *none* of the underlying factors which have been associated or have preceded the decline in business in the past,' said Mr Robert P. Lamont, Hoover's successor as Secretary of Commerce. 'Things are better today than they ever were,' said Henry Ford on 4 November. Indeed, there were some who, like President Hoover himself, with his in-built hostility to the Stock Exchange, almost welcomed the crash, as a return to financial sanity which would allow American industry to resume its forward march. Economists were not behind businessmen. The Harvard Economic Society, formed by a distinguished group of professors of economics to assist businessmen in forecasting the future, described the crash as a temporary phenomenon which would rapidly be made good by a recovery of share values to even greater heights.

The President took the appropriate action to counteract a recession, for there was no reason to think that it was any more. He cut taxes, and encouraged industry and state governments to continue with plans for capital investment, offered aid to agriculture through the Federal Farm Board, and urged the Federal Reserve Board to offer abundant credit. In the meantime, in the months after the crash, Congress debated, and passed, the Hawley-Smoot tariff which increased protection to American industry by 33⅓ per cent. The president also arranged a series of meetings with industrialists, trade union leaders, and representatives of the farmers to discuss the economic condition of the country; their conclusions were uniformly optimistic.

Indeed, for a short time after the crash it seemed as if optimism would be justified. The stock market made a recovery which continued until the end of May before it lost its impetus; the index of share prices rose to 180 as compared with 220 before the crash. To explain the recovery, one must assume that there were still those who trusted official reassurances, who believed that men like Henry Ford, Owen D. Young, Pierre du Pont and Andrew Mellon were both telling the truth and knew what they were talking about, and who could not believe that the great days of the Bull Market were over for ever. It was still their opinion that the state of the economy was, as the President liked to say, 'fundamentally sound'. There were even some who thought that the market was being artificially held back by deliberately organized bear operations. A notorious speculator, J.W.Livermore, had to issue a statement that in his modest dealings on the Stock Exchange he operated only as an individual, and nothing more.

It is difficult to know whether the President, his advisers, the industrialists, the bankers, really believed what they were saying and retained their faith in the recuperative powers of American industry, or whether they were simply conducting a public relations campaign. In any case, the stock market recovery of the spring of 1930 was precarious and short-lived. In the summer of 1930 the index of share prices fell to 100, its lowest since 1926, and thereafter reached even lower depths; by 1933, it reached 40. But by that time the stock market had lost the significant place in American life it had once occupied; for three years Americans had had more serious, even tragic, things to think about.

The hopes that were entertained by the President, his advisers, and the financial establishment that the collapse of share values would prove only a momentary and superficial setback to American prosperity seem all the stranger today because evidence of a serious fall in industrial activity had been accumulating since the summer of 1929. By June of that year American industrial production had reached its peak; it would not reach the same level again until 1939. But during the summer all the signs of coming depression began to manifest themselves. Production of steel, automobiles, freight-car loadings were all down. Building contracts had fallen by a billion dollars since 1928. Inventories had grown from $500 million to $18,000 million; there was a decline in consumer spending. Judged by such standards, rather than the dreams which inspired the speculation in Wall Street, the future was not promising; it was even less so because agriculture, which for many years had formed the weakest sector of the otherwise booming American economy, was now severely affected by the catastrophic fall which had taken place in world commodity prices.

The boom which had spread from the United States to Europe and the rest of the world from 1926 onwards was essentially an industrial boom. Agriculture remained a depressed occupation, a major source of weakness in the world economy and of the failure of effective demand which was one of the main causes of the depression. The insatiable demands of the belligerent countries for food and raw materials during the war had engendered a vast expansion of agriculture throughout the world, and the application of modern science and technology had increased agricultural productivity and reduced costs to an unprecedented degree; the combine-harvester and the tractor, the improvement in and increased use of fertilizers and insecticides, the breeding of new strains of wheat and other crops, all contributed to an immense increase in world agricultural production. From 1926 onwards the prices of agricultural products had been falling continuously if not disastrously; in the summer of 1929, as the industrial boom reached and passed its peak, they underwent a sickening and catastrophic fall.

The fall in commodity prices, which continued throughout the depression, produced some of its most calamitous features, reducing entire communities and entire nations to near subsistence level. It was responsible for that spectacle of poverty in the midst of plenty, of crops being burned and destroyed while entire populations went hungry, which struck the imagination of thinking and feeling men and women, and suggested to many that there was something at the very heart of the capitalist system which was both cruel and absurd. It was also a universal phenomenon, which emphasized more than any other the worldwide nature of the depression, and the intimate economic connections which bound up each country with every other; evicted farmers in the Middle West of America were victims of the same processes which made paupers of coffee-growers in Brazil, and the ruin of both contributed to the decline in industrial production. Governments however were slow to learn the right lessons from the universality of the depression. They responded to the fall in agricultural prices with tariffs, quotas and other restrictionist devices, and in so doing made even more intolerable the condition of those countries for whom agriculture provided their primary, sometimes their only, source of income.

By the beginning of 1930, the depression was already under way; however, no one at that time could have foreseen its intensity or duration, or the revolution it was destined to bring about in world affairs. But though the origins of the depression, as of the boom which preceded it, can be traced most clearly to the United States, and though the Wall Street crash provided the most spectacular evidence that times had changed, the first effects of the depression

[67]

were most evident elsewhere. In Germany, in particular, during the first six months of 1930, it brought about the end of parliamentary democracy and the introduction of a system of government by presidential decree which led directly, three years later, to the fall of the Weimar Republic.*

It lies outside the scope of this book to analyse the historical forces which were responsible for the fall of Weimar, and in particular the form which nationalism assumed in Germany and the very special features it derived both from the history and the national characteristics of the German people. But it seems safe to say that the explosive and destructive force it developed between 1929 and 1933 was the result of the intolerable strains imposed upon Weimar by the depression. It must be remembered that parliamentary democracy was a late and frail growth in Germany, and that Weimar from its birth onwards laboured under a vast burden of government indebtedness, which had only been made tolerable by the loans which Germany had been able to raise abroad. The impact of the depression on this already highly precarious structure was almost from the first a fatal one, and unleashed forces which were to prove uncontrollable.

It is significant that the end of the parliamentary regime in Germany, as opposed to the presidential one which followed it, arose directly out of the onset of the depression. Since June 1928, the government, headed by the moderate Social Democrat, Hermann Müller, had been based on a Grand Coalition, ranging from the Social Democrats on the left to the Democratic Party on the right. Its great achievement had been to give the dying Stresemann the chance, in the face of increasingly violent Nationalist opposition, to carry his foreign policy through to a successful conclusion. The collapse of the Grand Coalition, the last stable democratic government which Germany enjoyed, and the appointment of Heinrich Brüning as Chancellor, were directly due to the government's failure to find a parliamentary majority for the financial measures made necessary by the large growth in unemployment during the winter of 1929–30.

---

* Under Brüning Germany was governed by emergency decrees issued by the President, without the assent of the Reichstag, under Paragraph 3, Article 48, of the Weimar Constitution.

Despite Germany's economic recovery after 1926, unemployment remained heavy throughout the twenties, by the standards both of pre-First World War and of post-Second World War. It never sank appreciably below the figure of one and a half million; by the end of 1929 it had reached 2,851,000, and in the course of 1930 was to increase by another one and a half million. The figures for workers receiving unemployment relief were rather different. In December 1929 they were over 1,500,000; during January 1930 they increased by nearly a million. Financial measures before the Reichstag for the reform of unemployment relief had been based on an optimistic estimate of 1,200,000 in receipt of relief; the large and sudden increase in unemployment in the winter of 1929–30 made this hopelessly unrealistic, but even so it involved a deficit in the unemployment insurance fund of 321 million marks, which would have to be covered either by reduced benefits, or by increased contributions, or by a government subsidy, or by a combination of all three.

It was typical of a kind of political irresponsibility which had become endemic in Germany that, while all the parties, short of the Communists, were agreed on the necessity for financial reform, none of them, including the Communists, were willing to assume the unpopularity of putting it into practice. The cessation of foreign and particularly American lending after the Wall Street crash left the government with little room for manœuvre in dealing with the problem; its credit was exhausted, and in terms of orthodox finance there was no alternative to measures which would bear most hardly on the unemployed themselves. The Social Democrat Minister of Finance, Dr Rudolf Hilferding, was no revolutionary; he was as orthodox in his views as a Hoover or a Snowden, but he was flexible and ingenious, and made repeated attempts to find some way of alleviating the financial embarrassment of the Reich government. As early as May 1929, he had floated a 500 million mark bond issue, at 7 per cent, and on extremely favourable terms, which included exemption from income, property and inheritance tax. The issue was a resounding failure, producing only 170 million marks, a striking proof of how far confidence had already been shaken in Germany.

Later in the year, Hilferding's State Secretary at the Ministry of Finance entered into negotiations with the American banking house of Dillon, Read & Co. for short-term credits which would cover the government's needs until some permanent arrangement could be reached; initially the Americans responded favourably but the negotiations broke down under pressure from the aggressively nationalist President of the Reichsbank, Dr Hjalmar Schacht. In March 1930, in order to cover the government's current expenditure, Hilferding accepted a loan of 500 million marks from the already bankrupt colossus of contemporary finance, Ivar Kreuger, in return for granting the Swedish Match Trust a monopoly in Germany.

None of these expedients were sufficient to save Hilferding, who was exposed not merely to the difficulties created by the unemployment problem but to the relentless animosity to himself and the Coalition of the President of the Reichsbank, Dr Schacht. Hilferding's object was to solve the problem of unemployment within the framework of the existing parliamentary system. It was probably a hopeless task, more especially because the enemies of the Republic on the right wished to exploit the same problems in order to wreck the system. Of these enemies, probably the most effective at the beginning of 1930, both because of his position and of his personality, was the Governor of the Reichsbank.

Dr Schacht was one of the most remarkable figures in the world of international finance between the wars. In 1923, as Commissioner for National Currency, he had been largely responsible for bringing the run-away inflation of the mark to an end by successfully introducing the Rentenmark, a new currency backed, not by gold, but by a mortgage on the whole of German landed property. As a banker, he was capable of great technical virtuosity; politically, he was a fanatical nationalist. He deeply impressed Montague Norman, the Governor of the Bank of England, as the man who could restore financial stability in Germany; others disliked his overbearing personal vanity and a certain slyness and deviousness in his dealings. In some respects Schacht typified the worst vices of the German nationalists in the post-war period; to the task of restoring the old Prussian virtues of economy, probity and loyalty they were willing to apply every variety of bad faith. It is a curious fact that this conservative central banker was prepared, in pursuing his political aims, to adopt financial measures which, judged by the orthodoxies of the day, were revolutionary. General Groener wrote, 'Hilferding is a truly decent fellow, a great financial expert, stuffy but not particularly ambitious. His bitter opponent was Schacht, a man of consuming ambition and deceptive manners.'

Throughout 1929, Schacht used every means in his power to thwart the policies of the Reich government, both by the support he gave to Hugenberg's and Hitler's campaign against the Young Plan, and by restricting credits to the Ministry of Finance. When Popitz, State Secretary at the Ministry of Finance, approached Dillon, Read & Co. for a temporary loan, Schacht issued a statement denouncing the government for wastefulness and financial irresponsibility. The Americans, alarmed, inquired whether the Reichsbank had any objections to the proposed loan; Schacht replied in terms so violent that Popitz, who deeply resented Schacht's blackmailing of the government, resigned, and his resignation was followed by that of Hilferding himself, who was unwilling to allow responsibility for the failure of the loan to fall on his subordinate.

The government yielded to Schacht's demand that a sinking fund of 450,000,000 marks be established to cover its Budget deficits; the measure provoked intense dissatisfaction on the left as direct evidence of interference by the Reichsbank in government policy. Schacht then seized the opportunity to renew his campaign against the government which was offered by the opening of the second Hague Conference of January 1930 to give final approval to the Young Plan. Agreement proved difficult because of French alarm at the violence of the campaign against the plan in Germany. Briand had won thunderous applause in the French Chamber by comparing the death of Stresemann, whom the Hugenberg propaganda machine had attacked in the language of the gutter, with the murder of Erzberger and Rathenau by the German nationalists, and by crying: 'Does one have to die to prove that one desires peace?'

Schacht had refused to be a member of the German delegation to the conference. Nevertheless, he voluntarily appeared before the committee concerned with the establishment of the Bank of International Settlements to express the Reichsbank's refusal to participate in the Bank except on specific political conditions, including the final abolition of Allied sanctions against Germany in the event of failure to meet her reparations obligations. His intervention, which was in direct contravention of his promise to the government to maintain silence until the conference was over, very nearly wrecked the conference. The German government tried to solve the difficulty by substituting a consortium of German banks for the Reichsbank; it was finally overcome by forcing the Reichsbank by law to participate in the Bank of International Settlements. It was thought that Schacht would resign. For the moment he did not. He even seemed happy that the plan had been approved without his having to incur any responsibility. He finally resigned in May 1930, while the Reichstag was debating the Young Plan. Thereafter he pursued his plans by even more devious and sinister means.

Schacht's intrigues had been conducted in an atmosphere of steadily increasing financial difficulty for the Reich government. As unemployment rose, tax receipts fell, and made any fundamental reform of the unemployment insurance fund even more difficult. The Young Plan gave Germany an immediate saving on reparations payments of 700 million marks, but in January 1930, Hilferding's successor as Finance Minister, Moldenhauer, explained to the Reichstag that this would be entirely swallowed up by the Budget deficit for the fiscal year. Ready cash for current expenditure was only made available by accepting Kreuger's offer of a loan.

Under the strain of financial pressure, the Grand Coalition began to break up. In the Reichstag, Heinrich Brüning, the leader of the Catholic Centre Party, declared that he would only vote for The Hague agreements on the Young Plan if the government carried out a fundamental review of the Reich's finances. In March, Brüning sought an interview with President Hindenburg, in which he insisted on the urgent need for financial reform. The President agreed and promised that he would use 'all constitutional means' to this end. What this promise to Brüning meant was revealed in a sensational article in the Centre Party newspaper, *Germania*. To secure reform the President would 'assume whatever powers are appropriate and necessary ... The dissolution of the Reichstag, and Article 48, or both, are available if the parties fail.' Article 48 of the Constitution authorized the government, in case of emergency, to dispense with a parliamentary majority and govern by emergency decree.

On 12 March, the Reichstag voted on The Hague agreements and the President signed them, with 'a heavy but determined heart'. The government was now faced with the necessity of introducing the financial reforms required by Brüning and the Centre. The continued rise in unemployment made it certain that the insurance fund would incur increasingly heavy deficits which, unless they were covered by government subsidies, could only be met by reduced benefits or increased contributions or both. To one or other of these solutions the parties forming the Grand Coalition had strong objections; the majority Social Democratic Party, with the support of the Trade Unions, strongly opposed any reduction in benefits.

The last chance of reaching agreement was provided by a compromise put forward by Brüning which provided for a Reich subsidy to the fund, reduced benefits and increased contributions. It was almost unanimously rejected by a meeting of the Social Democratic delegation to the Reichstag. The government immediately resigned without appearing before the Reichstag. After two years in office, the Grand Coalition was at an end, and with it parliamentary democracy in Germany. Within a year, Hermann Müller himself was dead.

The Grand Coalition was the first political victim of the slump: Hermann Müller was the precursor of a long line of statesmen throughout the world who found themselves overwhelmed by what seemed an uncontrollable sequence of events. His fall, and the fall of his government, established a pattern which was to be repeated with uncanny regularity elsewhere.

No doubt there were features of the German situation which were lacking elsewhere and made it more unstable. In particular, there were the extremists both on the Nationalist right and on the Communist left whose fundamental object was to destroy the Weimar Republic; under the Grand Coalition they provided an opposition of 150 votes and were always ready to combine with any other party to overthrow the government. Hugenberg described the six million who voted against the Young Plan in the referendum as the embryo of a new, dynamic Germany. The impact of the slump in Germany was all the more violent because the country was fundamentally torn between those who wished to preserve the Republic and those who were determined to destroy it.

It may be that the forces of extremism in Germany would in any case have proved too strong in the end for any parliamentary regime. But in the struggle to contain them, the forces of moderation represented by the Grand Coalition were fatally enfeebled and paralysed by the rigid orthodoxy of their economic and financial views. It is significant that, in the crisis of 1930, the financial experts of all parties, except the Communists, were agreed on the imperative necessity of balancing the budget and making the unemployment insurance fund self-supporting; the only disagreement was about the ways and means by which this could be achieved and made politically acceptable. It occurred to none of them that, in such terms, there was literally no solution to Germany's financial problems; indeed, that the attempt to achieve one might only make matters worse. It is ironical that the only financial expert who would have been willing, given the power, to take unorthodox measures was the reactionary ex-president of the Reichsbank. Perhaps indeed in such matters the instincts of the ordinary German were a better guide than the rules of orthodox finance. Even the eccentricities of an autodidact like Gottfried Feder, economic adviser to the National Socialist Party, might come to seem preferable to deflationary policies so severe that, like Brüning's, they threatened to disrupt the German economy altogether.

The sum of the traditional economic wisdom available to statesmen faced with rapidly rising unemployment was that it was necessary to live within one's means and balance the budget. No one accepted these truths more unquestioningly and more wholeheartedly than Philip Snowden, Chancellor of the Exchequer in the British Labour Government; his reaction to the problem of mass unemployment in Britain was the same as Brüning's in Germany, and it proved equally unavailing. Snowden was obsessed by three fixed beliefs which he had absorbed from the textbooks out of which he had taught himself economics and he held to them with a passion and dogmatism more appropriate to a religious faith than an economic theory; they were Free Trade, a balanced budget, and the maintenance of the pound sterling at a parity of $4·85. Socialism, for Snowden, was a kind of luxury which could only be enjoyed after these three conditions had been satisfied; until then, the only safe rule for any country was to live, like a Yorkshireman who had experienced the evils of poverty, within its means.

It so happened that in his economic outlook Snowden was completely at one with the most experienced, the most influential and the most respected financier in Britain, the Governor of the Bank of England, Montague Norman; and not only with him, but with the Treasury experts who were responsible for advising the government on financial policy. By 1930, Norman had already been Governor of the Bank for eight years, an unprecedented period as the Bank normally only elected its governors for two years. As Governor, Norman had devoted himself to the task of restoring Britain to the gold standard at very nearly its pre-war parity with the dollar, even though this entailed a process of severe and continuous deflation which condemned British industry to stagnation. In Norman's mind, central banking was a wholly autonomous sphere of activity, and if in pursuit of its own best interests it might have unfortunate effects upon industry, this was no concern of his; he could hardly bring himself to admit that the rate of interest might affect business activity.

But the return of Britain to the gold standard was only one element of the Grand Design which inspired Norman's policies at the Bank and was so much a matter of almost mystical belief that he could hardly bear to explain its mysteries either to anyone else or even to himself. This was nothing less than the restoration of the gold standard throughout the world, as a preliminary to re-establishing the pre-war system of finance of which the City of London had been the centre and the Bank of England the central banker. It was an essential part of Norman's vision that it should be put into effect, not by governments, which were apt to be swayed by narrow and ephemeral nationalist interests, but by the central bankers of the world working together to apply the rules required by the successful working of the gold standard. The less governments interfered the better; for the rules of the game were built-in and automatic, and would only function if allowed to work themselves out to their inevitable conclusion. What Norman wanted, like General de Gaulle, was to restore 'the universal, automatic and impartial sovereignty of gold', and to this end he devoted himself to promoting the restoration of the essential features of the pre-war financial system; free trade, international lending, strong and stable currencies supported by strong and stable governments, the automatic operation of the trade-cycle through the machinery of the gold standard.

There was nothing mean or ignoble about Norman's dream, and

[75]

he pursued it with extraordinary tenacity. And since he himself was a man of mystery, carrying the avoidance of publicity, or even of the necessity of communication, to absurd and bizarre lengths, combining an unrivalled expertise in the techniques of central banking with the temperament of a romantic poet and a strong manic-depressive tendency which frequently led him to nervous collapse, he endowed his dream, in the eyes of others, with something of the power of his own, carefully cultivated, charisma. But it was not only a personal magic that he worked. What other central bankers, what governments, including his own, saw in Norman was the mysterious aura and prestige which, despite the decline in Britain's power, still clung to the Bank of England and the City of London, with their unrivalled experience and success in managing the financial affairs of the world's trading community; but it could be said that Norman, with his highly developed histrionic gifts, was in every way equipped to play the part of high priest of this mystery.

Up to the end of 1929, it could have been argued that Norman's Grand Design had prospered; the proof of its success was to be found in the economic recovery of Europe, the restoration of the gold standard, the stabilization of currencies, the return to normal political conditions. But behind Norman's hopes and objectives lay the assumption that the financial management of the world's affairs was essentially a matter for bankers, in which politics had no part and governments would not interfere; moreover, that the essential wisdom of the financier lay in allowing a delicate and self-adjusting mechanism to operate freely according to its own inherent laws. The machinery of the gold standard provided certain warning signals against the dangers of economic maladjustment; the duty of the banker was to interpret them correctly and take the appropriate action in extending or restricting credit, so that the disease would have the opportunity to cure itself.

In fact, however, in the post-war world these assumptions never corresponded to reality. Governments were no longer willing, and could not afford, to allow their economic affairs to be run for them by bankers; their job was to promote the economic strength and independence of their own countries by every means in their power, even if this meant disturbing the delicate balance of international finance. The most profound and permanent effect of the war had been the encouragement it had given to the growth of nationalism and this was as true in economics as in any other field. This was particularly true of the Central European successor states of the defeated Central Powers, whose financial stability Norman himself had done much to promote.

The fall of the Grand Coalition in Germany might have served as a warning, if any warning had been needed, that the world in which Norman believed had ceased to exist and had given place to an altogether different one. Norman himself might have seen the warning explicitly conveyed by the behaviour of his friend and ally Schacht, who, though a master of all the financial skills which Norman possessed, did not hesitate to exploit them in the service of his own particular political ends, which were those of fanatical nationalism. But Norman might have taken warning also from the behaviour of a country which had far less excuse than Germany for practising economic nationalism and taken note that the most important measure before the United States Congress in the early months of 1930 was the prohibitive Hawley-Smoot Tariff against foreign industrial products. Perhaps, indeed in his own strange way he did take note, though this could not shake the rigidity of his ideas. His moods of depression increased; the obscure nervous disorder which afflicted him all his life, wrongly diagnosed by Jung as general paralysis of the insane, intensified, and at moments of crisis he was apt to take to his bed.

Perhaps the most striking failure of the policies which Norman recommended to governments and to central bankers was to be found in Great Britain itself. Ramsay MacDonald's second Labour Government, which came into office in May 1929, had inherited a burden of unemployment which since 1922 had never fallen below one million, or ten per cent of the working population. This was what the eminent Cambridge economist, Professor Pigou, had termed 'the intractable million', which appeared to have become a permanent feature of British industrial life. There were many factors to explain this phenomenon, in particular the long-term decline of Britain's export industries, in which unemployment was largely concentrated; but certainly one of the most important was the policy of credit restriction practised by Norman and the Bank in order first to prepare for a return to the gold standard and afterwards to maintain it. The consequences were precisely as predicted by Keynes in *The Economic Consequences of Mr Churchill*; and indeed Churchill never forgave Norman for the policy which he urged upon him when Chancellor of the Exchequer. Churchill's attitude was that, being no financial expert himself, he had taken the best advice available, which was that of the Treasury and the Bank; but he felt that Norman had made a fool of him and, what was worse, had inflicted grave damage on the nation's economy.

But though unemployment had been heavy for so long, so that it formed the central issue of the 1929 election, during the Labour Government's first year of office it showed a tendency to rise alarmingly, as it did in Germany. In March 1929 it had stood at 1,204,000; by March 1930 it had risen to 1,700,000 and by July to two million. MacDonald had given special responsibility for unemployment to J.H.Thomas, the Lord Privy Seal; but Thomas had done little except to make the same kind of reassuring noises as were made in the United States after the crash and to make a wholly irrelevant visit to Canada which lasted for six weeks. 'I think the bottom has been reached,' he said in February 1930; on 12 March, 'Things can only improve'; and on 20 March, when unemployment reached the two million mark, 'The worst is past.' In uttering such phrases, however, Thomas was not merely expressing an unconsidered optimism. He was reflecting the opinions of his advisers, and they in their turn were reflecting the wisdom of the past, which was that at some particular part in the business cycle a level was reached from which the only change could be for the better; and the worse the figures became, the more likely it was that the turning point had been reached. The danger of such a view was that it offered the best of reasons against taking any positive action to improve the situation; indeed, any interference in the automatic process by which slump turned into boom might only postpone recovery by frustrating the free play of economic forces.

As unemployment rose, the Labour Government found itself faced with the same difficulties as the Grand Coalition in Germany; in Parliament, as in the Reichstag, they centred on the position of the unemployment insurance fund. In March 1930, the fund had to ask parliamentary authority to borrow fifty million pounds, and in June another sixty million. Again, as in Germany, it was felt that this could not go on indefinitely. The repeated appearances before Parliament, with requests for new loans, of Miss Margaret

Bondfield, the Minister of Labour, were a perpetual reminder of the rising unemployment figures and, as in Germany, concentrated attention on the problem of how to make the unemployment insurance fund self-supporting.

The failure of the government to produce more positive measures for dealing with unemployment, which after all was not merely an insurance problem, was the less excusable because the problem had been the dominant issue of the 1929 election and had provoked fierce discussion of possible methods of solving it. Yet the government was bound by the Labour Party's own programme of transforming society through the public ownership of the means of production, distribution and exchange; anything less was merely tinkering with the problem, and if there was any tinkering to be done it was better to rely on the advice of the recognized experts at the Treasury and in the City than on the unproven theories of economists like Keynes or politicians like Lloyd George. And indeed the election itself had demonstrated that the country decisively rejected such theories; the only party which had produced a comprehensive programme for curing unemployment had been the Lloyd George Liberals, who had been overwhelmingly defeated and reduced to less than fifty members in Parliament.

Nor when the Labour Government took office was it immediately apparent that urgent action was required. Unemployment at the level of about one million had become a permanent feature of the British economy; short of a socialist revolution, which politically was out of the question, the Labour Party was more concerned with protecting the unemployed than reducing their number. It even seemed for a time as if the economic situation might take a favourable turn without any positive action by the government. The unemployment figures, which had been exceptionally bad in 1928, had improved in the spring of 1929 and there seemed no reason for thinking that the improvement would not continue. In this situation, orthodox financial advice was unanimous that what was needed was a policy of credit restraint and government economy which would allow economic forces to work themselves out and do nothing to impair foreign confidence in the pound, which in the long run was the only guarantee of recovery. Such advice was the more readily accepted because it coincided with the deflationary views of the Labour Chancellor, Philip Snowden.

By March 1930, however, as the effects of the depression began to show themselves, so optimistic an outlook became harder to maintain. The unemployment figures were expected to fall after their seasonal rise during the winter, but in the spring they showed, instead of a fall, an increase of over half a million on the previous year. In April, Hubert Henderson, the Cambridge economist who was secretary of the Economic Advisory Council newly appointed by the Prime Minister, which included Keynes among its members, analysed the position as follows. First, Britain was faced by the long-term problem of the decline, both relatively and absolutely, in her export trade. Second, business activity was inhibited by a continuously deflationary trend due to a world scramble for gold as a result of the return to the gold standard;* until the Wall Street crash, however, this had been partly offset by the buoyancy of the American and European stock markets. Thirdly, the collapse of the stock market, together with the fall in commodity prices, had created a worldwide depression, which was superimposed on 'our special national difficulties'. This, he said, 'constituted the dominating fact in the immediate situation'. Yet Henderson was not despondent about the situation; he believed that the depression would of itself 'set forces in motion which will ultimately effect a cure, notably cheap money'.

MacDonald paraphrased Henderson's analysis by declaring that 'an economic blizzard' had struck. No doubt by such language he wished to emphasize the severity and unexpectedness of the depression. But it also unconsciously betrayed the attitude of mind of those who believed that no positive action was required or desirable. A blizzard, after all, is a natural event which will one day blow itself out; the most one can do is to endure, not wrestle with, the order of nature. Unfortunately, the rise in unemployment, by destroying the actuarial basis of the unemployment insurance fund, presented immediate problems which required, or seemed to require, immediate solutions; Miss Bondfield could not, after all, be permitted to go on raising loans for ever.

There is something deeply ironic about the form in which, initially, the depression forced itself upon the attention of govern-

* The return to the gold standard forced countries both to increase their gold reserves and to restrict credit in order to avoid pressure on them.

[80]

ments. They could afford to ignore, even while they deplored, the decline in business activity as something which would produce its own cure, and assure themselves, on the best authority, that no other cure was possible. They could even afford to ignore, though they might have wished to alleviate, the vast burden of human misery engendered by mass unemployment; this also could be regarded as unavoidable. What they could not ignore, given the principles of 'sound finance', was the actuarial condition of a fund whose recurrent deficits entailed recurrent loans, authorized by Parliament, without any assurance that they would ever be repaid or cease to be needed. After the spring of 1930, the energies of the Labour Government were increasingly drained away by innumerable parliamentary debates, cabinet meetings and consultations devoted to the intractable problem not of unemployment but of unemployment insurance.

The British government, however, was in a stronger position to deal with its problem than the German. By the spring of 1930, the German government had exhausted all its normal sources of credit, and had to depend on an adventurer like Kreuger in order to cover its normal expenditure. It was overloaded with debt, and Schacht at least had already envisaged the possibility of defaulting on the reparations payments due under the Young Plan; the strain of financing heavy deficits on unemployment insurance was to prove too severe for the survival of parliamentary government.

Britain's case was less critical. The restoration of the gold standard imposed a continuing strain on her economy and she seemed condemned to a rate of unemployment of at least one million a year. Yet she still remained an enormously rich country, which had suffered neither defeat nor inflation and was still able to lend abroad at the rate of £170,000,000 a year. It was still possible for her to contemplate without undue alarm the rising figures of unemployment, even though they might provoke periodic parliamentary crises.

In these circumstances, there were those both within and without the government who continued to urge that Britain should undertake a massive programme, to be financed by loan, of public expenditure on financial and agricultural development, on road-making, on house-building; the Liberals calculated that £1,000,000 expended by the government would set 5,000 to work. Outside the

[81]

government Lloyd George continued to press for the programme contained in *We Can Conquer Unemployment* and to promise parliamentary support if it were carried out. Inside the government was Sir Oswald Mosley, as Chancellor of the Duchy of Lancaster, a member of the Cabinet at thirty-two, a brilliant and arrogant patrician who had joined the Labour Party in the belief that positive and effective measures would be taken to combat unemployment and had prepared himself for such a task by reading Keynes. In 1925, together with John Strachey and Helen Young, he had composed a pamphlet, *Revolution by Reason*, which was read to the Independent Labour Party's summer school at the Countess of Warwick's house at Easton Lodge. It advocated government subsidies to industry, to finance minimum wages which would create additional working-class demand; nationalization of the banks, as a basis for 'a bold and vigorous expansion of the national credit'; and, if necessary, devaluation to a parity of 4·40 dollars. Strachey favoured a fluctuating exchange rate. Mosley's views were far ahead of those of the great bulk of his party; but he was a young man in a hurry and he had joined the Labour Party, and the government, in the firm, if naïve, belief that it would be possible to initiate decisive action on the lines which he proposed. He was soon to be disillusioned.

Both Lloyd George's and Mosley's programmes represented a radical departure from the economic orthodoxies of the time. Both owed much to Keynes, and were alike in identifying a failure of effective demand as the root cause of the depression, and deficit spending by the government as the quickest way to cure it. But Keynes himself had not as yet fully worked out a coherent theoretical basis for the pragmatic programmes which he advocated; in particular, in calculating the effects on unemployment of government expenditure on public works he still lacked the concept of 'the multiplier', first put forward in a famous paper published in 1931 by R.F.Kahn (now Lord Kahn), a pupil and colleague of Keynes's at King's College, Cambridge.

Revolutionary though Keynes's ideas were when judged by the standards of economic orthodoxy, as represented especially by the iron dogmatism of Philip Snowden, they commanded powerful support in the country, both among industrialists, who felt that their interests had been sacrificed for too long to the City of London, among trade unionists like Ernest Bevin, and among theoretical economists who, faced with the hard facts of mass unemployment, had begun to be sceptical about the underlying premises of *laissez-faire* capitalism. It may be asked why, in that case, such support was not welcomed by a socialist government for which the problem of unemployment was a crucial one? Partly the reason is to be found in the personalities of those who publicly sponsored direct government action to cure or alleviate unemployment; of Lloyd George, who had earned almost universal mistrust; of Keynes himself, regarded by many, for all his brilliance, as an intellectual flibbertigibbet; of Mosley, young, arrogant, immensely ambitious and with leanings towards authoritarianism which already aroused suspicion. These were not the kind of men whose ideas would recommend themselves to the leaders of any responsible political party, and especially to one as weak, irresolute and muddle-headed as Ramsay MacDonald.

But there was a deeper reason. The kind of programme advocated in *We Can Conquer Unemployment* was in no sense socialist. It was directed towards remedying the defects of an ailing system without destroying the system itself and therefore had no theoretical charm for a party dedicated, in theory at least, to the total transformation of society. On the other hand, it offended against economic dogmas which, as long as the system lasted, seemed as self-evident to socialists as they did to conservatives. The system, after all, had its own rules, consecrated by long experience; it was necessary either to obey the rules or to destroy the system.

Among other factors conducive to depression in Great Britain, Henderson noted in his memorandum for the Economic Advisory Council the 'scramble for gold' which followed the restoration of the gold standard. But Great Britain was not alone in feeling its effects; they were felt by every country, including the two which had become the world's largest importers of gold, the United States and France.

During the twenties, gold, instead of exercising a stabilizing influence on the world's economy, had itself become a factor tending to increase instability. This was partly because gold production was insufficient to cover the world's monetary needs. The world demand for new gold required an increase in production of about 3 per cent per annum, but between 1920 and 1930 production in fact only increased by 2·1 per cent. But gold itself suffered violent fluctuations in value relatively to other commodities. By 1920, it had lost three-fifths of its pre-war value as a result of the abandonment of the gold standard. By 1921, it had risen in value by 75 per cent, largely owing to the policy of credit restriction followed by the United States, at a time when the United States was also the world's largest creditor nation; as a result, stocks of gold in the United States rose from $2,284,000,000 to $4,507,000,000 between 1920 and the end of 1924. The general return to the gold standard between 1924 and 1928 brought a correspondingly increased pressure on the world's gold stocks as each country tried to increase its gold reserves. The United States lost a little of its gold to the rest of the world, while other countries gained. In particular, Germany by 1930 had almost doubled its gold reserves since 1925, while France gained enormously. After the end of 1929, the Bank of France ceased to buy foreign exchange as a backing for its note issue, and replaced what it already held with gold; Great Britain on the other hand lost almost all the gold she had gained up to 1925.

From 1930 onwards, the continued absorption of gold by France and the United States placed an increasingly heavy strain on the currencies of other countries, and was a major factor in the general financial crisis that ensued in 1931. That this was so is in itself evidence to what extent the post-war gold standard had ceased to function with the smoothness and effectiveness with which it had operated before the war. If it had obeyed the rules which were its theoretical justification, those countries, like Britain, which were losing gold, would have restricted credit until the loss of gold had been reversed, and indeed she had no choice but to do so if she were to remain on the gold standard; on the other hand those countries, like the United States and France, which were gaining gold, would have relaxed credit until gold began to flow out again. In fact, they did not. The result was world-wide deflation; it could be said that during the depression William Jennings Bryan's nightmare came literally true, and mankind was crucified upon a cross of gold.

CHAPTER FIVE

The Deepening Crisis

By the summer of 1930 it had become increasingly difficult to maintain the hope that the stock exchange crash in the United States was a passing incident, whose consequences would be purely temporary, perhaps even, as President Hoover thought, salutary. Anyone taking a dispassionate view of the world economic situation would have recognized that, in the brief space of a year, the situation had changed almost desperately for the worse; the fear, or the hope, began to grow in some men's minds that this was not a temporary setback to prosperity, but something so severe and so unprecedented that it might strike at the very roots of capitalist society. In 1929 it was estimated that, in thirty-three countries, total unemployment amounted to about 5,000,000. By July 1930 it had risen to 11,000,000, or more than doubled. By the end of 1930 it rose again to a figure estimated at between 19,000,000 and 25,000,000; 5,000,000 of this increase was concentrated into the last three months of the year.

But perhaps the most ominous sign of the deepening of the crisis was to be found in the worldwide fall in prices. 'The next phase, then, of the economic depression,' said the *Survey of International Affairs* in 1931, 'after the collapse of the stock exchange inflation, was the worldwide acceleration of the secular fall in prices.'* In the United States wholesale prices fell by 16 per cent; in Germany by 13 per cent; in the Netherlands by 20 per cent; in Great Britain by 18 per cent; in Japan by 21 per cent. The effect on business activity, on the businessman's expectations of profit which regulate his orders to manufacturers, was all the greater because no one could foresee when, and at what level, the fall would come to an end.

* The long-term fall in world prices had begun in 1925. Professor Toynbee's use of the word secular is perhaps an exaggeration.

The fall was sharpest in the prices of the staple commodities of world trade. Even by the end of 1929 this had been catastrophic; wheat had fallen by 19 per cent, cotton by 27 per cent, wool by 42 per cent, tin by 29 per cent, rubber by 42 per cent, coffee by 43 per cent. For large areas of the world, which were also its poorest, such a decline meant ruin, especially because it struck hardest at the world's debtor countries which, on a falling market, had to export larger and larger quantities in order to discharge their commitments to their creditors. These in turn reacted to such efforts by striving to protect their own dwindling market. In Germany agricultural protection was pushed so far, for reasons into which politics and class interest entered as much as economics, that by the end of 1930 the internal price of wheat was twice its price on the world market.

The effect of the rise in unemployment was felt most sharply in the leading industrialist countries, and particularly in the United States and Germany. In Britain the shock was less severe because of the high rate of unemployment which she had suffered ever since 1922; in her case the depression was not marked by the same sudden contrast between boom and slump, the descent from prosperity to poverty, as elsewhere. Even so, by the summer unemployment had risen to 2,000,000 and by the autumn to 2,200,000. France suffered least, because she continued, as long as the gold standard continued to operate, to enjoy the advantages of the undervaluation of the franc. But in the United States and Germany the effects were both so sudden and so great as to impose the severest strain on their social and political systems.

By the spring of 1930 there were already over 4,000,000 unemployed in the United States, and by the end of the year 6,000,000; during the course of the year the number of hours worked in industry fell by one-third. In Germany, unemployment rose to 5,000,000 by the summer of 1930 and to 6,000,000 by the end of the year; it was estimated that one man out of four of the insured population was out of work.

For the average man, the prospect was all the blacker because there seemed to be no immediate hope of improvement. In the United States, businessmen repeated their optimistic belief that the downward turn of the business cycle must inevitably produce an upward one, and picked different dates for the moment of recovery.

A poll of bank directors showed two-thirds in favour of October 1930; the remainder picked January of the following year. But such predictions were always accompanied by the warning that recovery would only come if there were no governmental interference with the immutable working of the trade cycle. For the man on the dole, with no prospect of work, this was as much as to say that he could expect no help from his leaders. Senator Lafollette asked the banker, Albert H. Wiggin, whether he thought the capacity for human suffering was unlimited. 'I think so,' said Wiggin; as things turned out, he was very nearly right.

Thus the victims of the depression were abandoned to the inscrutable mercies of economic law. During the summer, what this meant began to be visible in the United States and Europe. The long, grey, silent lines of the workless extended outside the labour exchanges and soup kitchens; children who never ceased to cry by day or by night were found, on medical examination, to be suffering from undernourishment; for thousands of men, life reduced itself to an endless and hopeless trek from factory gate to factory gate in the search for work, until the futility of it became intolerable, and even this occupation was lost to them. In a mining town in South Wales, on a summer's afternoon, the streets were crowded as if for an annual fair, but the lounging crowd was listless and apathetic; they were in the streets simply because they had nothing else to do. On the outskirts of American cities there sprang up encampments of the workless and homeless living in huts built of any materials that came to hand, packing cases, motor-car bodies, planks, tarpaulins, brown paper; it was as if the human rejects of a civilization were building their own cities out of its industrial waste. These encampments were christened 'Hoovervilles', and nothing could better illustrate the bitterness, resentment and contempt which were beginning to attach themselves to the name of the Great Engineer who only a short time before had been triumphantly elected President of the United States. In Germany also, around Berlin and other cities, there sprang up similar colonies of *Lauben*, or huts, of the same makeshift construction.

For many thousands of men and women such colonies were to provide the only homes they knew so long as the depression lasted, and the lives that were lived in them were infinitely grey, sickly and monotonous. They were like festering sores which openly proclaimed the failure of capitalism to provide even the minimum conditions of a decent life for millions of its victims. But unemployment, on a scale and of a duration such as it assumed in 1930, was not merely a matter of material impoverishment; it was a spiritual experience, a kind of capitalist purgatory, filled with the shades of men whom the economic system had rejected, and it broke men's spirits all the more because there was neither meaning nor justice in it. To find oneself rendered useless through no fault of one's own, without the means to support either oneself or one's family, condemned to a life of idleness without any of the resources which can make idleness a pleasure, is one of the bitterest experiences any man can suffer; from the summer of 1930 onwards, it was to be the common fate of the great, grey international army of the unemployed.

Nor was it only the direct victims of the depression who were affected by it. Others, observing what was happening to their fellow-men, began to wonder what kind of justification there was for a society which produced such results. The depression ceased to be merely an economic problem; it became a question mark directed at the values of western civilization and there were many who, finding no satisfactory answer, decided that there was no alternative other than to build a new society on totally different principles. On 6 March 1930, which had been declared International Unemployment Day by the Communist Party, there were violent demonstrations outside the White House which were broken up by the intervention of the police, and a crowd of 35,000 gathered in Union Square in New York to listen to the communist leader, William Z. Foster. 1930 saw the beginning of the alienation of large sections of educated middle-class opinion from the society of which it was a part, and it is doubtful if the breach has ever been fully healed.

Such feelings showed themselves, in every country, though in varying degree, in a growth of political extremism, which in turn gave rise to further doubts about the stability of the western economic and political system, so painfully restored in the post-war years. In the United States the Communist Party, though it never became a serious political threat, acquired a greater degree of popular support than it has ever known before or since. In Germany, extremism flourished both on the right and the left, with

John Maynard Keynes,
1883–1946.

Montague Norman,
Governor of the Bank of
England 1920–44.

Delegates to London
conference on Germany's
foreign indebtedness, July
1931. (*Front row, left to
right*) A. W. Mellon,
secretary to the Treasury
(USA), Pierre Laval,
(*centre*) Aristide Briand,
Ramsay MacDonald,
Henry L. Stimson,
Secretary of State (USA),
Arthur Henderson,
Foreign Secretary (Great
Britain).

Gustav Stresemann,
1878–1929, German
Chancellor 1923, Foreign
Minister 1923–9.

such effect that it led to the extinction of democracy. Even in Britain, despair at the failure to find a solution for the problem of unemployment drove Sir Oswald Mosley out of the government into unorthodox ways of protest which finally led him to fascism.

The recruits to political extremism were very largely the workless men who saw no hope of any improvement in their condition except in the overthrow of 'the system', either from the Right or the Left. Yet, except in countries which, like Germany, already suffered from a fundamental political instability, the seeds of revolution on the whole fell on barren ground. The explanation is to be found in the fact that the unemployed, though their numbers increased alarmingly, remained in a minority, while those who were lucky enough to remain in employment (who after all constituted the majority) were able to maintain and even improve their standard of life. Wages remained stable, and indeed there were those who pointed to this as one of the prime causes of the depression, and any inroads that were made on them were more than compensated for by the fall in prices.

Even among the unemployed, indeed, hopelessness rather than active indignation, passive suffering rather than aggressive militancy was the most characteristic reaction to their misfortune. This is confirmed by the innumerable memoirs of life on the dole which were published during the depression. Unemployment was regarded by most of those who suffered it as a form of natural catastrophe or divine visitation for which no human agencies could be held responsible; though frequently, in its victims, there was also the sense, when faced with the sufferings of wives and families, that unemployment might be the consequence of personal failure and inadequacy. This was the counterpart of the feeling among many employers that no one who really wanted work went without it. In Great Britain, nothing added more to the bitterness of political controversy about unemployment than the 'genuinely seeking work' clause, as a condition of receiving unemployment benefit.

Behind such feelings there lay certain intellectual assumptions, deeply embedded in the economic thought of the day, which appeared to deny even the possibility of positive and effective action to cure the problem of unemployment. The most important was the belief, which amounted to dogma, that in the economic system taken as a whole demand must always be equal to supply, and that this applied to labour just as much as any of the other factors entering into the process of production; the system as a whole was self-adjusting, and it followed that any action taken to stimulate demand was both unnecessary and positively harmful, because of the distortions it introduced in the automatic working of the system.

This assumption was based on the famous law enunciated by the French economist J.B. Say, which had dominated economic thought since he first stated it in the eighteenth century. Repeated, elaborated, reformulated in textbook after textbook, expounded from every university chair, propagated in business journals and leading articles, the unspoken dogma behind the practice of governments, financiers and businessmen, unchallenged even by those whom it condemned to a life of idleness and want, it had sunk so deeply into the consciousness of Western economic man that for the most part he did not even choose to think about it.

Say's Law was all the more acceptable because, in its classical form, it had the simplicity, elegance and perfection of a mathematical formula. It stated that total demand must be equal to total supply, because in fact demand was nothing other than the total payments made for all the resources entering into the economic process. What was a cost to the supplier was an income to somebody else; since total costs and total incomes were the same thing under a different name, how could they fail to be equal to each other? The process of production was at the same time a process of consumption and together they formed a vast system of double entry which, at the end of the day, could not fail to balance.

Since Say first stated it, his law had been given many formulations, and undergone many refinements, but, except by Malthus, who in this as in other respects was a kind of rogue elephant among economists, it had never been seriously challenged. It had become an axiom, self-evident once its terms were understood, which had entered into economic thought as profoundly as Pythagoras' theorem into Euclidean geometry, or the second law of thermodynamics into Newtonian physics; and just as these shaped the intellectual attitudes of men and women who had never considered the problems of mathematics or physics, so Say's Law influenced the minds of statesmen, administrators and businessmen who would never have claimed to be economists; indeed, as applied by

English classical economists in the nineteenth century, Say's Law
obtained such universal acceptance that almost no one dreamed of
doubting it. Keynes wrote:

Malthus, indeed, had vehemently opposed Ricardo's doctrine that it
was impossible for effective demand to be deficient; but vainly. For
since Malthus was unable to explain clearly (apart from one appeal to
the fact of common observation) how and why effective demand could
be deficient or excessive, he failed to furnish an alternative construction;
and Ricardo conquered England as completely as the Holy Inquisition
conquered Spain. Not only was his theory accepted by the city, by
statesmen and by the academic world. But controversy ceased; the other
point of view completely disappeared; it ceased to be discussed. The
great puzzle of Effective Demand with which Malthus had wrestled
vanished from economic literature.

Yet as mass unemployment grew, the contrast between theory
and reality became more and more baffling. Keynes himself,
whose *Treatise on Money* was published in 1930, was to succeed
where Malthus had failed, not only by an 'appeal to the facts of
common observation', but by providing the 'alternative construction' which had escaped Malthus; but even he was not yet ready
to offer a complete theoretical solution to the 'great puzzle of
Effective Demand'. But most people in positions of authority,
whether practical or academic, were paralysed in their efforts to
face the problem of unemployment by intellectual assumptions
which made it impossible for them to recognize that a problem
even existed. Unemployment undoubtedly seemed to exist, with
catastrophic results; but seen in the light of reason it was an
illusion, an impossibility, a nightmare; it followed both that it
could not continue to exist, and that it was impossible to do anything about it. Even those who, on empirical grounds, approved
of direct action to overcome the depression, continued to be
puzzled by the implications of Say's Law. Thus Hubert Henderson,
who had collaborated with Keynes on *We Can Conquer Unemployment*, wrote in his report as secretary of the Economic Advisory
Council appointed by Ramsay MacDonald: 'On classical assumptions the depression itself generates forces making for recovery,
such as low interest rates.' But what other assumptions were they
and how long did it take for the system's regenerative powers to
work? Whatever theory might say, there was more truth for the

THE GREAT SLUMP

unemployed in Keynes's remark: 'In the long run we are all dead.'

There was a striking contrast between the passivity of statesmen in face of the unemployment problem and their positive response to situations which did not impinge on their intellectual preconceptions. In the summer of 1930 the whole of the south-west of the United States was ravaged by drought which destroyed cattle and crops. Faced with a natural disaster of this kind Hoover, the organizer of a post-war famine relief in Europe, had no hesitation, and swiftly organized assistance, including Federal loans to the farmers. He would have considered a similar programme to assist the unemployed both futile and immoral.

The hopelessness and despair of the victims of the depression was the counterpart of the incapacity of their governments to find a solution for their problems. There was, however, one remedy which the combined financial wisdom of the world agreed to be indispensable before recovery could even begin; this was to reduce government expenditures and balance national budgets. This belief had no stronger supporter than the Democratic Governor of New York, Franklin D. Roosevelt, to whom many men's eyes were turning as an alternative to Hoover at the presidential elections of 1932. As prices, incomes and profits fell, and tax receipts with them, governments throughout the world found themselves threatened with growing Budget deficits, which could not be controlled except by heroic, almost sadistic, measures of economy and increases in taxation.

Statesmen rarely explained the economic processes by which such measures would achieve the desired end. It was accepted that a balanced Budget represented a return to 'financial wisdom', and as such would restore business confidence. There was a sense that the depression, for which after all no satisfactory explanation could be offered, was not so much an economic as a moral problem, a punishment for the laxity and extravagance of the boom; conditions would not improve until the world atoned for its frivolity. In some people, usually those who were well protected against personal suffering, this view of the depression as a natural consequence of a Gadarene rush after prosperity achieved an almost hysterical intensity, as in the case of Andrew Mellon, 'the greatest Secretary of the Treasury since Alexander Hamilton'. 'Liquidate labour,' he

[92]

cried; 'liquidate stocks, liquidate the farmers, liquidate real estate.'
He might as well have said: *Liquidate everything*!

The impact of unemployment in the United States and the human
suffering involved was all the greater because she was almost
totally unprepared for it. It had been assumed that, under the
American system, with its unprecedented capacity and opportunity
for growth, prolonged unemployment on any serious scale was an
impossibility. Moreover, there was something alien and 'un-
American' in the very idea of protecting the individual against the
effects of idleness, whether voluntary or not; it was an offence
against the spirit of enterprise and initiative which distinguished
America from the effete nations of Europe. How could America,
with its vast wealth and its vast spaces, ever be lacking in opportunity for anyone who was willing to work?

Thus the United States was less prepared, in mind and in her
institutions, for the depression than almost any other industrial
country. No other nation had in 1930 such feeble and confused
provisions for the jobless. There was no national, or even state
system of unemployment insurance, and relief was mainly on a
local basis, supplemented by private welfare agencies. But as the
depression deepened the burden fell increasingly on public funds,
which by 1930 accounted for four-fifths of the total cost of relief.
In the large cities they were administered by public welfare departments, but in smaller communities the principal agency was still
the poorhouse. Such a system contributed directly to making
paupers of the unemployed; they tried to avoid accepting relief
until all their resources were exhausted, their savings gone, their
furniture sold, the last line of credit withdrawn, until there was no
longer any alternative. The system was designed not for mass
unemployment but for the irreducible minimum of unemployables
and unfortunates that exist in any society. It had no relevance
or application to a system in which unemployment ran into
millions and for periods which could be counted in years not
months.

In the United States, in 1930, there appeared the visible signs of
mass unemployment which showed themselves all over the western
world, and in millions of households that appalling accumulation
of human misery which accompanied them. 'Every week, every

day, more workers joined the procession of despair,' writes Professor Schlesinger. 'The shadows deepened in the dark cold rooms, with the father angry, helpless and ashamed, the distraught children often hungry or sick, and the mother, so resolute by day, so often, when the room was finally still, lying awake in bed at night, softly crying.' A great fear began to descend on America, because this was the kind of existence which threatened anyone who was not fortunate enough to be in work; and, with fear, a growing sense of anger.

But the Great Engineer in the White House continued to believe in the virtues of the American system, and the wickedness of any measures which compromised the principles of unrestrained capitalist enterprise. He told working men to trust in 'the self-abnegating devotion of America's great manufacturers, and railways, utilities, business houses, and public officials', and declared that 'voluntary organization and community services were quite sufficient to take care of the unemployed'. When, reluctantly, and under pressure by demands for a special session of Congress, he appointed an Emergency Committee for Employment, his direction that unemployment was an entirely local responsibility left the committee with no function to perform. When its chairman, Colonel Wood, submitted a draft message to Congress, demanding a public works programme, and urged support of Senator Wagner's proposals for advanced planning of public works and a national employment system, the President rejected his advice. For him, such proposals struck at 'the roots of self-government'.

President Hoover was a tragic example of an intelligent, high-minded, extremely able man who was hopelessly trapped by intellectual orthodoxies which no longer corresponded to reality, so hopelessly indeed that he made no struggle to be free of them. The result was to induce a kind of paralysis of the will and to make him incapable of action. He compensated for this with words of optimism and faith which rang hollow in the ears of men who had no reason for either. They may even have rung hollow in his own ears, because the President was by temperament a pessimist. 'He always saw the dark side first,' said his Secretary of War, Henry L. Stimson. He had none of that overflowing self-confidence or personal vitality which give to others a sense of leadership; the contrast between his professions of faith and the reality by which they were confronted imposed an increasing strain on him, particularly because he was sensitive to criticism, and bitterly resented the charges of inhumanity made against him as one who would subsidize fodder for animals or fertilizers for crops but refused aid and assistance to human beings.

The White House became a mausoleum of Hoover's hopes and beliefs. The domestic atmosphere became intolerably oppressive; visitors commented on the air of gloom and anxiety which pervaded it, and its staff rejoiced when the Hoovers were away. H.G.Wells, when he visited the President in 1930, found him 'a sickly, over-worked and overwhelmed man'; meetings with him became 'like sitting in a bath of ink'. His relations with the Press reached 'a stage of unpleasantness without parallel in the present century', and this was only one aspect of the personal unpopularity and dislike which he came to inspire. His name was used as a symbol of everything that was shoddiest and shabbiest about the depression, for Hoovervilles, Hoover blankets, Hoover wagons, Hoover hand-kerchiefs, all *ersatz* mimicries which the unemployed substituted for the real thing. 'Is Hoover dead?' said a music-hall comedian, when told that business was looking up.

No one ever laboured harder or more conscientiously than Hoover for the wellbeing of the United States; no one failed quite so ingloriously. The White House has seen many personal tragedies, but perhaps none quite so complete as his.

The deepening of the depression in the United States had direct and calamitous effects, on both the economic and the political situation in Germany; and this in turn contributed to a further deterioration in conditions throughout the capitalist world. It was a significant feature of the depression that, the more governments tried to insulate themselves against its effects, the more evident their interdependence became; the more they tried to achieve self-sufficiency, the worse the blows they inflicted on one another. From the summer of 1930 onwards, political conditions were at the mercy of economic developments, which were beyond anyone's control, and as the political situation deteriorated new economic difficulties arose. A kind of politico-economic chain reaction was established, which led to successive crises in one country after another. The depression was a world phenomenon; statesmen

[95]

tried to solve it, so far as they made the attempt at all, as if each country were a law unto itself.

Perhaps the most serious single cause of this disastrous chain of events was the extreme weakness of the world's debtor countries, which, when the depression came, left them wholly exposed and unprotected. They depended upon a continuous flow of capital from abroad and when, as a result of the American stock market boom followed by the crash, the supply dried up, their position became untenable. The position was particularly serious for those countries which depended on exports of food and raw materials to service their debts, for the catastrophic fall in commodity prices, itself one of the main causes of the depression, meant that their burden of debt became increasingly higher at a time when it became more difficult both to secure fresh capital and to increase their exports.

Among the debtor countries, Germany occupied a peculiarly exposed and precarious position. She suffered from an acute and continuous lack of capital owing to the destruction of her financial and material resources as a result of war and inflation; the German banks alone lost two-thirds of their capital as a result of the war. At the same time, she had to meet the costs of her reparations payments which, since her creditors refused to accept them in kind, had to be transferred across the exchanges.* Since in fact Germany, between 1924 and 1930, had an unfavourable trade balance of roughly 500 million marks, this proved to be impossible except by borrowing abroad. Reparation payments amounted to 300 million marks; she also made net imports of gold of about 100 million marks, in the interest of stabilizing her currency and restoring the gold standard. The total sum of 900 million marks was met by foreign borrowing; 'it is not unfair to say that the payments of reparations abroad was effected not by Germany herself but by the foreign lenders who advanced her money in foreign currencies in exchange for claims on her future production.' It would also be fair to say that this could not have been effected in any other way.

The Young Plan, as finally ratified by The Hague agreement of

---

* Payments on reparations account had to be made in the currencies of the creditor countries and this threw a heavy additional burden on the international exchanges.

December 1929, appreciably reduced Germany's reparation payments and prolonged the period over which they were to be paid; indeed, if it had remained in force she would still be paying them, and this gives some measure of the confidence with which, at that date, financiers regarded the prospects of peace in Europe, and Germany's own financial stability; more especially because the ratification of the plan was accompanied by a loan to Germany to enable her to meet the first annual instalment of her payments.

But The Hague agreement also imposed obligations on Germany which, in the circumstances of 1930, were to have far more importance than the long-term financial commitments she had undertaken and which would never be carried out. If indeed Hugenberg, Hitler, Schacht and their followers had selected this aspect of the Young Plan as the basis of their campaign against it, rather than its long-term implications, it would have been difficult not to agree with them. For the plan obliged Germany, and she agreed, to maintain the gold standard 'under all circumstances' and to maintain 40 per cent of her reserves in foreign currencies. Given Germany's unfavourable trade balance, which continued even though in 1930 she achieved the remarkable feat of increasing her exports by 10 per cent, this was quite literally impossible to fulfil, except on the assumption that Germany would be able to continue borrowing abroad on the same scale as in previous years. By 1930 this assumption had already been falsified, and in that year her borrowing from the United States, her principal source of credit, fell to half of what it had been in 1928.

Nevertheless, in an attempt to restore Germany's credit both at home and abroad, the German Chancellor, Hermann Brüning, clung grimly to the policy of 'financial reform' for which he believed he had President Hindenburg's complete support. This took the form of a savage deflation in an attempt to reduce expenditure and balance the Budget, and in applying it, with an almost reckless severity, Brüning was doing what almost every financial expert throughout the world would have advised. It was a policy which was to prove disastrous both to Germany and to every other country.

One element in the disaster was the character of Brüning himself. He was conscientious, hard working, a skilful parliamentarian and party politician, a devout Catholic with a genuine interest in social questions which he had acquired through long years of association with the Catholic trade union movement. In normal times he might have served Germany well. But beneath his rigid exterior he concealed the heart of a German romantic and the spirit of unflinching *Gehorsamkeit*, of unconditional obedience, of a German non-commissioned officer. For him, as for Hitler, the Great War had provided his greatest spiritual experience, and he carried into civilian life the attitudes of the *Frontkämpfer*, and more particularly the unquestioning loyalty and obedience which was owed to the ex-Supreme Commander of the German armed forces, now President of the Reich. In applying his policy of deflation, Brüning conceived of himself as carrying out the will of the president; he expected of the president the same loyalty as he owed to him, and never suspected that the senile old man still commanded, in regard to himself, large reserves of craft and duplicity. For Brüning after all did not belong to the same landowning and military caste as the president; while the president never gave his complete loyalty to anything else, not his Kaiser, nor his people, nor the Republic, nor his Chancellor, each of which he unhesitatingly betrayed whenever the occasion demanded it.

Brüning carried his loyalty to the president so far that he accepted without question his views on agricultural policy, which faithfully reflected those of his class, to which, by 1930, he had become bound by a strong material interest. In the spring of the year he was presented, in recognition of his services to the nation, with what had once been the Hindenburg family estate of Neudeck in East Prussia; this national testimonial was organized by the Prussian Landowners' Association, of which Hindenburg's old Junker friend, von Oldenburg-Januschau, was president, though the money was largely subscribed by Rhineland industrialists and financiers. A nasty taint of scandal was, for those in the know, attached to the transaction; for in order to avoid death duties the deeds of the estate were registered in the name, not of the president, but of his son Oskar.

The president adopted his new responsibilities as a Prussian landowner with enthusiasm, and actively supported the landowners' claims to relief, in which economic arguments were supported by the demands of military strategy; German agriculture was not merely backward, inefficient and bankrupt, and therefore in need of relief, but its owners formed a military caste which was believed to be essential to the defence of Germany's eastern frontier against Poland.

The financial reforms introduced by Brüning in April 1930 were combined with measures for the protection and relief of agriculture east of the Elbe, to be administered through a government fund known as the Osthilfe, or Eastern Aid. These measures, by increasing German domestic food prices, imposed still further sacrifices on the mass of the German people. Elsewhere, the burden of the depression was to some extent alleviated by the heavy fall in the price of food; in Germany it was intensified by the maintenance of artificially high food prices by a policy of high protection. The scandal of the Osthilfe was further increased because the greater part of its funds went, not to the small farmer and peasant, but into the pockets of the large landowners. 'I cannot understand this policy,' said one critic of the Osthilfe. 'Do they want a social revolution?'

Brüning's package deal of deflation plus agricultural protection and assistance was passed by emergency decree on 12 April. By July, the financial situation had deteriorated so far as to make further economies necessary. With unemployment estimated at 2,000,000, as against the previous estimate of 1,400,000, the government faced a budget deficit of 750 million marks on unemployment account, and an additional 100 million marks for its public works programme.

On 7 July Brüning introduced further financial proposals demanding heavy sacrifices from all classes. Government expenditure was cut; there were increases in direct and indirect taxation, including supplementary income tax of 5 per cent, rising to 10 per cent on unmarried persons; a special contribution, the *Reichshilfe*, involving a reduction of 10 per cent in all public salaries; an increase in contributions to the unemployment insurance fund, producing a saving of 100 million marks on unemployment relief; and there were increases in municipal taxation.

This savage programme of deflation was again passed by emergency decree. The Reichstag, however, which had allowed the first emergency decree to pass without opposition, now made use of the constitutional provision permitting it to nullify the decree. Brüning replied by dissolving the Reichstag.

This has been described as 'one of the most fatal events in the history of the Weimar Republic'. It brought to an end the last Reichstag in which there was a parliamentary majority for the Republic, and plunged Germany into an acute political crisis which lasted until the appointment of Hitler as Reichschancellor. Today it is difficult to understand Brüning's reasons for this fatal decision, particularly as the Social Democrats had already signified that they were prepared, however reluctantly, for a renewal of the Grand Coalition.

Brüning, however, was convinced that his financial measures were unavoidable and that he alone was the man to execute them. Moreover, he was influenced by three beliefs, each of which turned out to be false. He believed, firstly, that he possessed the complete personal confidence of President Hindenburg, and that so long as he maintained the President's authority against the Reichstag he could continue to govern by emergency decree. He believed also that his financial programme would restore Germany's credit and, given time to work, would enable her to survive the economic crisis. And lastly he believed that, so long as the immediate financial difficulties could be overcome, the forthcoming elections would give him a majority in the Reichstag. He therefore postponed the elections until mid-September, the latest possible moment, and on 26 July introduced a new emergency decree, 'for the relief of financial, economic and social distress', which imposed additional taxation, provided credits for agriculture, and declared a moratorium on foreclosures on agricultural mortgages.*

It is hard to believe that anyone of Brüning's political experience and genuine ability could have miscalculated quite as badly as he did. Partly he was misled by his profound faith in, and respect for, the President, and his belief that this feeling was reciprocated. But he was also misled, like Hoover in the United States, by the belief that the depression, however severe, could not be more than a temporary phenomenon and that, so long as the strictest principles of financial orthodoxy were observed, it must necessarily come to an end.

In September the results of the elections demonstrated how

---

* This was designed to protect farmers against eviction for failure to meet interest charges on farm mortgages. Resistance to foreclosures had reduced parts of Germany to a state of civil war.

deeply Brüning had miscalculated the mood of the country. The Catholic Centre, Brüning's own party, did indeed gain 400,000 votes and six seats, but this was nothing like the sweeping vote of confidence for which he had hoped. The liberal parties, including Stresemann's German People's Party, suffered disastrous losses. The Social Democrats lost 600,000 votes and ten seats, but with 143 seats still remained the strongest party. The Nationalists, under Hugenberg, were punished severely for their leader's irresponsible and frequently ludicrous political antics. But the most startling result of the elections was the spectacular success of the two parties of the extreme right and left; the Communists polled 4,600,000 votes and won twenty-seven seats, the NSDAP 6,400,000 votes and 107 seats instead of their previous twelve.

The elections spelled the end of German democracy, and transformed the NSDAP from an insignificant parliamentary fraction into a national party, indeed *the* national party, second only to the SPD, but with all the revolutionary dynamism and fervour which the SPD so conspicuously lacked. From September 1930 onwards, until March 1933, the fundamental question in German politics was how long the National Socialists could be kept out of power. Their new importance, and the new situation which it created, was aptly symbolized by the election of Hermann Göring, ex-fighter ace and ex-drug addict, as President of the new Reichstag, a position which he immediately exploited to bring parliament into contempt and permit the Reichstag to become the scene of anti-Semitic demonstrations; while the composition of the National Socialist delegation, which included three convicted criminals and one murderer, Edmund Heines, showed that new and sinister forces had entered German political life.

The electoral success of the NSDAP was a victory for the lower depths of German society. Other events also revealed the alarming change which had taken place in German political life. Between 13 and 24 September there took place, before the Supreme Court in Göttingen, the trial of two young lieutenants, Scheringer and Rudin, accused and convicted of conducting National Socialist agitation in the Reichswehr. The trial showed how far National Socialism had already penetrated the politically neutral Reichswehr and gave Hitler the opportunity of haranguing the court, and the nation, on the basic principles of National Socialism and displaying himself as a national leader, entrusted with the destiny of the German people. On 5 October, a demonstration at Coblenz by the Stahlhelm, a war veterans' association, which provided the German Nationalists with a para-military force, was graced by the presence of General von Seekt, Chief of Staff of the Reichswehr, together with the German Crown Prince.

Both the trial and the demonstration were occasions for scandal and alarm, primarily because of the doubt they threw on the political reliability of the Reichswehr, which had hitherto given its support to the Republican regime. The doubts were justified, because the Reichswehr was already engaged on that course of devious intrigue and conspiracy which assisted Hitler to power. When Brüning's government was formed, his Minister of Defence, General Groener, assured a friend that 'all the trumps are in my hand, and the lead is on the left'; this was also the view, he said, of General von Schleicher, 'my Cardinal for political affairs'.

When the Reichstag opened on 13 October it was the scene of an anti-Semitic demonstration by the National Socialists. Brüning, as if still unable to learn the lesson of the elections, promised further cuts in expenditure, cuts in unemployment benefit and increases in contributions, and additional protection for agriculture; on 1 December the President signed a fourth emergency decree embodying these measures. Germany by now had entered on a period in which politics and economics were inextricably intertwined. Every increase in unemployment brought further measures of deflation; each measure of deflation further intensified the crisis.

Brüning himself was caught up in a chain of events which he could no longer control, because they no longer depended on Germany alone. The effect abroad of the National Socialists' electoral success had been disastrous, especially in France; of all the foreign press, which was almost universally hostile, only *The Times* offered reasons why the National Socialists should not be taken too seriously. No one was less inclined to take this advice than Germany's foreign creditors, who saw in the course of events reason to fear for the security not merely of their interest but of their capital and rushed to liquidate their holdings; there was a certain irony in this, because the policy followed by Brüning with such disastrous results was largely inspired by the motive of restoring confidence in Germany abroad, by methods which had the approval of every orthodox financier and banker.

The withdrawal, or failure to renew, foreign loans and credits, and the liquidation of foreign holdings had particularly severe effects in Germany, both because of the terms on which foreigners had normally extended credit to her and because of the nature of the German banking system, which made it peculiarly sensitive to movements of foreign capital.

To the foreign lender, the attraction of investment in Germany, after its political and economic stabilization, had been the very high rates of interest which could be earned; after 1925 they were at least twice as high as those offered elsewhere. From 1928 to 1929, however, this failed to maintain the constant supply of new capital required by Germany owing to the superior attraction of the New York market, where prospects of speculative gains were dazzling and call money could earn very high rates of interest without risk; after 1929, supplies of credit dried up as speculators licked their wounds and tried to liquidate their losses. Up to the end of 1930 the German banks lost one million marks of foreign exchange. But after the September elections, when investors began to fear about the security of their capital, withdrawals reached panic proportions and 700 million marks were lost.

The German banking system as a whole was ill equipped to meet withdrawals on such a scale. So far it had withstood the onset of the depression with greater success than industry. Bank profits stood at 69 per cent of their 1928 level, as compared with 33 per cent in industry, and bank shares had maintained their value better than industrial shares. But both the German banking structure and German banking practice had features which made them peculiarly sensitive to outside influences; indeed they were completely dependent on the maintenance of foreign confidence in the political and economic stability of Germany. Two-thirds of their own capital had been lost as a result of the Great War, and in the post-war period a large proportion of their capital was in foreign hands. Moreover, foreign investment had been primarily in the form of short-term loans, which required to be constantly renewed or replaced, as they had been employed by the banks to finance long-term investment in the expansion of German industry. Lastly, it was German banking practice to maintain a much lower liquidity ratio than was usual elsewhere, in some cases as low as 3 per cent as compared with the 10 per cent which was regarded as prudent in Britain.

The German banks in fact presented in concentrated form the characteristic features of the German economic system as a whole; that is to say, of a system which was rapidly expanding but depended on a constant import of foreign capital. Indeed, the banks had constituted themselves the main channel through which such capital flowed into German industry, and they had been among the leaders in encouraging and organizing the series of mergers, take-overs and cartels which had promoted the growth of large-scale industrial enterprises, particularly in the chemical, mining and textile industries, which were the characteristic feature of German industrial development in the post-war period.

In this, the banks had played an indispensable part; nevertheless, much of their activity had been, from the point of view of strict banking practice, of a highly speculative kind. In this respect perhaps the most typical, because the most daring and aggressive, German banker of the post-war period, was Jacob Goldschmidt, head of the Danat (Darmstädter und National) bank. In 1927 he had taken over the banking business of the largest German textile concern, the Nordwolle, from the Berliner Handelsgesell-schaft. The Nordwolle had grown out of a Bremen family firm owned by the three brothers Lahusen, who had been refused credits for further expansion, and had reacted by transferring their business to Goldschmidt, who shared their expansionist views. In 1931, the association of the Nordwolle and the Danat bank was to prove one of the weakest links in the entire German banking system.

By the end of 1930 Germany was threatened by a crisis which was at once political, economic and financial, and the German banks in particular were under increasing strain. It is doubtful if, at that moment, anything short of a miracle could have averted the crisis, and the miracle was not forthcoming. Brüning himself saw no hope except in continuing and intensifying the deflationary measures he had already taken; yet in fact they were themselves a major cause of the crisis.

Historians and economists alike have combined to condemn Brüning as one of the chief architects of Germany's ruin, though according to his own lights he acted from the best of motives. Yet at this date it should be possible to take a less severe view of his failure. Germany had recovered from the chaos and anarchy of the First World War by restoring her credit with her ex-enemies and by regaining their confidence. She could continue to maintain her credit, both moral and financial, only by continuing to fulfil the obligations she had assumed, including the obligation incurred under the Young Plan to 'maintain the gold standard under all circumstances'. This in fact made it impossible for her to follow any policy except one of severe, indeed intolerable, deflation. To have adopted any other policy would have been to admit that the unholy alliance of the extreme right and the extreme left, which opposed the Young Plan, was in the right; unless, that is, Germany's creditors had agreed, within less than a year of the signature of The Hague agreements, that it had already become impossible for Germany to fulfil its terms. To have disowned the Young Plan unilaterally* would have been to concede victory to the worst elements in Germany, and if he had done so Brüning would have been even more severely condemned by history than he is today.

There was probably no escape from the dilemma with which Brüning was faced; his error was that he believed implicitly in the efficacy of the measures recommended to him by every principle of 'sound' finance. In the last month of 1930 there occurred in Berlin an event which showed how greatly the mood of Germany had changed and the political situation had degenerated during the preceding twelve months. In 1929 the most popular bestseller in Germany (as in many other countries) was Erich Maria Remarque's *Am Westen Nichts Neues (All Quiet on the Western Front)*. It was a scarifying attack on German militarism and the evils of the trench warfare of 1914–18. The German public could read it in the reassuring knowledge that such horrors were things of the past, and could never recur again. In the same way English readers, in the same year, of Robert Graves's autobiographical account of the war in the West could take comfort from its title: *Goodbye to All That*.

* That is to say, without the previous agreement and consent of the other signatories to the Young Plan. It was of the essence of Brüning's policy that Germany's credit could only be maintained if revision of the Young Plan were carried out by consent.

But in December 1930, when the film version of *All Quiet on the Western Front* was shown in Berlin, Dr Josef Goebbels, the recently appointed National Socialist leader for North Germany, was able to call his storm troopers into the streets, and by riots and demonstrations force the authorities to ban the film, as an insult to the German army and the German nation.

In Great Britain, as in Germany, the deepening of the crisis and the rise in unemployment thwarted the government's calculations and increased the burden on the unemployment insurance fund. It had been expected, or hoped, that after a seasonal rise in the winter, the unemployment figures would show a fall in the spring; but by March they stood at 1,700,000, an increase of nearly half a million on the figures for the same month of the previous year, and the government was forced to increase the borrowing powers of the fund, first to £50 million in March, and in July, when the figures had risen by a further 200,000, to £62 million.

Orthodox reaction to the rise in unemployment and its consequences was, as in the United States and in Germany, to demand a return to the principles of 'sound finance' by a reduction in government expenditure together with a reduction in taxation. Businessmen, the Federation of British Industries, even the Archbishop of Canterbury, all denounced the burden of public spending as the main cause of the depression; in this they were in full agreement with the Socialist Chancellor of the Exchequer, Philip Snowden, whose first Budget, introduced in April, was described by the *Manchester Guardian* as having 'a puritanical rigour which has not been seen since the days of Gladstone'. Even Snowden, however, could not avoid new expenditure of £47,000,000, which included an additional £14,000,000 for unemployment insurance, and £5,000,000 as part repayment of the deficit of £14,500,000 incurred in the previous year; the new expenditure was to be paid for by new taxation.

Snowden's Budget marked the triumph of orthodox finance in the councils of the Labour Party, and the rejection not merely of a socialist answer to the problem of the depression but of any effective measures whatever for dealing with it. Given the choice between revolution or the traditional wisdom of the City, the Labour Government unhesitatingly chose the latter; its greatest contempt was reserved for those who believed there was anything in between. The counterpart of the Budget was the total inability of J.H.Thomas, as minister with special responsibility for unemployment, to devise any large-scale measures for dealing with the problem. Like its capitalist counterparts elsewhere, the Socialist Government believed that the depression was an inevitable result of the working of the capitalist system. They differed in believing that it could and should be cured by the total transformation of that system; but since, under existing conditions, this was manifestly impossible, they found themselves likewise condemned to wait until the depression cured itself.

To one member of the Cabinet, however, the policy of waiting on the mysterious workings of the trade cycle was intellectually and temperamentally unacceptable. The Chancellor of the Duchy of Lancaster, Sir Oswald Mosley, had a passionate belief that there were practical solutions for the problems of the depression and that the evils of mass unemployment were intellectually and morally indefensible. According to his private secretary, John Strachey, the strongest motive which had drawn him into politics was the hope of 'doing something for the unemployed', and in office he did not intend to sacrifice this hope to the orthodox obsessions of Philip Snowden, the passivity of Ramsay MacDonald, or the muddleheaded buffoonery of J.H.Thomas.

At the end of 1929 Mosley told the prime minister that he was thinking of preparing a memorandum on unemployment. In January he showed it to Keynes and Henderson, saying that it was 'his last word' on the subject. Both agreed that it was 'a very able document', not surprisingly perhaps, because it reflected many of Keynes's own ideas. Mosley then sent the document to MacDonald, who set up a Cabinet sub-committee to consider it.

Mosley's memorandum put forward a comprehensive plan which, if it had been adopted, would have revolutionized British economic policy. It covered both short-term and long-term measures to combat unemployment, the financial and credit policies required to support them, and the administrative machinery for putting them into effect. In the short term, Mosley proposed a pensions plan for the early retirement of workers in the declining industries, the raising of the school-leaving age to fifteen, expenditure of £200 million over three years on road construction, and grants to promote employment in the depressed areas. He calculated that, taken together, those measures would create work for 700,000 men annually, at a cost to the Exchequer of £10 million per annum, while the cost of the road programme would be raised by borrowing against the revenue of the road fund.

In the long term Mosley devoted himself primarily to the financial and credit policies necessary to support an expansionist policy of public works, industrial rationalization and internal development, and consulted Keynes about the possibility of borrowing on the scale that would be required. Keynes replied that this was primarily a technical question, which was a matter for experts, but that it would demand the creation of a national investment board.

The criticisms of Mosley's proposals made by the government's financial advisers may be regarded as a distillation of the economic wisdom of the day. They rejected Mosley's budgetary calculations of the cost of his retirements plan because he had averaged them over fifteen years, while the Treasury insisted that the whole of it should be paid in the first year; yet in fact even this would only have raised the total cost of his proposals to £19,500,000 in the first year, with a proportionate reduction later. The proposal to raise a large loan for unemployment grants was criticized on the ground that it would undermine confidence in the currency, and investment in internal development because it would curtail foreign lending. Snowden wrote in his autobiography that the finance of Mosley's plan 'would not stand a moment's consideration'; Lloyd George described it as 'an injudicious mixture of Karl Marx and Lord Rothermere'. Mosley's reply to such criticisms was that the views of the government's advisers implied that in fact nothing could be done to solve the problem of unemployment except to wait for it to cure itself: 'It is a policy of surrender, of negation.'

The difference between Mosley's ideas and those of his critics represents the difference between two distinct eras of economic thought; it is significant that Keynes was one of the few who gave Mosley his encouragement. In May, after a hostile report by its sub-committee, the Cabinet rejected the memorandum, and this was followed by Mosley's resignation, an event which may be regarded as both a personal and a national tragedy; personal, because it drove Mosley into political adventures which deprived him of any effective influence on British policy; national, because British parliamentary politics lost one of the few men who had the intellectual courage to face the real problems of the depression. It was also a tragedy for the Labour Party, for it meant that the government, chained by the views of its orthodox advisers, was no longer capable of any effective attempt to solve the problem of unemployment. It had condemned itself to what Mosley called 'the policy of surrender, of negation', and like every other government which adopted this course, its surrender was followed by its collapse.

CHAPTER SIX

Annus
Terribilis

The year 1931 was described by Arnold Toynbee in the *Survey of International Affairs* as *annus terribilis*. The title was well chosen. Today, a generation which is itself haunted by premonitions of approaching doom may find it hard to credit the great fear which overshadowed men's minds in that year, or at least may feel that it was absurdly exaggerated. For it was a fear, which to some people became a hope, that western civilization was on the point of imminent and total collapse, and that nothing could be done to avert its fall.

Professor Toynbee, a professional chronicler of his times, with wide and varied sources of information at his command, had no doubt of the reality of men's forebodings, nor was he inclined to dismiss them as unfounded. It seemed reasonable to him to compare the situation in 1931 with the collapse of the classical world order in the third century AD, and the comparison seemed all the more exact because in both cases collapse was due not to any external threat but to the disintegration of society as a result of its own internal weakness.

Toynbee was writing in the spirit of some ancient historian recording the details of a huge disaster which had occurred within his own lifetime. His words are worth quoting at some length because they express very vividly the apocalyptic sense of doom which filled many men's minds at the time.

The year 1931 was distinguished from previous years in the 'post-war' and the 'pre-war' age alike – by one outstanding feature. In 1931 men and women all over the world were seriously contemplating and frankly discussing the possibility that the western system of society might break down and cease to work. By the time when this possibility presented itself, western society had come to embrace all the habitable lands and navigable seas on the face of the planet, and the entire living generation of mankind; and, within narrower geographical limits, it had been in existence as a 'going concern', without any breach of continuity, for some twelve or thirteen centuries. Western civilization had been living and growing continuously, with only occasional and never more than temporary checks and setbacks, ever since the interregnum which had followed the breakdown of the ancient 'classical' civilization and the breakdown of the 'classical' super-state, the Roman Empire. In the West, that interregnum had closed at the turn of the seventh and eighth centuries of the Christian Era, with the emergence of a new order of society embodied in Western Christendom; and this small and rudimentary society was the geographical nucleus and the historical embryo of the 'Great Society' of 1931. During the intervening centuries, Western civilization had gone from strength to strength; and, while it had never been dispensed from the struggle for existence, or had been deprived of the perpetual stimulus of repeated challenge, it had always responded victoriously, and the Gates of Hell had not prevailed against it. In 1931, the members of this great and ancient and hitherto triumphant society were asking themselves whether the secular process of Western life and growth might conceivably be coming to an end in their day.

It would be easy to say, in criticism of this eloquent passage, that Professor Toynbee has always looked at history from too elevated a height, *sub specie aeternitatis*; and that, even during its greatest crises, ordinary men and women are too preoccupied with the ordinary business of living to ask if the world is coming to an end. But in fact, in 1931, the ordinary business of living was, for millions of men and women throughout the world, such that they were inevitably led to ask whether the system of society under which it was possible could or ought to survive.

One might also compare Professor Toynbee's words with the view of a much more sceptical and pragmatic observer of the human scene, who was less affected by analogies with the remote cataclysms of the past than by what businessmen were thinking and doing, and by how they expressed their expectations. Lecturing at Chicago in 1931, J. M. Keynes began as follows:

We are today in the middle of the greatest catastrophe – the greatest catastrophe due almost to entirely economic causes – of the modern world. I am told that the view is held in Moscow that this is the last, the culminating crisis of capitalism, and that our existing order of society will not survive it. Wishes are fathers to thought. But there is, I think, a possibility – I will not put it higher than that – that when the crisis is looked back upon by the economic historian of the future, it will be seen to mark a major turning point.

It would be interesting to know who told Keynes what was being thought in Moscow; but in his own beloved Cambridge there were already plenty of undergraduates who had come to the same conclusion, and some who were so committed to it as to come to decisions which finally turned them into spies and traitors. What drove them to this path was the spectacle of a world in which mass unemployment seemed to be a permanent and dominating feature; and *The Originating Causes of World Unemployment* was the title of a lecture to which Keynes's sombre words served as an introduction. What gave indisputable reality to the forebodings of Toynbee or Keynes, or to the prophecies of doom preached by communists in Moscow or Cambridge or Oxford or Harvard, and what linked them directly to the daily experience of millions of men and women, was the existence, and the apparently uncontrollable growth, of world unemployment on a scale never known before or since. On this scale it constituted a traumatic experience which shook the western world to its foundations, and it has never been quite the same since. The human suffering and waste it entailed was incalculable; but it was sufficient to amount, in the eyes of those who were directly affected by it or who felt themselves threatened by it, and of those with sufficient imagination to comprehend what it involved, to a moral and practical condemnation of the system under which it was possible.

But it was not only a source of condemnation; it was also, to many of those who, in government, in finance, in industry, were trying to administer the capitalist system, a source of profound intellectual bewilderment. For according to the accepted body of economic thought unemployment on this scale quite simply could not exist; yet the fact of it was there before men's eyes.

Keynes himself was saved from such a condition because he had, or believed that he had, discovered the true causes of unemployment and was in a position to offer a cure for them. Mass unemployment was indeed the predictable result of the capitalist system as it had operated in the post-war world, but this was for reasons which could be understood and therefore remedied.

The causes of world unemployment, he told his Chicago audience, were three:

(1) a decline in output leading to a decline in investment;
(2) a decline in profits leading to a decline in investment;
(3) a fall in prices, and a cessation of lending, which destroyed the credit of overseas borrowers, and made borrowing dearer for them just at the moment when they needed cheaper loans.

These conditions were, Keynes said, 'without any doubts or reservations whatever, the explanation of the world crisis'. But, he added, the explanation was only valid on one assumption; that a decline in the volume of investment leads to a fall in business profits. This assumption in turn involved an additional argument, which was fully stated in his book, *A Treatise on Money*, just published. Keynes warned his listeners that the argument was a long and difficult one and had not yet become 'part of the accepted body of economic thought'. His listeners might perhaps be forgiven if they felt that a cure for unemployment which required a general understanding and acceptance of *A Treatise on Money* was not likely to have much immediate effect.

Yet by 1931 'the accepted body of economic thought' was faced by a situation so unprecedented that the traditional rules and prescriptions of economic science and financial practice no longer seemed to have any application to it. The crisis was a crisis of confidence, and the approved means of restoring confidence were sound finance and a balanced budget; but how could these help if all they did was to reduce still further an already inadequate level of demand? The appropriate reply to a reduction, or cessation, of lending was to raise the bank rate; but what happened if a rise in bank rate, instead of attracting new money, was only taken as a danger signal which scared money away? In 1931 creditors were no longer interested in the rate of interest, however high; it was the safety of their capital which concerned them. And what if such measures, though sanctified both by theory and by experience, had political repercussions which only gave one more turn of the screw to an already intolerable situation?

In practice, the most that statesmen and financiers could achieve in 1931 were emergency measures and desperate improvisations which might temporarily fill the gaps which arose successively throughout the economic and political structure until they threatened to bring the whole system down in ruins. As the crisis became acute in one country after another, they flocked from capital to capital like birds of ill omen, and wherever they settled their arrival was taken as a storm signal which increased rather than alleviated panic. The travels of Dr Luther, President of the Reichsbank, in the summer of that year, might be taken as typical; from Berlin to Paris, from Paris to London, and from London back to Paris, assuming false names in the hope of escaping public notice, while in Berlin itself the situation progressively deteriorated.

The permanent shadow which lent a sense of helplessness and hopelessness to the efforts of statesmen was that of the steadily mounting figures of unemployment, which by the end of 1931 reached staggering proportions. It is estimated that, even in the prosperous years from 1925 to 1929, world unemployment was never less than six to eight millions, and this in itself was sufficiently disturbing to those who had to try and deal with the long-term difficulties of the problem. It was assumed, however, that on the whole the high level of unemployment was due to the dislocations caused by the war, and that as those were overcome the figures could be expected to fall. But during 1931 they rose to something between twenty and twenty-five million, and this represented an increase of some six million in that one year alone. Moreover, these figures were certainly incomplete, as they did not cover all countries, or all forms of unemployment in many countries. But even the incomplete figures pointed to the depressing conclusion that, in the words of the League of Nations Intelligence Service, 'there were some sixty to seventy million people deprived of the means of existence arising out of their own activity or that of those on whom they were dependent.'

The strain, economic and political, created by this huge mass of unemployment, was all the greater because it was very largely concentrated in the world's most advanced industrial countries. The great paradox of unemployment, of poverty in the midst of plenty, was all the more glaring because the poverty was worst where the plenty was greatest, and this seemed to justify the conclusion that the capitalist crisis was worst where capitalism was most advanced. In the United States, in 1931, unemployment increased by 4 million to nearly $10\frac{1}{2}$ million; in Germany from $4\frac{3}{4}$

million to over 6 million; in Great Britain it remained nearly
stationary at just over 2,600,000. Even in France, which until then
had escaped the worst effects of the depression, it rose from 72,000
to 347,000, and in Italy from 735,000 to over one million. To 'the
accepted body of economic thought' such figures were an outrage
and an affront; how much longer could it be contended, with any
show of plausibility, that capitalism was the most efficient means of
satisfying needs, if so large a proportion of the world's labour and
material resources were left to go to waste?

Yet, even so, the world's troubles in 1931 were only in part
economic, and Keynes might be accused of an oversimplification
in describing the crisis as a catastrophe 'due almost entirely to
economic causes'. For the economic crisis was at every point
accentuated and deepened by political factors, and even when it
appeared that there were economic or financial measures available
they were continually thwarted and frustrated by political com-
plications. One reason for this was that two of the countries to
which, since the war, the western world had looked for economic
and political leadership were temporarily prostrated by their own
troubles and were unable to play the part which the world had
come to expect of them.

For a century the western world had looked to Britain for its
economic and financial leadership; and when, after the First World
War, it became evident that Britain's resources were no longer
adequate to allow her to play this part alone, it seemed inevitable
that the United States should either share it with her or take it over
altogether. It now appeared that, for the time being at least, neither
Britain nor the United States could discharge the traditional
function of banker to the world economic system; they were hardly
able to save themselves, let alone the rest of the world.

In a third great industrial country, Germany, the economic
crisis became so acute during 1931 that it seemed her entire
financial structure would collapse, with incalculable consequences,
both economic and political, for the western world. The reconstruction and rehabilitation of Germany, to which both Britain and
the United States had made notable contributions, had been
regarded as essential to the restoration of 'normal', that is to say
pre-war, conditions in the capitalist world; her collapse threatened
a reversion to the chaos and confusion which had immediately

followed the end of the war and the disintegration of the new Europe which had so painfully been put together during the years of prosperity.

In this situation there was only one country, France, which during the crisis of 1931 had the resources to offer effective assistance and leadership; and one of the most remarkable features of that year was that for a short time it restored to France an economic and political hegemony of a kind which she had not enjoyed since the days of the *Roi Soleil*.

Such a development seemed to many people, especially in Germany, but also in Britain and the United States, both unnatural and intolerable, as if the course of history had suddenly been reversed. For France's predominance was based to a large extent on causes which were artificial and transitory. She had been protected against the worst effects of the depression by the devaluation of the franc and its stabilization at a parity considerably below its true value; and though there were already signs that she was beginning to lose the benefit of this advantage, for the moment it remained. A favourable balance of trade, the repatriation of French capital from abroad, the sale of the Bank of France's holdings of foreign exchange, had raised her gold reserves to nearly 80 billion francs, an increase of nearly 15 billion francs since 1928, providing a more than hundred per cent cover for her currency.

The significance of France's financial strength during the crisis of 1931 was that she was prepared to use it for primarily political ends; to her it seemed that the economic crisis offered her an opportunity which might never occur again. For the confidence she derived from her prosperity concealed reasons for profound disquiet about her long-term prospects, and particularly her relations with Germany. No country had followed with greater anxiety and alarm the growing strength of the National Socialists; for the total defeat of Germany in the First World War had signally failed to give France the security she desired. Defeat had been followed in Germany by an economic recovery which had allowed her to modernize and re-equip her industry, on a scale which made her potentially the most powerful country in Europe, while French industry remained relatively backward; demographically also, Germany enjoyed an advantage which increased every year. In population, in industrial resources and in technology, France was inferior and the violent campaign waged by the German Nationalists and National Socialists against the Versailles Treaty was an assurance that Germany would only accept her position of military inferiority as long as it could be maintained by force. The attempt made by Stresemann on the German side, and by Briand on the French, to find a genuine basis for understanding and cooperation had not reconciled the German Nationalists to the restraints and burdens imposed by the treaty; even the evacuation of the Rhineland had done nothing to abate the violence of the revisionist campaign. Indeed, it had come to seem to the French that every concession on her part only led to further demands by the Germans.

France had tried to compensate for her long-term weaknesses by an elaborate system of alliances with the successor states* of Central and Eastern Europe, but she had no illusions that they could permanently guarantee her security if Germany once recovered her freedom of action. By 1931 Stresemann was a dead man and Briand a defeated and dying one, and none of their successors were capable, even if they had so wished, of carrying their countrymen with them on the path of reconciliation. When France, therefore, momentarily found herself the strongest power financially, as well as militarily, in Europe, while Germany was on the point of collapse and compelled to turn to her for aid, she used her advantage for primarily political ends and insisted on political concessions by Germany in return for any assistance she might give.

Perhaps gold might buy what military victory had failed to achieve; M. Monet at the Bank of France was as much influenced by strategic considerations as if he had been Marshal Foch. Nor were personal factors entirely missing. He looked with hostility and suspicion on Montague Norman's plans for the reconstruction of Europe, of which the recovery of Germany was an essential feature; just as they had won Norman the friendship of Schacht, so they had earned him the enmity of M. Monet. In 1931 it was not an unwelcome feature of the situation in M. Monet's eyes that it gave him the opportunity of exposing the weakness of the Bank of England and of demonstrating to Germany that, if she wished for help, only France could give it.

* The newly created states, based on the principle of national self-determination, which had emerged after the war in Central Europe out of the ruins of the Austro-Hungarian Empire.

It was, no doubt, a shortsighted policy; the friendship, or compliance, of a potential enemy, especially one whose emotions are as inflamed as they were in Germany at that moment, is hardly to be won by such methods. But by a curious mischance, or fatality, it was also applied at a moment when every circumstance combined to make it difficult for any German government to accept it. For in Germany, also, Dr Brüning, in his effort to master the economic crisis, could not afford to ignore political considerations. He was determined, no matter what the cost to the German people, to fulfil the provisions of the Young Plan, and discharge the obligations Germany had assumed under it. He believed that this was the only way to show that those obligations were in fact too heavy for Germany to bear, while at the same time maintaining Germany's financial credit, and firm in his trust in the President, he was confident that he could carry out this double-edged policy.

But he also knew that the sacrifices it demanded of Germany were so heavy as to be intolerable unless some compensation for them were to be found elsewhere; indeed, the mounting agitation against his policy had become so violent that he had no alternative. He was thus driven to seek a success in the field of foreign politics of a kind which was precisely calculated to exacerbate all the suspicions and hostility of the French and increase their determination to obtain every advantage they could from their financial strength.

Thus the economic and financial crisis of 1931 was intensified and complicated by political issues. Financial measures which might have alleviated it were postponed or delayed by political differences. Economic difficulties forced statesmen into political measures which only aggravated the crisis. International cooperation, to meet what was in fact a general crisis, was thwarted and frustrated by political suspicions and passions.

And this intimate and inextricable intermingling of economic, financial and political issues was not merely a matter of chance or coincidence. It was of the essence of the crisis that it affected every aspect of the capitalist system and all its institutions, and it was the sense of its universality as well as its intensity which gave rise to the fear in many men's minds that the system as a whole was at the end of its tether. Moreover, the close association between politics and economics marked a permanent change in the working of the capitalist system as it had developed in the nineteenth and early twentieth century. It had been of the very essence of that system that economic forces should be free to work themselves out without political interference; the crisis of 1931 demonstrated that this was an ideal which no longer corresponded to the facts of contemporary life and that economic policies were in the last resort only a special aspect of politics.

Yet the year began well. In January it was announced, after months, indeed years, of preliminary negotiations, that the World Disarmament Conference would open on 2 February 1932. The only preliminary problem that remained to be settled was the negotiation of a Franco-Italian naval agreement which would complement the three-Power agreement of April 1930 between the United States, Britain and Japan. It is difficult today, with knowledge of subsequent events, to understand the high hopes and expectations which were inspired by the announcement. Yet throughout the twenties general disarmament had been regarded as the surest means of liquidating the aftermath of the First World War, not only politically and militarily, but economically. There were those who thought that armaments were at the root of the western world's economic troubles; security, peace and business confidence were merely different aspects of one fundamental problem. In President Hoover's view, general disarmament provided the most important single cure for the depression. This followed from his belief that the depression was mainly the consequence of the political and economic uncertainties arising out of the First World War, and that for these disarmament was the most effective remedy.

Otherwise, however, there were not many reasons for satisfaction. In the United States, at the beginning of the year, as unemployment rose to the five million mark, a demonstration by the unemployed in New York led to disorders which were suppressed by the police. The crop failure of 1930 had caused intense distress in agricultural areas; the effect of the fall in commodity prices was intensified by natural disaster, and it was all the more acutely felt because now it struck at even the most prosperous farmers. In January, tenant farmers at England, Arkansas, both white and black, and armed with rifles, rioted and looted a foodstore. A young communist in New York called Whitaker Chambers wrote a story, 'Can You Hear Their Voices?' in *New Masses*, based on newspaper reports of the incident. Reprinted in the Soviet Union, it was accepted as the authentic voice of a starving agricultural proletariat, foretelling the doom of capitalism. In the following month there were widespread disorders throughout the central and south-western states. In March the number of unemployed approached six million, and since public funds were exhausted the burden of relief was thrown almost entirely on to private and charitable sources. In the richest country in the world, as distress increased, the means of relieving it declined.

In Britain also the year opened with industrial unrest. New Year's Day was marked by a miners' strike in South Wales; later in the month, a strike in the Burnley cotton mills was followed by a general lock-out of the Lancashire cotton weavers. Unemployment rose to 2,600,000, an increase of over a million on the previous year, and in February it was necessary to authorize additional borrowing of £20 million by the Unemployment Insurance Fund. In May the government, alarmed by the financial outlook, appointed a committee, under the chairmanship of Sir George (later Lord) May, secretary of the Prudential Assurance Company, to inquire into the country's financial situation and propose means of improving it. But it was not only the government that was alarmed. Britain had long had an unrivalled reputation for the prudent management of her finances; the difficulties with which she was now faced seemed to many people abroad an ominous omen of the collapse of the entire world order which she had taken so large a part in constructing. For many people in the world, Britain *was* capitalism, and if Britain was no longer a going concern, neither was the capitalist system.

There were equally ominous signs in Germany. In February there were serious disorders in the Ruhr and the following month an emergency decree was issued aimed at the suppression of political violence. Parliamentary government was rapidly becoming impossible owing to the tactics employed by the Nationalists and National Socialists, and on 11 February their entire parliamentary delegations marched out of the Reichstag; on 26 March it was adjourned, but fears that it might be recalled, and so add a political to the economic crisis, played a considerable part in reducing foreign confidence in Germany during the summer. Unemployment, in February, had risen to nearly five million; the budget

Barney Baruch, Wall Street operator and adviser to three American Presidents.

(*right*) Sir Oswald Mosley in 1930.

Herbert Hoover, President of the United States 1929–33.

Hjalmar Schacht, President of the
Reichsbank 1924–30 and 1933–8.

Charles E. Mitchell, Chairman of the
National City Bank, Director, New
York Federal Reserve Bank.

Pierre Laval, Jimmy Walker (Mayor of New York), and Albert H. Wiggin,
Chairman of the Chase National Bank, in New York, October 1931.

deficit for 1931–2 was estimated at over one billion Reichsmarks.

The effects of the depression were most striking in the United States, Britain and Germany, because they were leading industrial countries on whose activity and prosperity the entire capitalist world depended. But by 1931 the crisis knew no geographical limits. There were revolutions and *coups d'état* in Spain, Portugal, Brazil and Peru. In China internal political troubles were complicated by the catastrophic fall in the price of silver on which her currency was based, and to these troubles were added the calamity of the worst floods in her history. And, almost unnoticed, during the summer the Japanese announced the murder of an obscure officer, Captain Nakamura, in Manchuria and thus prepared the way for the outbreak of war in the Far East. France alone seemed exempt from the universal epidemic of misfortune.

It was against such a background of deepening and darkening crisis that Dr Brüning undertook a diplomatic initiative which, he hoped, might appease nationalist sentiment in Germany. In March the European Powers were formally notified that a customs union between Germany and Austria was under consideration and had already been discussed in Vienna between the Austrian Chancellor, Dr Schober and the German Foreign Minister, Dr Curtins. The project had advantages for both the interested parties. To Austria it offered economic opportunities which would provide some compensation for the loss of the Hapsburg Empire of which Vienna had been the financial and commercial centre. To Dr Brüning it offered the chance of extending German influence in a way which would be particularly gratifying to German nationalist sentiment.

The proposal was, indeed, strictly limited to economic relations between the two countries; if it had wider implications it would be a serious breach of international agreements guaranteeing the sovereignty and independence of Austria. Yet no one, either in Germany or in France, could overlook the fact that an economic union was likely in the long run to have political results; or to forget the fact that an earlier customs union, the North German Confederation, had provided the foundation of a united Germany under Prussian domination. To the French, the proposal was a direct threat to the security system which she had erected in Eastern Europe, and she, her ally Czechoslovakia, and Italy immediately protested against it in Vienna. Nor was the Customs Union the only, though the most important, cause for French alarm; there was also the launching, in May, of the pocket battleship *Deutschland*, and the bitter conflict between Germany and another French ally, Poland, with regard to Germany's eastern frontier.

Yet despite such issues, it was not politics but finance which opened the next, and most acute, phase of the crisis. On 11 May the annual balance sheet of an Austrian bank, the Credit-Anstalt fur Handel und Gewerbe, was published. It showed that in the year 1930–1 the bank had lost 140 million Austrian schillings, or very nearly its total capital of 145 million schillings.

Professor Toynbee, in his review of the year 1931, compared the failure of the Credit-Anstalt with the murder of the Archduke Franz Ferdinand at Sarajevo in July 1914. Both events were in themselves of relatively minor significance, but both set off a chain reaction of disasters which was out of all proportion to their origin; each had such an effect only because of the immensely precarious and unstable condition of the society in which it occurred.

Indeed, there was no reason why a bank failure should in itself have affected anyone except those who were immediately involved. Between 1928 and 1930, 357 banking and savings institutions had become insolvent in Germany, without any significant after-effects. The Credit-Anstalt, however, was something rather different. Founded in 1855 by the Austrian branch of the Rothschilds, it was the oldest and most respected bank in Austria. In 1929, under government pressure, it had taken over an agricultural bank, the Boden Credit-Anstalt, which was already in financial difficulties, and after the take-over was responsible for seventy per cent of all Austria's banking assets and liabilities. The troubles of the Boden Credit-Anstalt, combined with a certain degree of mismanagement and extravagance in the conduct of its own affairs, proved too much for the Credit-Anstalt, and immediately its huge losses were known there were panic withdrawals not only from the Credit-Anstalt but from all the Austrian banks.

The panic brought to light a situation which applied not only to the Austrian banks but to the German banks as well. Against its own capital of 145 million schillings, it had borrowed 1,800 million schillings of foreign money, of which 700 million were in the form

[122]

of short-term credits. These, however, had been invested in Austrian industry and represented assets which could not be realized so long as the depression continued. Moreover, the value of the bank's assets had been heavily reduced by the decline on the stock market. This pattern of inadequate internal capital in relation to foreign holdings, of assets frozen in industry, and a sharp fall in share values was later to be found repeated in Germany.

The run on the banks began on 12 May and by the end of the month the Credit-Anstalt had lost 25 per cent of its foreign credits. To find new finance, the banks rediscounted bills with the National Bank of Austria, whose holding of bills tripled within four days. The banks were also forced to buy foreign exchange from the National Bank, while there was also a large internal demand for foreign exchange owing to growing fears of a devaluation of the schilling; in three days the National Bank's cover for the currency in gold and foreign exchange fell from $83 \cdot 5$ per cent to $67 \cdot 5$ per cent.

The Austrian government and the National Bank acted promptly to assist the Credit-Anstalt, which was responsible for financing the greater part of Austrian industry, but their own resources were not sufficient to halt the panic. It became necessary to look abroad for help, and the government now found itself faced with French pressure to surrender its plans for a customs union with Germany, as the political price for a loan. The government refused and turned to London for a loan; on 16 June a new government was formed, to which help was forthcoming from the Bank of England, in the form of an interim advance of 150 million schillings until other arrangements could be made.

This was Montague Norman's last unilateral attempt to save the crumbling edifice of Central European finance, which he had done so much to restore after the war. He realized that the Austrian financial crisis could not be localized unless it was quickly halted, and his offer of an interim loan was a desperate effort to prevent it from spreading to other centres, in particular Germany. And in its immediate object of saving the Credit-Anstalt his initiative was successful; but owing to the delay imposed by France's refusal to give financial assistance without political assistance, it was already too late to achieve the larger objective of preventing panic from spreading to Germany. Moreover, his generous action exposed the

Bank of England itself to danger. At the Bank of France, M. Monet regarded it as a deliberate attempt to thwart France's political aims, and took his revenge by opening an attack on sterling. The Bank of France sold the larger part of its holdings of sterling on the international exchanges and thus contributed directly to forcing Britain off the gold standard later in the year.

But first it was Germany's turn to become the centre of the crisis, which moved from country to country like a tornado. The fall of the Credit-Anstalt had made foreign investors sharply aware that the German banks were in many cases in a very similar position; they displayed the same characteristic weaknesses of over-expansion, inadequate capital, assets frozen in industry, and depreciated investments. Attracted by the high rate of interest, foreign investors had poured vast sums of money into Germany; now they became alarmed about the security of their capital. Their fears were increased by a series of financial failures in Germany, notably of two large insurance companies, which occurred immediately after the fall of the Credit-Anstalt. Moreover, some investors were under a pressing necessity to cash their foreign balances. The foreign debts of the Credit-Anstalt amounted to $76,000,000, of which $27,000,000 were owed in Britain. These assets were now frozen, and the creditors were forced to restore their position by withdrawing balances from Germany.

Immediately after the announcement of the Credit-Anstalt's losses, the run on the German banks began. German securities fell heavily on the New York Stock Exchange, and, from 11 May to the end of the month, $11,000,000 worth of short-term credits were withdrawn. Gold was exported to cover foreign withdrawals and the Reichsmark declined sharply on the exchanges. In June the run continued. In the first week of that month the Reichsbank lost 180 million RM (£9 million) in gold and foreign exchange, and in the second week 540 million RM (£27 million); the discount rate was raised from five to seven per cent. By the end of the third week in June, withdrawals had reached panic proportions; in two days, 19 and 20 June, the Reichsbank lost 150 million RM, and quotations for discounting private bills were suspended. In all, in the three weeks ending 23 June, the Reichsbank lost 974 million RM in gold and 93 million RM in foreign exchange, and its holding of discounted bills rose to 534 million RM.

[124]

The Reichsbank's losses were a consequence of the withdrawal of foreign credits from the German banks, in particular the five big Berlin banks, which had provided the channel through which foreign investment had poured into Germany. The most hard hit was the Danat (Darmstädter und National Bank), which lost 97 million RM of foreign credits, but the Dresdner and the Deutsche Banks, and the Commerz -und Privatbank also suffered severely, together losing a total of 166 million RM. The exception was the Berliner Handelgesellschaft, which under the direction of Carl Fürstenberg and Otto Jeidels had pursued an extremely cautious and conservative policy, refusing to accept any credits terminable at less than six months. Their caution had indeed lost them valuable customers to the other banks, in particular to the Danat; but it justified itself during the crisis of 1931, as the Berliner Handelsgesellschaft, while suffering losses, was never threatened with insolvency like its competitors, which during the month of May lost in all 263 million RM.

Events in Germany itself did nothing to allay the panic. On the same day on which the Credit-Anstalt's balance sheet was published, it became known that the great Karstadt department store was in difficulties. On 30 May the Hardstern insurance company announced a loss for the financial year of 28 million RM. A further blow to confidence was given, on 5 June, by the publication of a second emergency decree for the protection of Germany's economy and finances. This imposed a reduction of 4-8 per cent in public salaries, reduced unemployment relief and increased taxation. But, as in the case of the proposal for an Austro-German customs union, Brüning was again anxious to pacify the nationalist opposition, and the decree promised the German people a reduction in reparation payments; on the following day, the government announced its intention of demanding a revision of the Young Plan.

Brüning had been warned by the President of the Reichsbank and the State Secretary at the Ministry of Finance that the announcement could not fail to administer another blow to confidence in Germany; he replied rather naïvely that it was only designed for internal consumption. The text of the declaration was published while Brüning and his Foreign Minister were in London, where it was made clear to them that the damage to Germany's credit, particularly in the United States, would be far greater than any relief that might be obtained in the form of a reduction of reparation payments.

The warning proved correct. The declaration was interpreted abroad to mean that Germany was approaching national bankruptcy, and in the four days following its publication the Reichsbank lost 400 million RM of foreign exchange. There were also other reasons for alarm. On 5 June a member of the Berlin Municipal Council stated that the Danat was bankrupt, and his remark was printed in the communist paper *Welt am Abend*; the Danat immediately issued a denial, together with a threat of legal action, but the position of the bank remained under suspicion.

Politics also played its part. On the night of 10 June the parliamentary delegations of the National Socialists, the Nationalists, the Social Democrats and the Communists united to demand the recall of the Reichstag, with the object of debating and either rejecting or amending the emergency decree. The recall of the Reichstag at that moment threatened to add a political to the economic crisis and increased the uncertainties of the situation. On the two following days the Reichsbank lost 220 million RM and 114 million RM; the raising of the discount rate on 13 June brought some relief and the bank's losses fell on 15 June to 60 million RM and on 16 June to 80 million RM. There was a further improvement when the Social Democrats, the Volkspartei and the Centre Party withdrew their support of the demand for the recall of the Reichstag; on 17 June the Reichsbank's losses were only 10 million RM and on the following day they were insignificant. It seemed for a moment as if panic might be subsiding.

But Germany's financial position was by now so fundamentally unstable that any further mishap could renew the flight of capital. In all, from 1–17 June the Reichsbank had lost 1,400 million RM, or nearly half its total reserves; it was fast reaching the point when they would not be sufficient to provide the minimum legal cover for the currency. And on 17 June itself it was announced that the great textile combine, the Norddeutsche Wollkämmerei (the Nordwolle) was bankrupt. The Nordwolle had transferred its account to the Danat in 1927 because the Berliner Handelsgesellschaft refused to finance its further expansion; thereafter, under the management of the three brothers Lahusen, and with the backing of Jacob Goldschmidt of the Danat, its affairs had been conducted with a boldness that verged on illegality. The Lahusen brothers had speculated heavily in their own shares, in order to maintain their value, and had concealed both profits and losses through their Dutch subsidiary, Ultramare. When the Nordwolle's losses were revealed on 31 June, they were shown to amount to 200 million RM; their largest creditor and their largest shareholder was the Danat.

On 19 June there were renewed withdrawals of foreign credits. The Reichsbank lost 70 million RM, and by the evening its reserves barely exceeded the forty per cent minimum currency cover required by law. The Reichsbank could no longer fulfil its legal obligations. From now on, to all the other reasons for panic was added the spectre of inflation, which had haunted all German minds since the traumatic experience of 1923. Nor was the Reichsbank any longer able to finance, out of her own resources, the withdrawals of foreign capital on which the entire structure of German industry was dependent. Germany was on the point of collapse, for reasons which were both national and international, and were at once financial, economic and political, and she could no longer save herself by her own efforts. Her only resource was a foreign loan with which to meet the renewed withdrawals of capital; but how was such a loan to be raised when the crisis was itself the result of a total loss of confidence abroad in her financial and economic prospects?

In this critical situation Dr Luther, the President of the Reichsbank, turned once again to the Bank of England, which had for so long been Germany's friend and supporter. On 20 June Luther telephoned Montague Norman to ask whether he was willing to grant the Reichsbank a rediscount credit; Norman refused, not only because the risk involved, given Germany's economic and financial situation, was too great, but, even more perhaps, because the granting of a credit to Germany at the moment would have provoked an even stronger attack on the pound by the French. In the hope of persuading Norman to change his mind Luther announced that he would visit London the following day.

By now the Reichsbank was not only under pressure from abroad but was faced by an internal crisis also. The suspension of quotations for rediscounting private bills threatened to bring about a credit restriction which, superimposed on Brüning's deflationary policy, would bring the whole of German industry to a standstill. It was to come into force on 20 June, but the Reichsbank hesitated to take such a step, which would have had the gravest consequences both internally and externally, and for the moment contented itself with subjecting bills presented to it to a sharper scrutiny. But further credit restrictions could not be postponed much longer unless a loan was forthcoming. The Bank of England's refusal made this unlikely, and everything appeared to depend on Dr Luther's projected visit to London the following day. Yet, at this moment, help was at hand, though not in the form, or from a quarter, which had entered into German calculations. Late in the evening of 20 June the American Ambassador in Berlin informed the German government that President Hoover wished to propose a moratorium, for one year, on all international political debts, in particular German reparation payments and the war debts of the Allied powers to the United States. The Ambassador asked that, in order to provide a justification for the President's proposal, a telegram should be sent by President Hindenburg, calling attention to Germany's desperate financial position. Later that evening the telegram was despatched and on the night of 20–21 June President Hoover published his message.

For the moment it seemed as if Germany was saved. For years she had claimed that reparations constituted both an act of historical injustice and an intolerable financial burden; and the Nationalists had pressed this claim with such violence that it had become the source of a protracted crisis in the politics of the Reich. The Hoover moratorium promised Germany immediate economic and political relief. It was so interpreted both in Germany and abroad, and from 22–4 June foreign withdrawals from Germany almost ceased.

CHAPTER SEVEN

After the Moratorium

The Hoover moratorium, announced to the world on 21 June, was greeted as a great and generous act of statesmanship, and for a moment it seemed as if the announcement alone might, by restoring confidence, halt the crisis which was dragging Germany to ruin. To the Germans, especially, President Hoover appeared as a *deus ex machina*, who at one stroke had relieved them of the heavy burden of reparations which, they believed, had crippled them financially and economically ever since the signature of the Versailles Treaty. The President was not far from agreeing with them; he also believed that reparations were a fundamental factor in the general dislocation of the world economic system which was a legacy of the First World War, and that to abolish them was to take a decisive step towards solving the world crisis. His action in proposing the moratorium, though unexpected and dramatic, was not unpremeditated. He had been gravely disturbed by the gloomy reports about the deterioration in the economic situation which he had received both from his ambassador in Berlin, a former Federal Reserve banker, and from his Secretary of the Treasury, Andrew Mellon, who was visiting Europe and kept him fully informed of the pessimistic conclusions he had come to. The moratorium was conceived both as an emergency measure to alleviate Germany's immediate crisis and as a preliminary to a general settlement of the problem of inter-governmental debts which would remove one of the greatest obstacles to recovery.

The President was not alone in his belief in the importance of reparations as a determining factor in the economic crisis. The problem of inter-governmental debts, like the disarmament problem, had occupied the minds of enlightened statesmen for years, and there was a widespread feeling that, unless they were overcome, there could be no return to normal economic conditions, by which was meant the conditions that had prevailed before the First World War. In Britain especially, opinion had been profoundly influenced by J. M. Keynes's tract, *The Economic Consequences of the Peace*, and an entire generation had grown up to regard reparations as both a political crime and an economic blunder. Now it seemed as if the President had, temporarily at least, made a return to economic sanity possible, and, with one important exception, his proposals were welcomed in all the financial capitals of the world.

The immediate effect, therefore, of the President's proposals was to halt the drain of foreign capital from Germany. The moratorium represented a saving to Germany on reparations account in 1931–2 of 162 million RM; at the same time her financial resources were strengthened by the grant of a short-term rediscount credit of $100,000,000, shared equally between the Federal Reserve Bank, the Bank of England, the Banque de France and the Bank for International Settlements. Confidence was momentarily restored, and on 22 June, the day after the President's announcement, the Reichsbank suffered only insignificant losses.

It is possible that, if the moratorium had come immediately into effect, the restoration of confidence might have been lasting. Nevertheless, it rested very largely on a misunderstanding; it was one of those 'psychological' reactions to which bankers and statesmen attach so much importance but which rarely last long if they are in conflict with facts. For the immediate cause of the pressure on Germany was not due to doubts about her ability to pay reparations; it was due to the doubts of Germany's commercial creditors about the safety of the capital which they had poured in a golden stream into Germany and about the underlying soundness of the German economy. What was in doubt was Germany's ability to pay not her political but her commercial debts. No doubt these two problems were in the long run interrelated, but there was no real reason to think that the solution of the one would lead immediately to the solution of the other.

Moreover, the President's proposals had another weakness, which quickly became apparent as the days went by. They were, after all, only proposals, which could not come into force without the agreement of the other signatories to the Young Plan; owing to the critical situation of Germany, they had been made by the President unilaterally and without prior consultation with Germany's other political creditors; but without their consent his gesture would prove only a gesture.

At least one of those creditors, and in some ways at the moment the most important, did not regard the moratorium with the enthusiasm which it had inspired elsewhere. To the French it had none of the advantages which it offered in German, American or British eyes; indeed, on inspection, it looked suspiciously like an Anglo-Saxon plot to save themselves at France's expense. Moreover, it threatened to deprive France of the political advantage created by Germany's weakness, and on this occasion, as on many others before or since, she was determined to use financial strength as the servant of political policy. President Hoover might feel generous; France did not; and she felt even less inclined to pay for the President's generosity.

The French deeply resented the President's unilateral announcement; she regarded it as an affront both to her financial predominance in Europe at that moment, and to the facts of the situation, which were that she alone was in a position to give effective financial assistance to Germany. Moreover, she was being asked to make by far the heaviest sacrifice under the moratorium, as she was entitled to 52 per cent of the annuities payable by Germany under the Young Plan. On the other hand, she had the least to gain; she had not followed the rush of the Americans, British, Swiss and Dutch to pour their money into Germany and stood to lose little by a German financial collapse.

French hostility to the moratorium, and the consequent delay in securing general agreement to it, quickly deprived it of its initial effect as a stimulant to confidence and blighted the hopes that had initially been founded on it. By 27 June, the breathing space it had afforded Germany was already coming to an end; but to the Germans themselves this was not yet apparent, nor were they as yet prepared to draw the right conclusions from the temporary relief they had been afforded. On that day an emergency meeting of the central association of the German bankers was held; it was attended also by Dr Brüning and Dr Luther. The prevailing mood was one of self-satisfaction that Germany's ex-enemies had at last recognized the folly of reparations. The Chancellor described the moratorium as an event of world historical importance, which

[131]

would lay the foundation for economic recovery; but only on condition of the strictest economy in national expenditure and rigid observation of the policy of deflation. The President of the Reichsbank attributed the nervousness of Germany's creditors to political factors, and in particular to anxieties about the burden of reparations. The bankers' representatives were equally agreed that politics, in the shape of reparations, and not the weaknesses of capitalism, in particular any mistakes of their own, were responsible for the crisis. Only one dissentient voice disturbed the harmony of the meeting, which was in sharp contrast to the bankers' disagreements whenever they were asked to put their own house in order. A provincial banker from Bavaria suggested that one important contributory factor in the economic crisis was the abnormally high rate of interest prevailing in Germany, due not merely to her continuing lack of capital, but to excessive competition for deposits between the German banks. He proposed a general lowering of interest rates, to which the banks, savings banks and other credit institutions would contribute by a self-denying ordinance against internecine competition.

There is an air of unreality about these proceedings, of men unable to face the truth, which is curiously reminiscent of the deliberations of American bankers during the Wall Street crash. But the complacency of the German bankers was not permitted to last for long. On the same day that they acquitted themselves of blame, the withdrawal of credits was resumed, and the Reichsbank lost 40 million RM of foreign exchange. The sole resources which the Reichsbank now possessed to meet the pressure from abroad was the recently granted rediscount credit of $100,000,000; her remaining reserves were barely sufficient to provide the minimum cover for the currency, to which it was committed, not only under German law but by international agreement.

But the situation of the Reichsbank only reflected the pressure upon the private banks, in particular the five large Berlin joint stock banks. Their monthly figures, published on 30 June, showed that during the month they had lost 100 million RM of foreign credits, without any corresponding reduction in their outstanding loans. The largest loss of credits had been incurred by the Danat, which lost 355 million RM; its first-class liquidity rate (that is to say, of securities which would be discounted by the Reichsbank) had fallen from 30·5 per cent to 22·2 per cent. It was apparent, especially to the nervous foreign investor, that if withdrawals continued at the same rate for only a few weeks longer, the banks would be unable to meet their liabilities. The outlook was all the more alarming because the provincial banks, the savings banks and the giro centres were in a similar situation. The figures of the Rhineland Landesbank showed that while credits had fallen by 51 million RM, outstanding loans had actually increased.

In the first week of July, foreign pressure on the banks increased, and between 6 and 8 July the Reichsbank lost 190 million RM in foreign exchange. On 7 July it was announced that France had at last, reluctantly and only with reservations, accepted the terms of the moratorium, but by then it was too late for the news to have any reassuring effect, for the continued withdrawals were not, as the bankers had claimed, due primarily to political factors but to a general loss of confidence in German industry and German finance as a whole. In the City of London, which had maintained an optimistic view of the German situation and had refrained from joining in the rush of withdrawals, opinion was shaken by the failure of the Nordwolle, though the extent of its losses were not yet known. Confidence received a further blow from the rumours, originating in the Swiss press, which had begun to circulate about the difficulties of the Danat. On 6 July the Reichsbank and the Danat issued a joint denial, through the official Wolff news agency, of 'the rumours circulating abroad about a Berlin bank', which were described as 'completely unfounded'.

As rumour and panic increased, Germany found herself again on the brink of financial catastrophe. Up to the beginning of July the Berlin banks and the Reichsbank had taken the view that the only way to restore confidence was to meet all demands without limit. The joint stock banks had been able to do so because the Reichsbank had continued to provide the foreign exchange required to meet withdrawals from abroad. But some banks were already approaching the point where the securities they offered for rediscount no longer satisfied the conditions required by the Reichsbank. In the middle of June Jacob Goldschmidt, of the Danat, had proposed to the Dresdner Bank that they should make a joint demand to the Reichsbank for a guarantee that it would continue to rediscount bills even if they fell below the required degree of liquidity. The Dresdner Bank agreed, but only on condition that they were joined in their demand by the Deutsche Bank, the largest of the joint stock banks. Goldschmidt was unwilling to accept this condition, as he was afraid that the proposal would be interpreted by the Deutsche Bank as an indication that he was at the limit of his resources.

Thus, when their foreign creditors resumed their withdrawals the joint stock banks had no assurance of continued support except through normal banking channels, while the Reichsbank subjected securities offered for rediscount to increasingly severe scrutiny. The Reich government, which during June had become increasingly concerned about the position of the banks, refrained from taking any action and contented itself with an assurance from the Deutsche Bank that it would come to the assistance of any other of the Berlin Big Five which found themselves in difficulties.

From the beginning of June, however, the government was forced to abandon its neutral attitude and to intervene increasingly in the banking crisis, initially because of the repercussions of the failure of the Nordwolle. Brüning had been warned of its situation as early as 13 June; it was known in the City of London even earlier. But the Nordwolle's losses were not known until 1 July, when an investigation of the affairs of its Dutch subsidiary, Ultramare, revealed that they amounted to 200 million RM.

The failure of the Nordwolle could not be treated as a normal commercial failure, however large, because of its effects abroad, and particularly in London. Germany's English creditors had hitherto largely refrained from withdrawing their money from Germany. It was now feared that, as a result of British losses in the Nordwolle, British credit also would be withdrawn, and increase even further the pressure which was driving Germany to disaster.

On 1 July the German government let it be known in London, through an unofficial intermediary, that it would act swiftly in the case of the Nordwolle, and in the next few days discussed with the Reichsbank, the Berlin banks and the Nordwolle's German creditors, plans for restoring the company's credit. At the same time, it proposed that the largest German industrial and financial corporations should form a joint guarantee fund of 500 million RM for German industry; it was hoped that such an exhibition of confidence would have an effect abroad and help to stem the continuing drain of credits. The proposals failed, however, because several large industrial concerns refused to cooperate; and when the guarantee fund was forcibly established by emergency decree, it failed to impress investors abroad because it had lost its voluntary character.

While these discussions proceeded, the situation deteriorated. On 5 July the Reichsbank was only able to meet the demands for foreign exchange, while maintaining the minimum legal cover for the currency, by drawing on an American credit granted to a subsidiary, the Gold Discount Bank; throughout the crisis the Reichsbank, haunted by memories of the inflation, was anxious above all to maintain confidence in the currency, and in this it succeeded to a remarkable extent. By 8 July the position of the Danat had become desperate, and at length Jacob Goldschmidt had to do what he had so long avoided, and turned to the Deutsche Bank for help; what he proposed was a merger between the two banks. The Deutsche Bank refused; the example of the Credit-Anstalt's merger with another insolvent concern, the Boden Credit-Anstalt, was not an encouraging precedent. The next day, 9 July, the Deutsche Bank was informed that the Danat could no longer meet its liabilities, and Goldschmidt, at his urgent request, met the Reichschancellor, Dr Brüning and his financial advisers; the Reichsbank president, Dr Luther, was not present, because he had already left Berlin for London, Paris and Basle, in a desperate attempt to raise a new rediscount credit for Germany.

His deputy, Dr Freyse, declared that the Reichsbank was prepared to assist the Danat by continuing to discount its bills, even though they did not meet with the requirements imposed by the Reichsbank, but only on condition that Dr Luther was successful in the object of his journey; he also required a government guarantee against loss. Until the result of Dr Luther's journey was known, the Reichsbank was prepared to continue financing the Danat for a further two or three days.

Thus the Danat was offered a reprieve; but only a short one. Dr Luther was everywhere unsuccessful. He travelled under an assumed name (perhaps in imitation of Montague Norman) in the hope of avoiding public notice, but his alibi was quickly penetrated by the Press. In London, Montague Norman refused a credit on the grounds that the German situation had become better and not worse since the Hoover moratorium, and that the Bank of England's own resources were strained as a result of the assistance given to Austria; and he warned Luther that his reception in Paris was likely to be unsympathetic. Norman believed that the situation was by now beyond the control of the central banks and he advised Luther to seek government intervention to prevent further withdrawals from Germany. For Norman, who believed so profoundly that finance was a matter for central bankers and not for governments, to give such advice was something like a cry of despair and was evidence of how near to collapse was the system he had done so much to maintain and promote.

That evening Luther flew to Paris. From there he telephoned to Berlin to say that it would not be easy to find a solution and recommending even severer credit restrictions as a means of reviving confidence in Germany. The next morning he was exposed to the full flood of French resentment against Brüning's adventures in foreign politics and left in no doubt that in French eyes, as so often before and since, finance was the handmaiden of politics. In turn, M. Monet, the governor of the Banque de France, the representatives of the French banks, and M. Flandin, the Finance Minister, made it clear to the unfortunate Luther that while France, and only France, had the financial means to help Germany, and was even willing to do so, no assistance would be forthcoming unless Germany accepted France's political demands, and Brüning and his Foreign Minister, Curtins, came immediately to Paris to negotiate an agreement. The demands were high. Germany must abandon her plans for customs union with Austria, she must put an end to nationalist agitation against the Young Plan and demands for a revision of her eastern frontier. In particular, she must abandon the construction of her second 10,000-ton battleship, even though this came within the limit permitted by the Versailles Treaty. The first, Panzerschiff 'A' (later pocket battleship Deutschland) had been launched, and the Reichstag had immediately voted the credits for Panzerschiff 'B' (Ersatz-Lothringen). The French asked for a complete reversal of Brüning's foreign policy, and to this Luther could make no reply. He left Paris empty-handed, except for a prolongation for three months of the recently granted short-term credit which was due to terminate on 16 July.

In the meantime, Brüning had turned to the United States for help. On the evening of 10 July an urgent request for financial assistance was sent to Washington through the American ambassador. Nor was international socialism neglected as a prop for capitalism; in a pressing letter the German Social Democratic Party begged the British Labour Party and the French Socialist Party to use their influence to overcome the political obstacles that stood in the way of financial assistance. The government also attempted, unsuccessfully, to persuade the large banks to form an association which would guarantee the position of its weaker members.

It was now too late to save the Danat. On 11 July the Reichsbank, whose reserves had fallen in two months from 2·6 million RM to 1·6 million RM, while its portfolio of bills discounted had risen from 1·8 to 3·3 million RM, introduced further credit restrictions. The Danat no longer possessed any securities which would satisfy the requirements of the Reichsbank, and when it asked the Reichsbank to rediscount bills to an amount of 250 million RM its request was refused. The other joint stock banks also refused assistance, with the exception of the Deutsche Bank, which in return for 30 million RM placed at its disposal bills which were rediscounted by the Reichsbank. This was, however, far too little to be of real help; on Friday, 11 July, Goldschmidt informed Brüning that the Danat would not open for business on the following Monday.

The position of the Danat at that moment reflected, in an extreme form, the weakness of the German banking system as a whole. Its total capital was 60 million RM, but in fact its real value was much lower, as over half its shares was held by the bank itself. Over 50 million RM had been lost in the Nordwolle. Yet despite this, even by the end of June the bank's assets were in theory more than sufficient to cover its obligations. In the eight previous weeks it had lost 650 million RM of foreign credits, or about one-third of the total before the run on the bank began. As against this, it possessed assets of first- and second-class liquidity which amounted to nearly 90 per cent of its obligations; if they could have been realized, it is clear that the bank could have withstood a very much longer run than the two months which had elapsed since the failure of the Credit-Anstalt had shaken the confidence of foreign investors. The fatal weakness was that very nearly two-thirds of its nominally 'liquid' assets was represented by short-term loans to German industry which, under the conditions of the depression, were effectively frozen.

The sin of the Danat was that it had pushed to extravagant extremes practices which were common to the great majority of German banks, though there were shining exceptions. For this, the chief responsibility fell upon Jacob Goldschmidt. An interloper from the Stock Exchange in the banking world, he had been a colleague of Schacht's in the National Bank before its amalgamation with the Darmstädter, had acquired for the Danat large holdings in German industry and thereby attracted valuable customers, and had taken a leading part in promoting the concentration of German industry into large units, like the Vereinigte Stahlwerke, the great German steel combine. He planned the creation of a great German automobile combine on the model of General Motors, and had been the most active of all German bankers in promoting foreign investment in Germany. Though the Danat was only fourth among the five leading Berlin banks in respect of share capital, it held second place in respect of foreign credits.

Goldschmidt was the image of the aggressive, progressive, 'expansionist' banker who saw no limits to the development of German industry, and with it of the Danat, so long as unlimited foreign capital continued to be available. Like the 'expansionist' bankers of the American boom, he made the mistake of taking a consistently optimistic view of the development of the trade cycle, even after it exhibited every sign of depression, both at home and abroad. If he had been right in his view he would have been regarded as one of the great creative figures in German finance; when he did not succeed, he became a laughing stock and a by-word for failure, and his failure, together with the scandal of the Nordwolle with which it was associated, helped to feed the fires of Nazi propaganda against the type of Jewish financier who, according to the National Socialists, was dragging Germany into the abyss.

Goldschmidt's best epitaph, as of many bankers of his age, both in Germany and America, is to be found in a parody of the prologue to Schiller's *Wallenstein*, which circulated in Berlin at the time:

You know him well, bold leader of the market!
The idol of the bulls, scourge of the bears,
The irrepressible child of Fortune,
Who, borne aloft by the Inflation,
Gloriously mounted the steps of the Exchange
And in the insatiable grip of speculation
Fell victim to unbridled gambling lust.

Goldschmidt's message was not the only bad news the government received on 11 July; on the same day they were informed that the Rhineland Landesbank was bankrupt. Its failure revealed yet another aspect of the crisis. The bank's obligations amounted to over 200 million RM, chiefly in the form of deposits from the Rhineland savings banks; these had been lent to local authorities which were already overburdened with debt, and could not be recovered. The situation called for immediate action, as the Landesbank was a state institution operating under public authority, and its credit involved the credit of the state itself; accordingly, the Reichsbank extended an immediate credit of 30 million RM, but only on condition that the Prussian government took over the administration of the bank.

The position was now desperate. Despite every effort to meet the demands of Germany's foreign creditors, withdrawals continued, and it was feared that when, on Monday, 13 July, the Danat failed to open, the other Berlin banks would come under even greater pressure. The failure of the Landesbank showed that the panic was no longer confined to German creditors abroad but extended to her internal creditors also and, through the intricate network of the provincial banks, the savings banks, the giro centres and public authorities, was beginning to affect Germany's entire financial structure.

The weekend of 11–12 July was spent in feverish attempts to prevent the panic from spreading. On the evening of 11 July there was a joint meeting of the financial committee of the Cabinet, the President of the Reichsbank, who had that day returned from his travels, and the representatives of the banks and of industry. The bankers were informed that no further help could be expected from the Reichsbank; its reserves were now down to the lowest level compatible with discharging its legal obligations, and it was also under strong pressure both from Montague Norman in London, and from Harrison of the Federal Reserve Bank, to introduce still further credit restrictions.

The American and British demands were made in the belief that the financial crisis was primarily due, not to foreign withdrawals, but to a flight of German capital from Germany. In fact, so long as the foreign withdrawals continued, the only real solution to the problem lay in achieving some form of agreement, if necessary supported by a government guarantee, between Germany and her foreign commercial creditors. Such an agreement had not yet been feasible, because of the conflict of interest between Germany's political and commercial creditors. Before the Hoover moratorium, a standstill agreement on commercial debts, primarily to America, Britain, Switzerland and the Netherlands, would have meant that Germany's available resources could have been applied to paying her political debts, primarily to France; it would have meant that Germany's commercial debtors would have been called upon to pay the cost of reparations. In fact, of course, this is what they had been doing throughout the boom years, but by now their own resources were exhausted. Only when France, on 7 July, at length signified her agreement, even with reservations, to the Hoover moratorium, did a standstill agreement on commercial debts become a practical possibility.

Such a solution was not yet in sight. Neither Germany's statesmen, nor her financiers and industrialists, were as yet prepared for a step which might appear both as a declaration of national bankruptcy and a breach of the most fundamental principles of the capitalist system. The meeting of 11 July failed to reach any decision. On the following day, 12 July, the government and the Reichsbank decided on one more desperate appeal for a rediscount credit to the Bank of International Settlements at its next meeting on Monday, 13 July. There remained the immediate question of what action should be taken with regard to the Danat. While this question was being discussed, Dr Brüning was informed, by Wasserman of the Deutsche Bank, that not only the Danat but the Dresdner Bank was on the verge of collapse.

The Cabinet discussed the situation from 4 p.m. on the afternoon of 11 July until 2 a.m. on the following morning. An emergency decree empowering the government to regulate the affairs of the banks was telephoned, for immediate approval, to President

Hindenburg at Neudeck. It gave the government power to close the banks and the stock exchange and to take individual banks under its own supervision. It was also proposed that the government should guarantee the banks' creditors, but it proved impossible to agree whether this should apply equally to foreign and domestic creditors and after discussion with the representatives of the bankers a decision was postponed.

At 6.30 a.m. the Cabinet and the bankers met again. In the meantime, it had been decided to invite Schacht to take over the administration of the Danat as the representative of the government. The meeting again revealed wide differences of opinion and provoked a strong protest against the terms of the emergency decree by Wasserman of the Deutsche Bank, who insisted that they should apply only to the Danat, and not to the banks in general. Brüning dismissed the bankers until they could reach agreement and speak with a common voice, and the Cabinet meeting was resumed in the presence of Schacht, who also disagreed with the terms of the emergency decree.

The discussion with the bankers was resumed on the night of 12 July; the long and agitated weekend now had only a few more hours to run and still no final decision had been taken on what action the government should take. Guttman, of the Dresdner Bank, now stated that the government had been misinformed with regard to the position of the bank and that it was able to meet its obligations. It was therefore decided to restrict the terms of the emergency decree to the Danat alone. It was also decided, at the request of the banks, to declare a bank holiday for the following day. Later, however, the bankers raised 'psychological' objections against a bank holiday and, once more at their request, the decision was reversed.

Thus when Monday, 13 June, dawned, the government's intervention in the banking crisis was restricted to the Danat, which closed its doors under an emergency decree which guaranteed its obligations, except to its two partners, Goldschmidt and Bodenheim, and placed the bank under the supervision of the government. Immediately the news was known, it quickly became clear that the bankers had gravely miscalculated in their advice to the government. The closing of the Danat provoked a general panic and a run on the other banks which it proved impossible to halt. By midday the Berlin banks and savings banks were unable to meet demands in full and had to restrict payment to 20 per cent. The Berlin savings banks, which in the previous week had a surplus of deposits over payments, had by the end of the day paid out 7 million RM and had only 1 million RM left to meet demands on the following day.

Thus the government's intervention had had precisely the opposite result from that which had been intended; that is to say, it had added an internal run on the banks, hitherto avoided, to the pressure exerted by their foreign creditors. That evening, also, the government learned that its last frail hope had vanished, when it learned from Dr Luther in Basle that he had again failed in his attempt to obtain a rediscount credit. In the opinion of the members of the Bank of International Settlements, Germany's foreign debts were primarily a political problem, to the solution of which they could make no contribution. And to the general problem of Germany's debts was now added, as a result of the internal run on the banks, the problem of an acute domestic shortage of means of exchange;* the bankers themselves urged the government to reintroduce the Rentenmark, which had helped to stabilize the currency after the inflation of 1922, as an alternative to the Reichsmark. In these circumstances there was no longer any alternative to the step which the government had tried so hard to avert. A general bank holiday was declared for the following days, the 14 and 15 July, all banks and credit institutions were closed, with the exception of the Reichsbank, and all commercial payments of any kind were suspended.

Immediately after the announcement of the bank holiday, many of Germany's foreign creditors, particularly in Switzerland and the Netherlands, terminated all their outstanding credits. On the other hand, several British and American banks informed the Berlin banks that they wished to maintain their existing balances with them. But it was clear that the two days' holiday would only afford Germany a brief respite and that, unless preventive action were taken, the crisis would break out again in an even more dangerous form when they were over.

* Restrictions on withdrawals from the banks and savings banks meant that payments could only be made with whatever cash people had in their pockets.

CHAPTER EIGHT

German Bank
Holiday

The closure of the banks, and the suspension of cash payments, gave the German government two days in which to set the affairs of the banks in order, at least to such an extent that they might open their doors again without a repetition of the panic of Monday, 12 July. Immediate action could no longer be postponed because the suspension of cash payments had brought the whole of German economic life to a halt, and unless it could be quickly resumed there could be no escape from the catastrophe with which Germany was threatened. Even the problem of Germany's foreign creditors was now less urgent than the task of providing the means of exchange on which a country's industry and commerce depend.

For such a task, the government was not well prepared. Throughout the crisis, the information it had received from the banks had proved to be unreliable, and they had been unable to agree among themselves on any common policy to recommend to the government. Brüning came increasingly to feel that they were incompetent at managing their own affairs and that it was time for the government to take the initiative, without relying upon the bankers' advice.

The bankers themselves took advantage of the breathing space to make one last effort to avert government intervention, and Solmssen, of the Deutsche Bank, as president of the German Bankers' Association, on 15 July put forward a demand for the dismissal of Luther and the appointment of Schacht as president of the Reichsbank, on the grounds that German industry, and particularly the banks, had totally lost confidence in Luther.

There was a kind of ineptitude in this demand which was characteristic of the bankers' behaviour throughout the crisis. For by law, as the bankers knew, the government had no powers to dismiss the president of the Reichsbank; as a guarantee of its independence, he was appointed by its board of directors and could only be dismissed by them. Nor was there any reason to think that the appointment of Schacht in his place would be of any advantage to the bankers, in the matter that interested them most. They believed that the crisis had arisen primarily because of Luther's refusal to continue to provide foreign exchange with which to satisfy their foreign creditors; this was in fact precisely the policy which, in his recently published book, *The End of Reparations*, Schacht had recommended if, as was the case, the Reichsbank's reserves threatened to fall below the minimum legal cover for the currency.

The bankers might also, in their own interests, have taken wider considerations into account. Since the beginning of the year, Schacht had already made contact with the National Socialists, in the persons of Hitler and Göring, and was now one of those who was anxious to make them respectable in the eyes of German industry and finance. There was a very large proportion of the Berlin bankers, including Solmssen himself, who had everything to fear from such a combination.

The government rightly refused to consider the bankers' demand; indeed, it may only have increased Brüning's exasperation with them. Only the previous day he had been given a particularly glaring example of how little their information was to be trusted. On 12 July he had been assured by the Dresdner Bank that it could meet its liabilities; two days later, he was informed that the bank was insolvent, so that now it had to regulate the affairs of the Dresdner Bank as well as those of the Danat.

The government found itself faced with three main problems. The first and most urgent was the resumption of cash payments, because until this was possible Germany's economic life was paralysed. No wages or salaries could be paid; the state could collect no taxes; and the only monetary transactions which could be carried out were those for which the individual had sufficient cash in his pocket. Moreover, the longer this situation continued the worse the effect upon Germany's creditors. Yet payments could not immediately be resumed in full, and between 16 July and the beginning of August the government issued a series of seventeen emergency decrees carefully regulating payments until conditions at length returned to normal.

The second problem was that of Germany's foreign credits. Her Swiss and Dutch creditors had already terminated all their outstanding credits and it was to be feared that when the banks reopened withdrawals would continue on an even greater scale.* The government now had no alternative to introducing exchange control and on 15 July, against the opposition of Schacht, it issued an emergency decree bringing all foreign exchange transactions under the control of the Reichsbank and forbidding all dealings in futures and precious metals.† On 18 July further restrictions were imposed. All holdings of foreign exchange had to be notified, and if required, sold to the Reichsbank, and severe penalties, including heavy fines and up to ten years' imprisonment, were imposed for failure to comply with the regulations.

Exchange control was a decisive step away from what had hitherto been considered one of the essential conditions of a free economy and was decisive proof of how far the attempt to restore the gold standard had failed. Its most obviously dramatic feature was the heavy penalties; they converted into a crime, punishable by law, activities which, until then, had been regarded as the prerogative of any free person who could afford to indulge in them. In imposing them, Brüning was largely influenced by regard for public opinion. The Nordwolle scandal had shown that there had been large-scale exports of German capital abroad in order to evade the heavy burden of German taxation and such practices had inspired widespread and violent indignation. A referendum was impending in Prussia, initiated by the Stahlhelm, and supported by the Nationalists, the National Socialists and the Communists, on the question of dissolving the Prussian Landtag. If the Nationalists' demand was successful, there was the danger that the largest German state, commanding the most powerful police force in the Reich, would come under the control of the radical right. Agitation against financial chicanery in high places was a favourite theme,

* The Swiss and the Dutch had refused to renew their outstanding short-term loans and required immediate repayment when it fell due. This gravely weakened the position of Germany's other foreign creditors.

† The normal method of ensuring against exchange fluctuations by purchasing foreign currency for forward delivery at fixed prices.

often with justification, in both right- and left-wing propaganda, and Brüning could not afford to be accused of having any sympathy with those who might try to evade the exchange control regulations.

In the following weeks they were extended and elaborated. Payment of interest on foreign capital, or repayment of terminated credits was permitted, but payments for imports were severely restricted. The restrictions indeed were so severe that between 1930 and 1931 German imports fell by a half, and by 1932 by over two-thirds. The effect was to give Germany during those two years a large export surplus. This was absorbed by the repayment of foreign credits, and at the same time provoked retaliation by other countries against German exports.

Discrimination against imports, however, by adding to the cost of living, added yet another burden to those which the German population was already being asked to bear. It added another turn of the screw to the human suffering entailed by Brüning's deflationary policy, which, while it depressed incomes, was at the same time combined with the maintenance of exorbitantly high food prices, at a time when throughout the rest of the world they had fallen precipitously. Even so, protectionist interests were not satisfied. Indeed, Schule, the Minister of Agriculture, wished to manipulate exchange control to exclude particular food imports, particularly butter, from the German market, but his proposals were rejected by Brüning.

Exchange control, however, was essential to protect the Reichsbank's diminishing reserves. By the end of July, at 1·6 million RM, they were just sufficient to provide the minimum legal cover of 40 per cent but by the end of August they had fallen to 39·3 per cent, and by the end of the year they were to fall to 24·8 per cent. But the introduction of exchange control meant that Germany had freed herself from the necessity of maintaining a minimum cover; she was now insulated against the fluctuations of the market and in practice operated two different currencies, one for foreign and one for domestic use, and with only an artificial relation between them. It is a significant reflection of the state of economic thought at the time that no one drew from this the deduction that it was now possible to relax Brüning's deflationary policy. This was not thought of as either an advantage or a disadvantage of exchange control and in the discussions which its introduction provoked the question never arose.

The third problem which faced the government was the steps to be taken to permit the banks to resume their normal functions and in particular the measures to be applied to the Danat, and, as it was now revealed, the Dresdner Bank; in addition, on 20 July the government learned that the Bremen banking house of J. F. Schröder was in difficulties. Schröder had been heavily involved in the failure of the Nordwolle, and had also incurred losses in Norddeutsche Lloyd and Deschimag, the machine tool combine; it held a dominating position in the industry and trade of Bremen, which would have faced serious difficulties in the event of its failure. This was averted by the joint intervention of the government, the free city of Bremen and Bremen industry, which took over the bank's losses. They were at first under-estimated, and the government's liability was limited to 20 million RM. This was later increased to 48 million RM. Finally, the true losses were revealed as 90 million RM, of which the government undertook responsibility for 68 million RM.

Between 26 July and 3 August, the government devoted ten sessions of the Cabinet to the affairs of the Danat and the Dresdner Bank. In addition to the Cabinet and its financial advisers, representatives of German finance and industry took part in the discussions, together with the American economist Sprague and the Swedish banker Wallenberg. By now Brüning was determined that the discussions should not be limited to technical questions; his own feelings, and the pressure of public opinion, led him to insist on fixing personal responsibility for the banks' mistakes. He did not hesitate to express his loss of confidence in the bankers: 'It is difficult,' he said, 'to obtain even approximately accurate information from bankers'; and again, 'After our recent experiences, it is useless to expect advice from them.' The only representative of the banks in the discussions was the immensely respected Dr Melchior, a partner in Warburg's and German representative on the board of the Bank of International Settlements, to whom Keynes has devoted a deeply sympathetic portrait in his *Essays in Persuasion*.

Brüning was determined that a reform of the banking system should not be thwarted by leaving its execution in the hands of those who had been responsible for its breakdown, and that it should be accompanied by changes in personnel; 'the reform of the banking system requires the most far-reaching changes in the leadership of the banks, otherwise it will not achieve its effect.' And with regard to public opinion, he stated: 'If the directors of the banks which have been hit should continue in office, public opinion would be provoked to a storm of indignation, which could not be fully appeased.'

In fact, the problem of the Danat proved easier to solve than that of the Dresdner Bank. It had intimate and powerful connections with West German industry, in particular with the great steel combine, the Vereinigte Stahlwerke, which Goldschmidt had played a leading part in promoting. The chairman of the combine, Albert Vogler, and its largest shareholder, Friedrich Flick, came forward with a plan, which was also supported by Krupp and the Rhineland coal industry, to restore the bank's capital by taking over its shares, the money to be provided by the state and repaid over 5–10 years. The plan was approved by Sprague and Wallenburg and by the government's own financial advisers. Thus it proved possible to reconstruct the Danat without direct government intervention.

The reconstruction of the Dresdner Bank proved more difficult. Various proposals were considered which might prevent, or limit, direct government intervention, but owing to the Dresdner's large foreign indebtedness there was no solution to be found except by a large injection of new capital. This was provided in the form of preference shares, to an amount of 300 million RM, which were taken over by the government. Thus the government, with a 75 per cent share of the Dresdner's total capital of 400 million RM, became the effective owner of the second largest German bank, a form of state ownership which was widely satirized as 'the nationalization of losses'.

An even more difficult problem was provided by the savings banks. It was calculated that they would require one milliard RM of new finance if they were to meet all demands in full after the bank holiday, but that by restricting payments initially this sum could be reduced to 500 million RM. The savings banks proposed that the money should be provided by permitting them, like the joint stock banks, to rediscount bills with the Reichsbank, but the problem arose that they had no bills to offer which would meet the strict standards of liquidity demanded by the Reichsbank. The difficulty was overcome by the creation of a new credit institution, the Acceptance and Guarantee Bank, which would act as an intermediary between the savings bank and the Reichsbank. Its acceptance of a bill under government guarantee would give it the required standard of liquidity, and the Reichsbank agreed to rediscount such acceptances, on the condition only that it was not itself under pressure from Germany's foreign creditors.

The Acceptance and Guarantee Bank was founded with a capital of 200 million RM, of which 80 million was subscribed by the government and 20 million each by the Gold Discount Bank, a subsidiary of the Reichsbank, and the Deutsche Bank; it had powers to lend to all banks (including the Danat), savings banks and giros, but in fact 70 per cent of its advances went to the savings banks and giros. By the end of 1931 it had made advances amounting to 1,625 million RM, and in 1932 to 1,326 million RM, but as the financial crisis passed its advances diminished until by 1936 they amounted to only 7 million RM.

The Acceptance and Guarantee Bank was a brilliant improvisation, which successfully achieved the purpose for which it was founded; that is, to provide a sound financial basis for the German savings banks. But it also added another burden to the weight of interest rates under which the German economy laboured. The bank charged 2 per cent for its services, over and above the Reichsbank's rediscount rate, which at the beginning of August was 15 per cent. On 11 August it was reduced to 10 per cent and in September to 8 per cent. The high rate of interest charged by the Reichsbank was influenced by the advice of the distinguished economist, Wilhelm Röpke, whom the president of the Reichsbank had taken into consultation. He advised that a high rate of interest was preferable to credit restrictions, because the one was automatic and impersonal, while the other lent itself to bureaucratic interference.

The intervention of the government in the banking crisis was undertaken against its will, under the urgent pressure of events, and on the basis of imperfect information and conflicting advice. But in its immediate object of getting the German banking system, and indirectly the German economy, to work again it was remarkably successful and Brüning never showed to greater advantage than he did during the banking crisis. He was right to reject the advice of the bankers, wise in his choice of his own advisers, and determined that the government's intervention should not be used as a cover for the bankers' mistakes.

Yet the measures he took were founded on a profound misapprehension. Most of them, especially exchange control and discrimination against imports, were conceived of as essentially temporary expedients; indeed, the very necessity of government intervention was regarded as an abnormality which could only be justified by the depth and urgency of this crisis and which would cease once the crisis was over. No government could have been less inclined than Brüning's to introduce socialism into the banking system; in fact, under the pressure of the crisis, it introduced a greater measure of nationalization, even if it was the 'nationalization of losses', than any German government before or since.

Nor did the measures it took pass away with the crisis. Exchange control, in particular, survived for twenty-five years, and in the hands of Schacht, when he once again became president of the Reichsbank, became one of the foundations of the system of economic autarchy created by the National Socialists.

Indeed, it has been argued that, by his interference with the independence of the banking system, in particular his *de facto* nationalization of the Dresdner Bank, Brüning helped to pave the way for the economic dictatorship exercised by Hitler, and acted a kind of Kerensky of capitalist reaction. But this, at least, is not one of the sins, or errors, which can be laid to Brüning's account. One of Hitler's earliest actions was to return the banks into private hands and release them from the restrictions laid upon them by Brüning; Hitler had other methods of making finance and banking do as he wished than by establishing government control of them.

In one respect, however, Brüning's intervention could be said to have been a further blow to democratic government, or so much of it as remained in Germany. What finally threatened the German economic system with bankruptcy was the imminent collapse of the savings banks, and the suspension of cash payments which this involved. But the difficulties of the savings banks were hardly of their own contriving. Their liquid assets consisted of their deposits with the provincial state banks; these, however, had been used by the state banks to make advances to the German municipalities, which in turn had used them to finance projects of urban development and improvement. However socially desirable these projects may have been, they held no prospects of immediate financial return. The funds of the savings banks were effectively frozen, as the municipalities were themselves bankrupt, and it was impossible for them to meet the demands made upon them by their depositors.

The position was particularly acute in the Rhineland, the largest industrial concentration in Germany, owing to the failure of the state bank of the Rhine province. Its largest debtors were the municipalities of Cologne and Dusseldorf. Cologne especially, under its Lord Mayor, Konrad Adenauer, had engaged in particularly grandiose plans of civic improvement, inspired both by his love of his native city, and by the hope of making it a gateway and a bridge between Germany and the West. He had carried out a programme of enriching and beautifying Cologne with parks and open spaces, sports arenas, playing fields and swimming baths, a green belt involving the compulsory purchase of its former fortified zone, magnificent exhibition halls for trade fairs, a great expansion of the university and attendant academic institutions.

By 1927, Cologne's debts already amounted to 700 million marks; its example was one which many other German municipalities followed. When the depression came, Adenauer continued his policy of urban development as part of a public works programme in aid of unemployment which he unsuccessfully urged Brüning to adopt on a national scale.

The loan of savings bank deposits by the state banks to the municipalities had no sound financial basis, and in fact contravened their charter as public banking institutions.

One of the reforms introduced by Brüning, as a protection against a repetition of such errors, was to make it illegal for the savings banks to lend to local authorities, and thereby, at a time when tax receipts were falling and the cost of the obligations imposed on local authorities by the state were rising heavily, to cut them off from the only form of credit available to them. No doubt the municipalities, by their extravagance, and the huge indebtedness they had incurred to the savings banks, were largely responsible for their own financial difficulties. But they had also been made responsible for heavy expenditure, especially in the fields of education, welfare and unemployment relief and Brüning's reforms made it

[151]

financially impossible for them to carry them out; in this respect, they were a heavy blow to local autonomy and self-government and helped to undermine democracy in Germany.

But the banking crisis also struck at the roots of democracy, as it operated in Germany, in a much wider and more general sense. It seemed to reveal that those who were responsible for one of its most vital functions, that is to say, the financial system, were both incompetent and untrustworthy, and added further fuel to the propaganda of both right and left against 'the system' and against the *bonzen* – the bosses – who manipulated the economy to their own profit at the expense of suffering millions. If there was one single cause to which the fall of Weimar can be attributed, it was the lack of faith which infected its committed supporters, as contrasted with the fanaticism of those who were determined to destroy it, and the banking crisis helped to erode still further what little faith remained.

CHAPTER NINE

After the
Bank Holiday

Introduction of exchange control, and the measures taken to regulate the German banks, had averted the prospect of total financial collapse in Germany, and given her a brief respite from the drain of capital abroad, but there was no guarantee that it would not be resumed at any moment. Her Swiss creditors indeed had terminated all their outstanding loans immediately after the announcement of the closure of the banks, and were to threaten further reprisals because of the effects of exchange control on the Swiss tourist industry. The nightmare which faced Germany was that of being forced into declaring a moratorium on all her foreign debts, an announcement of national bankruptcy which would have destroyed her financial credit beyond all hope of repair.

Yet the German government had dangerously little room for manœuvre. On his travels round the financial capitals of Europe, Dr Luther had pressed for the immediate grant of a long-term loan to Germany, without political conditions. He had learned, in London from Montague Norman, in Paris from Monet and Flandin, in Basle from the Bank of International Settlements, that a loan on such terms was out of the question. The French were the financial masters of Europe, and a loan would be forthcoming only on the political conditions prescribed by them.

Nor was it possible to look beyond central banks and governments and turn to private sources for a loan. In the United States this was forbidden by law; the City of London already had large sums frozen in Germany and was itself under increasing strain; French investors shared the view of the government and the Banque de France that any loan to Germany must be accompanied by political guarantees.

In its attempt to raise a foreign loan, the German government found itself involved in an insoluble contradiction. On the one hand, it desperately needed to re-establish confidence abroad in Germany's financial and political stability; this required that she should strictly observe her existing obligations, particularly those she had assumed under the Young Plan, and avoid any measures likely to increase existing international tension. On the other hand, such a policy only increased the fury of nationalist agitation at home and, in an attempt to appease it, led the government into foreign adventures which inevitably created mistrust and resentment abroad, especially in France, the only country capable of offering direct financial assistance.

For Germany there remained only the possibility of negotiating an agreement with her creditors by which they voluntarily postponed their claims until Germany's financial and economic position had improved; and in achieving this object she once again found help forthcoming from the United States. On 16 July President Hoover proposed that an international conference be called to discuss the problem of Germany's foreign debts and the measures required to restore her to financial stability. The President's motives were by no means disinterested or entirely determined by Germany's need of assistance. The announcement of the German banking holiday had provoked a severe fall on the Continental stock exchanges, and particularly in Amsterdam. There, a particular feature of the fall had been large-scale bear operations, especially against the shares of Kreuger and Toll, which suffered losses of up to 40 per cent. The President was afraid that the fall in share prices might spread from Europe to the United States, and by his proposal of a conference hoped to give some reassurance to the market.

The proposal was agreed to by both Britain and France, though each had reservations about its usefulness and its prospect of success. Britain in particular was by now becoming acutely aware of her dependence on French goodwill, such as it was, and insisted that, before the conference opened, Brüning and Curtins, his Foreign Minister, should visit Paris in order to improve Germany's relations with France. Brüning yielded to British insistence, yet without, it would seem, fully understanding the reasons for it or the attitude which Britain was likely to adopt at the conference; at a German cabinet meeting on 17 July it was decided that the discussions in Paris should be strictly limited to financial and economic matters and that all political commitments should be avoided.

There was in Brüning's attitude to France's political demands a kind of rigidity which was characteristic of the man, and was also the product of a peculiar combination of despair and hope. Throughout the discussions and meetings provoked by the German financial crisis, Brüning greatly impressed the representatives of her foreign creditors by his honesty, frankness and integrity; yet at no time did he show any sign of comprehending their view that the crisis itself was in part inspired by the anxieties and uncertainties created, particularly in France, by German foreign policy. The explanation of his attitude is to be found in the belief, firstly, that he could not afford to make concessions abroad without being engulfed by the nationalist opposition at home; but, secondly, the belief that, despite and in some respects because of the crisis, he was beginning to come within sight of his goal and, given only a little more time, would be able to give demonstrative proof of success. The first belief was almost certainly true; the second, even more certainly, was almost wholly an illusion.

Given Brüning's attitude, the Paris meeting inevitably proved fruitless. The French Prime Minister, Laval, was, as he remained throughout his life, a profound and sincere believer in Franco-German cooperation; but he was as much under the pressure of French public opinion as Brüning was of German. The French offer of financial assistance was immediate and generous: a long-term loan, maturing in ten years' time, of 500–1,000 million dollars, to be underwritten in Paris, New York, and London. This meant, in fact, that the burden of the loan would have fallen almost entirely on the shoulders of the French. But the political conditions attached to a loan were once again made explicit: no revision of the Young Plan, abandonment of the Austro-German Customs Union, the maintenance of Germany's existing Eastern frontiers. These were in fact conditions which were already written into existing treaties, to which Germany was committed. But the French also wished the Germans to deny themselves rights to which they were entitled: the right to construct battleships of under 10,000 tons, and the possibility of treaty revision granted by Article 19 of the Versailles Treaty.

The French conditions, in fact, amounted to a German guarantee of the *status quo* for a period of ten years; and there can be little doubt that, if the Germans could have been persuaded, or bribed, to accept them, they would have provided a basis for a revival of both political and financial confidence. It was equally true, however, that, as Brüning claimed, no German government could have agreed to them and survived.

Thus, when the London conference opened on 21 July, it was already clear that the fundamental obstacle to a long-term loan to Germany was not financial but political. It became equally clear that neither Britain nor America felt inclined to bring pressure to bear on France to reduce her political demands, or, even if they did, could not do so because they could not afford to. Britain's weakness at the conference, indeed, was startling evidence, for all those who had once believed in her financial predominance, of how greatly things had changed in the course of a few months. In April, Montague Norman could still propose at Geneva the creation of a great 'international organization for the conscious direction of money . . . towards the borrowers whose relief and rehabilitation are a grand object of policy', and in making the proposal he had primarily in mind the needs of Germany, Eastern Europe, Australia and South America; and he could still afford to provoke French hostility by coming to the aid of Austria. But by July those days were over, and the Bank of England itself had become a financial satellite of the Banque de France.

Thus the London conference could do no more than accept a proposal by the American Secretary of State, Stimson, that all interested governments should recommend Germany's private creditors to come to a standstill agreement with regard to their claims upon her. Direct financial assistance was limited to a renewal of the joint $100 million credit granted to Germany in June, while measures were discussed for maintaining the existing volume of credits to Germany. The only immediate success achieved was to secure yet another short respite for Germany by recommending the appointment by the Bank of International Settlements of a committee of experts to consider Germany's credit needs, while representatives of Germany's creditors should meet to discuss a standstill agreement on her short-term obligations.

But time was now pressing. Between the bank holiday in Germany and the end of July, the German government gradually relaxed the restrictions imposed on the German banks and by 5 August payments in full had been resumed. Only voluntary restraint by Germany's creditors, and their willingness to observe the recommendations of their governments, now prevented a renewal of foreign withdrawals and the end of the month saw statesmen and financiers in migratory flight from capital to capital in the effort to create reassurance and alleviate panic. On 25 July, Mr Stimson left London for Berlin, and on the 27th, when he returned to London and immediately left for New York, he was followed in Berlin by Ramsay MacDonald and Arthur Henderson. While the London conference was still in progress, two German bankers, Schliepe of the Deutsche Bank and Melchior of Warburg's, had arrived in London to discuss the standstill negotiations with representatives of the City. On 27 July two members of the joint Anglo-American commission of creditors continued the discussions in Berlin. The British member, Frank Tiarks, was a director of the English banking firm of Schröders, which had only been able to survive the freezing of its assets in Germany with the help of an immediate loan from the Bank of England. For the Germans, the Reichsbank nominated men whose reputations had emerged unscathed from the panic, and who had pursued a cautious and conservative policy with regard to foreign credits: Schliepe, Hans Fürstenberg of the Berliner Handelsgesellschaft, Loeb of Mendelssohn's, Spiegelberg of Warburg's. Though the Danat and the Dresdner Bank carried by far the heaviest burden of indebtedness, they were not represented in the discussions.

The German bankers asked for a total standstill on all withdrawals for a period of six months, which Tiarks strongly opposed. Agreement was finally reached on a compromise which provided in principle for a complete standstill, but permitted a small quota of repayments in particular cases.

The committee of experts recommended by the London Conference met at Basle on 8 August, under the chairmanship of Albert H. Wiggin, of the Chase National Bank. Its primary task was to determine the extent of Germany's indebtedness and the possibility of transforming her short-term into long-term credits. On 13 August, the members of the standstill committee also arrived in Basle to conduct parallel discussions on the terms of a standstill agreement. The committee of experts worked under great pressure, and by 15 August had agreed on the terms of its report; by a piece of good fortune, the writing of it had been entrusted to the British representative, Sir Walter Layton, editor of the *Economist*, and it provided both an admirable analysis of the German crisis and the reasons why the committee had no long-term solution for it.

The Layton report emphasized that the German crisis was only a particular phase of the worldwide economic crisis, and that without general economic recovery there was no permanent solution for it. The distinguishing feature of the situation in Germany, however, was her acute dependence, which would continue for some time to come, on foreign capital and especially on short-term credits. Until general recovery was achieved, the immediate object was to avert the total financial collapse of Germany, and this was all the more necessary because of the vital part which Germany played in the world economy; without economic recovery in Germany, there could be no real or permanent recovery elsewhere.

One valuable service which the report performed was to reveal, for the first time, the true extent of Germany's foreign indebtedness, of which, until then, only estimates had been available. In all, it amounted to 23 milliard RM, of which 8 milliard RM were short-term credits maturing in under six months. Against this, the Reichsbank held reserves in gold and foreign exchange amounting to 1·67 milliard RM. German holdings abroad amounted to 8·5 milliard RM of which 1·7 milliards were in the form of short-term credits, but of this only 1·5 milliards could be realized immediately, as the remainder was tied up in current trade transactions. Germany's remaining asset was her favourable trade balance, which was estimated to produce an export surplus of 2 milliard RM in the second half of 1931. The report's analysis made it clear that even if Germany mobilized all her immediately available foreign assets, it would be impossible for her to repay her short-term creditors in full.

The report also examined the use Germany had made of her imports of foreign capital. Between 1924 and 1930, these had amounted to a total of 18·3 milliard RM, and over half of this, or 10·3 milliard RM, had been devoted to the payment of reparations. For Brüning this was perhaps the most significant part of the report. It lent powerful support to the German claim that Germany, even if willing, was incapable of fulfilling her reparations obligations out of her own resources, and brought him a step nearer to the goal to which his whole policy had been devoted, that is to say, of ending reparations with the consent and agreement of Germany's political creditors. Such an achievement would not merely relieve Germany of the burden of reparations, and correct what Germans believed to be a great historic injustice; it would also demonstrate that the aims of German policy would be most successfully achieved not, as the nationalists claimed, by unilateral action, if necessary by force, but by negotiation. Brüning was encouraged in thinking that the goal was now in sight by the impression he had formed, during Stimson's and MacDonald's visits to Berlin, that both Britain and the United States now favoured an agreed end to reparations.

But though Brüning might be encouraged in his long-term views, the Wiggin Committee could not offer any direct solution for Germany's problems. The report might show that, under the prevailing conditions of trade, the burden of reparations was unbearable; but reparations were essentially a political problem, requiring a political answer, which was outside the competence of the committee. Its analysis of Germany's indebtedness, short-term and long-term, pointed unmistakably to the conclusion that there was no real answer to her problems other than to provide her, in the shape of a long-term loan, with a fresh injection of the capital which she lacked; but the question of a long-term loan to Germany also involved political risks, and might simply result in throwing good money after bad. Germany's export surplus created the possibility of building up a large favourable balance of payments; yet the committee could not be very hopeful that this would continue, at a time when the volume of world trade was rapidly contracting and when every increase in German exports provoked the danger of trade reprisals by other countries.

The committee was driven to the gloomy conclusion that economic recovery, not only in Germany but elsewhere, depended on a general improvement in political relations, of which, at that moment, there was little prospect. This was true not only in respect of particular political problems, like those which divided France from Germany; it was true also in the much larger sense that, in the committee's view, economic recovery demanded the removal or lowering of all those barriers which had grown up between nations since the war, and in this sense the reparations problem only added, in the case of Germany, one more complication to a situation which applied throughout the world. Indeed, the committee came near to asserting that the worldwide restrictions on the free mobility of goods constituted a contradiction within the capitalist system which, unless it could be cured, might prove fatal.

The Layton report was a classical statement of the conditions which, according to orthodox economic thought, were required if the world economy was to be restored to health; they were conditions which there was little prospect of establishing at that moment, and they never were established even when at length capitalism began to take its slow road to recovery. The report was published on 18 August, and the standstill agreement between Germany and her creditors was signed the next day. Under the agreement, 6·3 milliard RM of short-term credits to Germany were prolonged for a period of six months, and thus Germany was for the time being freed from the danger of a renewed financial panic. In the circumstances this was the most that could be achieved. Yet the agreement, while affording relief, also administered a profound psychological shock to the beliefs and assumptions on which capitalism was based. One of those beliefs was that the prompt settlement of debts voluntarily incurred was essential to the working of the system; the standstill agreement was an acknowledgement that, as between a whole nation of debtors and her creditors, this no longer applied.

One German, the banker Melchior, was quick to draw the conclusion. 'What we have just experienced,' he said, 'is the destruction of the fundamental principles of capitalism. Yet the system demands the strictest observation of those principles. This is the first time that I have had to refuse to fulfil obligations to which I had voluntarily committed my name, simply because the state required me to refuse. The capitalist system in Germany will not survive such a deviation from its principles. For the deviations will constantly increase, and the system will accordingly disintegrate.'

In the most obvious sense, of course, Melchior was wrong. The capitalist system in Germany did survive the financial crisis and the standstill agreement. But it survived only in a form which preserved its most hideous vices while losing most of its virtues, of which the kind of morality represented by Melchior was one of the most admirable. Moreover, the capitalist system which survived the *annus terribilis* of 1931 was one which was passing into a new stage of development, in which what had been regarded as its fundamental principles did in fact cease to apply. In this sense, at least, Melchior's instinct was truer than that of most of his fellow bankers. What is apparent throughout the German financial crisis is that, under the pressure of events, men took decisions which they believed to be only temporary expedients, hardly to be justified in view of longer term considerations, but acceptable as providing a breathing space until the crisis had passed and the world had returned to normal. By 'normal' was implicitly understood the conditions which had prevailed before the First World War. Among these expedients can be counted the Hoover moratorium, the introduction of exchange control by Germany, the restrictions imposed upon the German banks, the standstill agreement on Germany's debts. All were in flagrant contradiction of those 'fundamental principles' of established economic thought which Melchior invoked; all survived the crisis for which they were intended to provide relief. The Hoover moratorium was not a temporary suspension of reparations payments; it was the final end of them. Exchange control became a permanent and indispensable feature of the Germany economy. The new banking regulations became the basis of German banking legislation. Even the standstill agreement was still in force at the beginning of the Second World War. In March 1932, when Germany's outstanding 'short-term' credits had been reduced to 5·4 milliard RM, it was renewed for twelve months and in succeeding years was repeatedly extended, until by 1939 the balance had been reduced to 7 million RM. The problem of Germany's short-term debts was solved by unintentionally converting them into long-term ones.

Immediately, the standstill agreement and the publication of the Layton agreement coincided with a momentary improvement in Germany's position, and on 19 August the Reichsbank was able to reduce the discount rate from 15 per cent to 10 per cent. In Hungary and Austria also the financial position improved; Rumania, however, suffered a financial crisis which reproduced precisely the panic from which Austria and Germany had just emerged. In the United States also conditions continued to deteriorate. Cotton prices fell by over a quarter, and the Federal Farm Bureau proposed that one-third of the year's crop should be destroyed. In the states of Oklahoma and Texas over 4,500 oil wells were closed as a means of restricting production, and martial law was declared. In Toledo, Ohio, 70 per cent of bank deposits were frozen as a result of bank failures. But even such evidence of economic decline was overshadowed, in August, by events in Britain, which led first to the fall of the Labour Government and subsequently to the abandonment of the gold standard. For by the second half of 1931 the crisis had reached a stage in which it swept like a hurricane from capital to capital, and it was now the City of London at which it struck.

CHAPTER TEN

The Fall of the Labour Government

The German financial crisis was, for many others besides Melchior, a profound shock to accepted ideas of how the capitalist system worked. It had reduced one of the most powerful capitalist countries to the verge of bankruptcy, which had been avoided only by the suspension, on a nationwide scale, of commercial obligations which had been voluntarily incurred. Moreover, this had been achieved by transferring to others the burdens which Germany herself could not discharge. By its own standards, not only of efficiency but of morality, the system seemed to stand self-condemned, and indeed it was difficult for many people to separate these two aspects of what had happened. As the crisis migrated from Germany to Britain, there developed a note of nervous hysteria, as if people could no longer trust the rules to which they had been so long accustomed, and indeed some of the principal participants in its development were actually reduced to a state of mental and nervous prostration.

Just as capitalist principles demanded the prompt repayment of debts, so they required that those who failed to do so should be punished. The German standstill agreement required that all repayments should be suspended, whether the borrower was able to repay or not, and this was the burden of Melchior's complaint. His own bank, Warburg's, or Fürstenberg's Berliner Handelsgesellschaft, which by prudent management were in a position to meet their obligations, were compelled to become defaulters, just as the Danat or the Dresdner Bank were, which had no alternative.

No doubt such arrangements were unavoidable if Germany was to be saved from total collapse; but they tended to discredit still further a system which had already departed so far from the model it professed to follow as to become unrecognizable. Moreover, they tended to restrict still further the flow of capital which was essential to Germany's recovery. Their effect, wrote Professor Robbins, was 'an almost complete paralysis of investment of any kind – a paralysis which was all the more damaging in that it hit sound concerns even more severely than the unsound. Concerns which could have repaid all that they owed were prevented from doing so. Concerns which had no hope of repaying were kept alive. The result was, as might have been expected, deflation and the intensification of the depression.'

There was another sense in which the German crisis emphasized how far capitalism had diverged from its classical model which still dominated orthodox economic thought. It was, in theory, a basic principle of that model that business decisions were taken by individuals and private individuals in accordance with the laws of a free market, and with the minimum of interference by governments. The sum total of those decisions produced the maximum of efficiency and hence of profit. The beauty of the system was that it contained built-in restraints and correctives, with automatic penalties for those who disobeyed the rules, and always tended to a position of equilibrium; political interference could only disturb the smooth working of the system, by distorting its delicate balance of rewards and punishments.

But in Germany it appeared that, under the actual conditions in which capitalism operated, the sum total of individual decisions might produce a situation in which only government action could enable the system to function at all. It was the Reich government, not individuals or private institutions, which had averted total collapse, by means which were in flagrant contradiction of the 'principles of capitalism' as they were generally understood; indeed, private institutions had proved singularly incapable of providing any solution for the problems created by their own errors, and equally loath to accept their consequences.

The principal conclusion reached during all those feverish meetings of statesmen, bankers, and financial experts which took place during the summer was that, things being what they were, the impartial working of economic law could contribute little or nothing to an improvement in the situation; this conclusion was acknowledged by the Layton–Wiggin committee when it recognized that a solution to Germany's financial problems was dependent on political decisions which would lead to a general improvement in international relations.

The trouble was, however, that the economic crisis itself aggravated all those forces which tended to create, not an improvement, but a deterioration in international relations. *Sauve qui peut* not *Love one another* was the normal national reaction to the crisis.

Over and above such theoretical considerations, there was a widespread sense that not merely the system but those who directed it had failed. The crisis brought to light practices in banking, finance and industry in which folly and greed seemed equally compounded and bankers and financiers in Germany, as in the United States after the Wall Street crash, became the objects of a popular indignation which helped to swell radical agitation against 'the system'. The series of financial scandals, culminating in the collapse of the Nordwolle, which punctuated the German crisis made it only too easy for workless men to believe that the true cause of their misery lay in the wickedness and corruption of their leaders.

Yet if the German crisis gave a shock to established ideas, the feeling that no one could know what would happen next, it was tempered, especially abroad, by the reflection that Germany was after all a very special case. Though she played a leading part in the world economic order she was a relative newcomer, almost an interloper, among the great industrial nations and she had expanded at a speed which placed an increasing strain on her established institutions. Moreover, she had lost a disastrous war and had lost much of her territory, her wealth and her industrial resources as a result, while the accumulated capital of the entire middle class had been wiped out by the inflation. And in particular it could be said, with much force, though not with complete truth, that reparations, combined with the refusal of her political debtors to accept payment in goods, had placed her under an intolerable burden and it was inevitable that, in the circumstances of 1931, she should collapse beneath it.

There were many other reasons which could be given why Germany in particular should have been brought so near to collapse by the depression. Her political history since the war had been violent and turbulent, marked by revolution, counter-revolution, civil disorder and political assassination and, in her case, in 1931, the economic crisis had coincided with a violent political crisis which had already destroyed the basis of democracy and had given her a system of government by emergency decree which was only one stage removed from dictatorship. Her political instability played a decisive part in undermining her financial credit abroad, and foreign doubts and suspicions had only been increased by Brüning's disastrous attempt to appease the national opposition by his foreign policy. Germany, in 1931, might in many respects, despite her industrial power, have been more reasonably compared with some unstable South American republic than with her older European neighbours. No doubt the German financial crisis had revealed grave weaknesses in the capitalist system, but it could as reasonably be attributed to her exceptional circumstances as to the working of the system itself.

None of these arguments could be applied to Britain, the country to which the acute stage of the crisis was now transferred. Germany might be regarded as a latecomer, a *parvenu*, of the capitalist world; but Britain, in a sense, *was* capitalism. She had invented it, and had been the first country to apply its principles logically and con- sistently, enjoying its benefits and suffering its miseries. She had endowed it with its puritan morality and given it its economic theory. She had created the two instruments which were essential to its growth and development overseas: the British banking system which had made London the financial centre of the capitalist world and the British navy which had kept the seas open to its trade and commerce. A financial crisis in Britain, to which she responded in a way which contradicted and reversed her established image, was from the point of view of the capitalist system as a whole something of an entirely different order from a financial crisis in Germany and made it certain that capitalism, if indeed it survived the depression, would never again be what it had been, either in conception or in practice.

A part of the confusion in men's minds in the summer of 1931 was due to their unwillingness to accept that the past could not be restored and their inability to conceive what form the future would take. In this sense, 1931 was a decisive turning point both in the development of capitalism and in men's conception of how it worked or could be made to work, and the most drastic evidence of this is to be found in the events of that summer in Britain. Not, indeed, that this was immediately apparent. The story of the summer is very largely one of how men arrived at decisions they did not intend for reasons they did not understand and it took many years before the meaning of what they did began to emerge. There are certain aspects of it indeed which still remain obscure but this element of confusion is an essential part of the events themselves.

One fact that must still continue to surprise us, even today, is the general unawareness, in the summer of 1931, both of the British government and of the country as a whole, that any crisis was impending. Britain indeed remained in the grip of a depression which in her case had continued for longer than in any other country. In July, unemployment stood at 2,700,000 or 22 per cent of the insured population; production was 8 per cent lower than it had been in 1913; exports had declined by 10 per cent in value. But this was a situation which had persisted for so long that the British had become almost inured to it, or could see no way out of it; and there were compensating factors, in the shape of the fall in prices, the growth of new industries, especially in the Midlands and the South of England, the new pleasures made available by technological innovations like the radio and the motor car, which for many people, perhaps indeed the majority, provided the basis for considerable contentment and satisfaction.

The government also had reason for a subdued optimism. The Prime Minister, Ramsay MacDonald, although his powers were already on the decline, had been active in trying to promote an agreed settlement of Germany's financial problems. At the London conference, he had been disappointed in his hope of arranging a long-term international loan to Germany, but he had no reason for thinking that the failure would rebound upon Britain. When on 1 August Parliament adjourned for the summer recess, and MacDonald travelled to Lossiemouth to seek relaxation on the golf course, neither he nor the members of his Cabinet had any apprehension that the German financial crisis might spread to Britain, and in this we might perhaps find somewhat surprising evidence of how tenuous the communications were between the government and financial circles in Britain, and of how real an independence from the government the Bank of England and the City of London enjoyed.

This corresponded, of course, to the orthodox view that the separation of powers between the government and the Bank should be, as nearly as possible, complete. In practice, under a Conservative Government, it was tempered by the elaborate network of personal relationships which existed between members of the government and the City of London; they had been to the same schools and the same university, their families had intermarried, they hunted and shot and fished and dined together, in effect they were members of one family and their ideas and their information were mutually available to all. Under a Labour Government, this umbilical cord was severed. In 1931 there was not a single member of the Labour Cabinet who had any personal and practical experience of the working of the financial world. For their information they relied entirely on the Treasury, which in turn reflected at secondhand the views of the City, but it would seem that, in July 1931, they had received no warning of what might be impending. If there is a certain dreamlike and unreal quality about the events of August 1931 in Britain, it is partly at least because the direction of affairs, in the crucial field of finance, was in the hands of men who knew almost literally nothing except what others chose to tell them.

MacDonald's mind, indeed, was upon domestic matters rather than international finance. The government was concerned with the increasing cost of unemployment insurance, the prospect of a large Budget deficit and the Opposition's demand that the problem should be solved by a severe reduction in government expenditure, including cuts in the social services. They had solved this difficulty neatly by the appointment earlier in the year of a committee, under the chairmanship of Sir George (later Lord) May, secretary of the Prudential Assurance Committee, to recommend economies in public expenditure; the appointment of the committee was a purely delaying measure, designed as a political concession to the Opposition, and the government did not take it very seriously. In making the concession, Snowden had said contemptuously in Parliament: 'I have no objection to setting up a committee. The government has already set up seventy-two, and one more will not hurt.' The committee's report was published on 31 July, and once again, before dispersing for their holidays, the Cabinet took refuge in delay by appointing a committee to consider the report 'during the recess'.

What concerned MacDonald, as head of a minority government, more than the report were the prospects of maintaining a majority in Parliament and in this respect he had good grounds for optimism. Indeed, in the last six months, there had been a considerable improvement in the government's position. At the beginning of the year Beatrice Webb had written in her diary: 'Everyone expects the Government will be out before the Budget.' By June she could write: 'Barring accidents, the Government will now go on indefinitely.' The change had come about because in the meanwhile MacDonald had been assured of the support of Lloyd George and his rump of thirty Liberal supporters, and was preparing to strengthen the government by the appointment of Lloyd George as Chancellor of the Exchequer in place of Snowden. Thus on 1 August MacDonald could leave London with the feeling that the future of the government was secure and that the accession of Lloyd George would give it a vigour and dynamism it had hitherto lacked. Three weeks later, the government, hopelessly divided, had fallen, and the Labour Party was in ruins.

Even today it is not easy to find the explanation of the crisis which struck Britain so suddenly in August 1931, as unexpectedly as that other crisis for which she was equally unprepared in August 1914. And in 1931 there is not even a Sarajevo to which one can point unhesitatingly as at least the proximate cause of what followed. But just as the outbreak of war, and Sarajevo itself, were the product of a complicated network of processes, some of long-term historical significance, some transitory and almost fortuitous, so in 1931 we can trace an elaborate interplay of circumstances which combined to bring about the fall of the Labour Government.

Perhaps the first signs of the approaching crisis in Britain can be found, as in the case of Germany, in the fall of the Credit-Anstalt. In the spring there had been a slight but perceptible improvement in Britain's economic and financial situation, and Montague Norman had still felt strong enough, though for the last time, to come to the aid of Austria and to support the crumbling financial structure of Central Europe. To Norman this was vital to all his plans for creating a Europe of strong and stable currencies and one of the distinctive features of British banking policy since the war had been the degree to which it had become involved in the financial rehabilitation of Central Europe. Yet Norman seems to have underestimated the consequences which the collapse of the Credit-Anstalt was to have on Britain, as a result of the freezing of British credits to Austria. During the German banking crisis which followed the collapse of the Credit-Anstalt he continued to advise British investors that Germany was, in the long run, 'a good bet', and deserved their comfort and support, and when Lazard's found themselves in difficulties as a result of their commitments in Germany he came to their help with an immediate loan. Indeed, throughout the German crisis and until the end of July he seems to have been seized by a kind of unreasoning optimism; his highly-strung temperament was stimulated by the demands made upon him by the endless succession of meetings, conferences, interviews, telegrams, telephone calls, and perhaps the sheer drama of the situation hid some of its threatening aspects from him.

Norman also for a time seriously underestimated the offence given to France by his assistance to Austria and the hostility of the Banque de France was an added source of weakness to Britain. The French resented Norman's assumption that the Bank of England still had the power to thwart their aims in Central Europe. They resented his sympathy with Germany, and his friendship with and admiration for Schacht, and had taken offence at a lighthearted remark of his that what the Credit-Anstalt needed was 'a foreign butcher' and that 'Schacht was the right type of butcher'. Norman's own dislike of the French, and of French banking methods, was so strong that he could never bring himself to stay in France for pleasure.

Norman's optimism was so far justified that up to 15 July the Bank of England had been gaining gold. At that date, its reserves stood at £165 million, or £15 million above the minimum cover for the currency prescribed by the Cunliffe Committee in preparation for Britain's return to the gold standard. That day, however, there was a sharp fall in the sterling rate of exchange, and Norman received an anxious telegram from Harrison, Governor of the Federal Reserve Bank of New York: 'We are surprised and concerned at sudden drop in sterling exchange today. Can you throw any light on this?' Norman replied laconically: 'I cannot explain the drop.'

Norman was never very good at explanations; he preferred to veil himself in mystery. On this occasion he might have thought it worthwhile to be more forthcoming, but it is possible that he may have been genuinely puzzled by the fall and may have felt in it a warning of impending disaster. One explanation of it, offered later, was that it was provoked by the publication, two days earlier, of the report of the Macmillan Committee on Finance and Industry, with its estimate that in March 1931 London was in deficit on its short-term lending abroad by £254 million. It also revealed the decline during the depression in Britain's 'invisible' exports, in the form of earnings on banking, shipping and insurance, which in normal times gave Britain a favourable balance of payments. Since 1929 shipping had declined by £50 million and interest on foreign investment by £70 million. No doubt these were depressing figures, but there is no particular reason why they should have caused a sudden fall in sterling, particularly because in fact the foreign press made no mention of the report, or its figures, in the week following its publication and it was almost totally ignored in the British press.

The more likely explanation is to be found in the closing of the German banks on 14 and 15 July and the introduction of exchange control by the Reichsbank on 15 July. Foreign investors whose assets were thereby frozen in Germany, and who wished to maintain their liquidity, were forced to withdraw funds from other markets, and the strain fell most heavily on London because that is where most of the money was. For Britain, despite her post-war decline, was still the world's greatest trading nation and held more foreign exchange for commercial purposes than any other country in the world; she was also the world's greatest money market. In particular, large French funds had accumulated in London between 1924 and 1926, before the stabilization of the franc; large balances were also held in London on foreign Central Bank account. By an accident, the German crisis coincided with the time when, owing to the working of the French income tax system, there was always a large demand for funds in Paris.

The same reason which impelled foreigners to withdraw funds from London, that is to say, the freezing of assets in Germany and

Central Europe, also made it difficult for London to meet their demand; £90 million of British assets were frozen in Central Europe. But this was only part of Britain's predicament. She had continued to act as the world's banker even though her own resources no longer qualified her to play the part; indeed, she had financed the depression abroad at a time when no other country would do so and when she herself suffered from a restriction of credit. She had found the means to fulfil this function by borrowing on short-term abroad and employing such funds to finance a much larger volume of foreign loans. In the summer of 1931, her short-term loans amounted to £407 million, against which she was owed £153 million. In normal times her assets could be regarded as adequate cover for her liabilities, but in July 1931 the times were not normal, foreign lenders were themselves under pressure and were nervous and apprehensive, and moreover a large proportion of Britain's short-term loans abroad could no longer be realized. The position, therefore, was potentially one of great weakness, and the weakness was all the greater because, at the time, no one knew how much the total of British indebtedness abroad really was. Banks and finance houses had acted independently of each other, and their total indebtedness had reached a far higher level than any of them would have considered prudent if they had known what others were doing.

When the drain in London set in, the potential dangers of the position became quickly apparent. From 15 July until the end of the month, the Bank of England lost £33 million in gold and £33 million in foreign exchange. On 26 July Norman sent a director of the Bank, Sir Robert Kindersley, to Paris to negotiate an immediate credit of £25 million, while a credit of an equal amount was obtained from the New York Federal Reserve Bank.

There was nothing in itself unusual or alarming in such arrangements, and indeed it had become normal for the Bank of England to look to New York and Paris, with their huge unused reserves, for support when it was under pressure. When the credits were announced on 1 August it was taken for granted both in Paris and London that, as *L'Information* put it, they made the position of sterling as the leading international currency 'impregnably secure'.

Norman, however, felt no such reassurance. He was by now disabused of his former optimism and he had been made sharply aware of how deep-seated French hostility was by a letter received on 23 July from Francis Rennell (later Lord Rennell of Rodd), the British manager of the Bank of International Settlements. Rennell reported the malicious glee with which Pierre Quesnay, of the Banque de France, had described how Norman's policy was misrepresented in Paris and the intrigues conducted against his efforts to arrive at an agreed solution of the crisis. As so often with Norman, the disappointment of his hopes led to nervous collapse. On 27 July he made the last entry in his diary for two months: 'Danger of suspension of gold payments.' The next day he left the Bank 'feeling queer', took to his bed, and when he was well enough to leave it went on holiday to Canada until 23 September. He was therefore absent from the Bank during the whole of the political and financial crisis of August and September, leaving the direction of affairs in the hands of the Deputy-Governor, Sir Ernest Harvey, and Norman's most trusted colleague among the Bank directors, Sir Edward Peacock, who was also financial adviser to King George v.

There was something uncannily appropriate in Norman's breakdown, which coincided with the collapse of the entire financial structure he had tried to build up after the war. His own reputation followed the downward course of sterling, and almost overnight he was transformed from the enigmatic yet omnipotent archpriest of the mysteries of finance into a figure of popular obloquy and contempt. Winston Churchill in a letter from Biarritz to Eddie Marsh at the beginning of July expressed a feeling which was later shared by millions of his fellow countrymen: 'Everybody I meet seems vaguely alarmed that something terrible is going to happen financially. I hope we shall hang Montague Norman if it does.'

In addition to raising credits in Paris and New York, the Bank of England had added to its available reserves by increasing the fiduciary issue, which was not required to be covered by gold, by £15 million. Up to this point the financial crisis had been, and was generally regarded as, a technical matter which could be left to the bankers and financiers; hence, presumably, the government's lack of concern. Indeed, it was not as yet a crisis of confidence, as, for instance, the German crisis had been; the pressure on the Bank of England, and on sterling, had been very largely a consequence of the strain thrown upon foreign investors by the German crisis and by their need for liquidity. Some part of it also should probably be attributed to deliberate withdrawals, for political motives, by France. But there were not as yet any doubts in most people's minds about the Bank of England's ability to stand the strain or of the stability of sterling.

Nor had there been as yet any suggestion that there was any direct and immediate connection between the sudden flight from gold and the condition of the British economy. It is true, of course, that for some years foreign observers had taken a pessimistic view of both its actual and prospective performance. 'For years,' Professor Robbins wrote later, 'continental observers had been coming to the view that the British system was dying of ossification,' and it was commonly believed that if Britain were exposed to financial strain, she would not take the deflationary measures required to maintain the gold standard. This view of Britain as a country burdened by the weight of the past, archaic, inefficient and self-indulgent, suffering from a loss of nerve which made her unable to face the harsh decisions required for her, had been given persuasive force in an immensely popular book, *England's Crisis*, by the French writer André Siegfried, which had considerable influence on public opinion abroad. But this was a long-term historical view, with no immediate bearing on the international exchanges, and up to the end of July there was not any inclination to believe that London was no longer a safe place to hold money in sterling or any other sound currency.

Such considerations perhaps help to explain the *insouciance*, almost frivolity, with which the government treated the publication of the May report on 31 July. It had not thought it worthwhile to accompany the report with any comment of its own or with any declaration of policy with regard to its recommendations. These were in the hands of the Cabinet's economy committee, which would consider them during the recess. It consisted of MacDonald himself, Snowden, Henderson, the Foreign Secretary, J. H. Thomas, the Dominions Secretary, and Graham, the president of the Board of Trade. Intellectually, the committee was supremely ill-equipped for its task. Neither MacDonald nor Henderson had any knowledge of finance or economics. J. H. Thomas was the licensed clown of the Cabinet, who had already proved his incompetence as minister with special responsibility for unemployment. Graham was a profound admirer of Snowden's, whose rigidity of mind was impenetrable to any ideas that were even faintly tinged by unorthodoxy. It was this body of men which had to face the financial and political crisis which followed the publication of the May report.

Its effect was all the more explosive because, for twelve days, it had the field to itself and received no comment or reply by the government. Arnold Toynbee reports a remark of an 'eminent authority' that 'it was an incredible folly ... to allow the May report to be published without any commentary or declaration of policy.' When at length the government did issue a statement, it was too late and the damage was done.

Both the majority and the minority reports of the committee agreed that the Budget deficit for 1932–3 would amount to £120 million; this included both the normal Sinking Fund provision of £50 million and the whole of the borrowing for unemployment insurance, amounting to £50 million. The majority insisted on economies amounting to £97 million, including £67 million on unemployment insurance, and £17 million on teachers' salaries and the pay of the armed forces.

But it was not so much the figures of the May report, alarming as these were, which gave it its impact, especially abroad. It was, rather, its insistence that the Budget deficit was the direct consequence of government extravagance, especially on the social services; the deficit was not merely a problem of accountancy, it was not even a problem which allowed alternative solutions; it was a moral problem which could only be solved by a conspicuous demonstration of those puritan virtues which were embodied in the principles of 'sound finance'. The minority report, while conceding the amount and the seriousness of the deficit, saw in it the evidence not of government profligacy, but of deflation, and proposed to adjust it by taxing those classes, particularly the rentiers, who had benefited by it; the majority were determined that the only cure was to be found in reducing government expenditure to a level which corresponded to the fall in prices. The feverish negotiations which followed the publication of the report, within the Cabinet, and between the Cabinet and the opposition parties and the trade unions, centred on whether increased taxation or government economies should be given priority in balancing the Budget; in fact, the difference between the conflicting parties finally narrowed itself to £10½ million, a figure wholly out of proportion either to the profound moral significance which was attached to it, or to the scale which the flight from the pound assumed.

The May report was no doubt a stupid and a cruel document, which firmly placed the burden of balancing the Budget on the shoulders of those least able to bear it. 'The most foolish document it has ever been my misfortune to read,' said Keynes. 'Composed of prejudice, ignorance and panic,' is the verdict of A.J.P.Taylor in his history of post-war England. Few people today would accept either its theoretical basis or the moral implications which were drawn from it; few would believe that it presented either a correct analysis of Britain's difficulties or the proper cure for them. Yet it also represented the combined wisdom of the banking and financial community of the day, and as such carried an authority which, for most people, was unchallengeable. Its theoretical basis was that British costs must be reduced to a level that brought them into equilibrium with the fall in prices; and as such it represented the orthodox deflationary view. But to this extent at least it conflicted with the view of the Macmillan Committee that the real cure was to be found in international action to raise prices until they were in equilibrium with costs.

This was also Keynes's view, and indeed the view of everybody who still placed any faith in the possibility of international action to solve the problems of the depression. But, as the Hoover moratorium and the London Conference had shown, there were formidable political obstacles to international cooperation of this kind, and Keynes, as a result, believed that until it could be achieved it might be necessary to adopt other, and purely temporary measures, such as, for instance, a revenue tariff. In this, he would have had the support of Lloyd George, of the Conservative opposition, and of large sections of the business community. But this kind of empirical approach was not open to the government, or to the economy committee, because of Snowden's fanatical and ideological commitment to free trade; any deviation from it would have caused his resignation and provoked the political crisis which it was the government's purpose to avoid.

Indeed, in trying to meet the problem created by the May report, the government's liberty of action was strictly confined by its intellectual limitations. Socialist theory provided it with no answer to the flight from the pound, except that this was the inevitable result of a capitalist organization of society which had broken down and must be replaced. But neither the government, nor the Labour movement as a whole, contemplated so radical a cure; anything else they regarded as mere amelioration of a system self-condemned in the long run to destruction; for immediate action they were dependent upon the guidance to be derived from the existing orthodoxies, of which the May report was an authoritative statement.

This attitude was reinforced by the effect of the May report abroad. There the report's condemnation of the government's extravagance, and of the inflationary effects of its expenditure on the social services, convinced foreign investors that Britain was suffering from a profound internal crisis, the product of deep-seated evils which threatened its whole financial structure, including the stability of the currency. This was indeed the explicit message of the May report, and it had all the more effect abroad because it reinforced a lesson which British bankers and financiers had been preaching to foreigners for years. Since the war, British financial policy, under the influence of Montague Norman, had been directed towards restoring financial stability to Europe, but aid had been combined with insistence that the principles of sound finance must be followed, that budgets must be strictly balanced, and government expenditure confined within the strict limits of what a country could afford. It now appeared that Britain herself did not obey her own rules and was threatened with the same dangers against which she had so often warned others. Inflation to the foreigner was a spectre which made their blood run cold, and the May report, by the sombre picture it drew of its effects in Britain, introduced an element of panic and hysteria into the flight from the pound which up to then had been lacking.

The May report transformed a crisis of liquidity into a crisis of confidence. After its publication the flight from the pound, which had been temporarily checked by the announcement of the credits raised in Paris and New York, was resumed, and the Bank of England was inundated by reports from all over Europe that foreign investors expected immediate action by the government to balance the Budget. On 5 August Keynes wrote to MacDonald: 'It is now nearly certain that we shall go off the existing parity at no distant date. When doubts as to the prosperity of a currency such as now exist about sterling have come into existence the game is up.'

This represented a change in Keynes's own views, for until then he had believed that devaluation, whatever theoretical advantages it might have, did not present itself as a practical answer to Britain's problems. For to most people, including the Labour Government and the National Government which followed it, voluntary devaluation as a deliberate act of policy was almost literally *unthinkable*; it conjured up the nightmare of a chaos of unstable and competing currencies which would postpone indefinitely whatever hopes remained of a revival of world trade and an end to the depression. One of the few people in a position of authority who openly accepted the possibility of devaluation was Ernest Bevin, who in his addendum to the Macmillan Report had argued that if credit expansion was incompatible with the maintenance of the gold standard at the existing parity, Britain should go off gold.

The government, however, could afford to ignore Keynes or Bevin, who were both regarded as each in their own way economic mavericks. But it was impossible to ignore the letter which at the same time Sir Ernest Harvey, the Deputy-Governor of the Bank of England, addressed to Snowden. Sir Ernest stated that, despite the French-American credits, the situation had deteriorated. The Bank of England had lost £60 million in the last four weeks, and had virtually no reserves left. In the Bank's view, the Budget must be balanced immediately, if devaluation was to be avoided. The letter ended on the ominous note that the Committee of the Bank had directed him to find means of informing the leaders of the opposition of the facts in regard to the loss of gold and foreign exchange, though 'not to act in any way which you would regard as embarrassing to the Government'. The letter itself was sufficient embarrassment. Snowden immediately summoned MacDonald from Lossiemouth, and the Prime Minister arrived in London to be informed by Harvey and Peacock that Britain stood on the edge of bankruptcy.

There is a curious air of unreality surrounding the twelve days that intervened between the return of MacDonald to London on

11 August and the resignation of the Labour Government on 23 August. Most of the country (with the exception of the unemployed) was happily on holiday and had no reason to think that anything had happened to disturb their pleasures. In London harried and anxious men believed, half-believed, or professed to believe that Britain was faced with ruin, which was demonstrably not true. Abroad, foreigners continued to withdraw their money from London and thus to force Britain towards a decision which everyone thought it their interest to prevent. On the other hand, the Labour Party and the radical press refused to take the May report seriously or to accept for a moment that it could, or should, have any influence on Britain's conduct of her own affairs.

MacDonald, however, could not afford to adopt such an attitude, especially because the terms of his alliance with Lloyd George included a promise of retrenchment in government expenditure, and the reception of the May report both at home and abroad left him no alternative to putting the promise into effect immediately. For him, the crisis presented itself in political terms: what was the minimum level of economies which would satisfy the opposition and the foreign investor, and what was the maximum level which his own supporters could be persuaded to accept? In any case, he was already of the opinion that, whatever the economies were to be in what he was convinced was a national emergency, they should have the support of all three parties and the Labour Party should not be left to bear the responsibility of imposing them alone.

MacDonald arrived back in London on Monday, 10 August, and on Tuesday conferred with Snowden, and representatives of the banks, including the Bank of England. The bankers had arrived at the conclusion that the crisis had 'reached a point which, in our opinion, is threatening the depreciation of the currency with all its consequent evils'. It had become a crisis of confidence, which could only be halted by immediate action by the government to balance the Budget and 'improve our balance of trade'.

On the following day the Cabinet economy committee met, to be informed that the prospective Budget deficit was even greater than the May report had estimated and was not £120 million but £170 million; this figure was accepted as the correct measure of the problem which had to be faced, and by 19 August the committee had evolved a formula to meet the situation as presented by

Snowden: £78·5 million of economies and £89 million of new taxation. The greater part of the economies was derived from savings on unemployment insurance, but did not include a reduction in the standard rate of benefit, as demanded by the May report (20 per cent), the Treasury (10 per cent), and by the bankers, who regarded it as essential to the restoration of foreign confidence. Indeed, the standard rate of benefit had assumed an almost mystical importance; it is significant that what finally split the Cabinet, and obstructed all-party support for its proposals for balancing the Budget, was a figure of £12 million derived from a 10 per cent reduction in the rate.

The days following 19 August were spent in a desperate, and unsuccessful, effort to achieve agreement, within the Cabinet, and between the Cabinet and the opposition leaders and the Labour movement as a whole on the government's proposals. These varied sometimes almost from hour to hour and no one ever seems to have been quite sure what the actual figures were which they were discussing. MacDonald himself fell into a condition of physical and mental exhaustion, and his efforts met with a decisive failure on Thursday, 20 August, when both the opposition leaders and the General Council of the TUC rejected a revised schedule of economies, amounting to £57 million. The opposition considered them inadequate, in particular because they excluded £20 million of savings on the rates of transitional unemployment benefit; the TUC thought them excessive because they considered that the Budget deficit should be met by increased taxation and not by reduction in expenditure. For the TUC Bevin expressed what became the official Labour view of the crisis. It was, he said, 'the result of the manipulation of finance by the City, borrowing from abroad on "short-term" and lending it on long-term . . . As is usual, the financiers have rushed to the government . . . by attributing the blame for the trouble to the social policy of the country and to the fact that the Budget is not balanced.'

MacDonald left the meeting with the TUC in 'furious' despair, and was near to collapse. The Cabinet agreed with him that it was intolerable to submit to dictation by the trade unions; 'the General Council are pigs,' wrote Sidney Webb to his wife. It had now become exceedingly unlikely that MacDonald could achieve the object he had consistently aimed at, of balancing the Budget by measures which would secure all-party support, including that of his own; the alternative was some kind of national government, to which he had already vaguely referred. But decisions could not be delayed much longer. The credits raised in Paris and New York had failed to halt the flight from the pound and were rapidly becoming exhausted; inquiries made in New York had shown that the possibility of obtaining further support depended on the approval by Parliament of an adequate programme of economies.

On Friday, 21 August, the Deputy-Governor of the Bank told MacDonald that the delay in approving the necessary economies had increased the flight from the pound, and that on the following Monday, unless a decision had been reached, sterling would almost certainly have to be devalued, which was something which no party at that moment was prepared to consider. The only alternative was to secure a government loan, as by then the pressure on sterling was too acute to be halted by inter-Central Bank credits; it was the credit of the country itself, and of the government, which was now at stake and this could only be restored by reducing the burden of expenditure on unemployment relief.

On Saturday, 22 August, MacDonald made his last attempt to secure the Cabinet's agreement to such a programme. He was reluctantly authorized to ask the opposition leaders whether they would agree to a revised schedule of economies of £68 million, and, if they did so, to inquire in New York, through the Bank of England's agents, J. P. Morgan & Co., whether such a figure would meet the conditions for a loan.

The opposition leaders accepted the new proposals, on the condition that the loan was forthcoming, and between Saturday and Sunday the Cabinet awaited the reply to the telegram despatched to Morgan's; it did not arrive till Sunday evening, and in the meantime MacDonald had informed the King that the government would probably break up that day. It was essential that a new government should be formed immediately, if the pound was to be saved, but as yet it was still not clear what form it would take.

On Sunday evening, at 8.45 p.m., as the members of the Cabinet walked anxiously in the garden at 10 Downing Street, Morgan's reply was received by telephone at the Bank of England, and a copy of the message was taken by Harvey to Downing Street. It stated that a public loan to the government was not possible until

Parliament had approved the proposed economies, but that a short-term credit of £40 million could be raised in New York if Paris would contribute an equal amount. When Harvey arrived in Downing Street, MacDonald hastily snatched the telegram from his hand and disappeared into the Cabinet room. Soon the Deputy-Governor of the Bank heard voices raised in indignant protest; it seemed to him that 'pandemonium had broken loose'. It was the noise of the government breaking up and that night MacDonald submitted the Cabinet's resignation to the King; on the following day, 23 August, it was announced that the formation of a national government was under consideration.

CHAPTER ELEVEN

The Fall of Sterling

In the National Government which was formed in Britain on 25 August, Ramsay MacDonald remained prime minister, and was accompanied by three members of the Labour cabinet: Snowden, who continued as chancellor, J.H.Thomas and Lord Sankey. The rest of the small Cabinet of ten was made up of four Conservatives and two Liberals. MacDonald parted from his former colleagues more in sorrow than in anger. He said that he expected to be denounced and reviled for breaking up the Labour Government, but initially at least it was expected that he would receive a substantial degree of Labour support. Indeed, only on this assumption could the National Government hope to achieve the specific object for which it had been formed: that is to say, to restore confidence abroad in its ability to defend the pound.

The decisive telegram from New York which had brought about the fall of the Labour Government had made it clear that a loan would be forthcoming only on condition that the measures required to balance the Budget were passed through Parliament with the support of all three parties. What was required of Britain was a kind of act of national contrition for its supposed extravagance, especially on unemployment relief, and for this the support, or the agreement, of the Labour Party was essential. It was all the more essential because the economy measures were expected to be extremely unpopular, and it was thought that Labour opposition would provoke the risk of a general election in which Labour would benefit by their unpopularity.

There was another element of confusion in the National Government's position. It was assumed that it had one purpose and one purpose only: to defend the pound. MacDonald had assured the Labour Government that there were no other questions of policy involved, and the political parties would not be required to surrender, or compromise, their respective points of view on other matters. The government had been called into existence to overcome the immediate financial crisis, and when once this had been satisfactorily disposed of the parties would revert to the *status quo ante*. It is doubtful, however, if MacDonald's partners in the government saw matters in quite the same light. The Trade Unions' rejection of the Labour Government's proposals had made it clear that there was the possibility of a fundamental split in the Labour movement, and the formation of the National Government, which brought it into the open, created for the Conservatives the prospect of being able to turn it to their advantage.

It would have been surprising, indeed, if there had not been considerable confusion about the precise basis, and significance, of the National Government. The emergency it had been formed to meet had developed with such intensity and speed that it had taken everyone unawares, and during most of August it had been Germany which was the cause of anxiety and alarm. Throughout August some of the leading political and financial figures were absent from the scene. Montague Norman was recuperating in Canada; Baldwin was on holiday at Aix, Lloyd George undergoing a prostate operation. And elsewhere August and the beginning of September were by no means uneventful. The Chilean fleet mutinied and was bombed into surrender; there were riots and a general strike in Spain, a rising in Brazil, an attempted *putsch* in Styria. In the United States cotton prices fell by nearly 1d to 3½d a pound and the Federal Farm Bureau recommended the destruction of one-third of the crop. Martial law was declared in Oklahoma and bank deposits were frozen in Toledo, Texas, as a result of the closing of the oil wells. American external trade had declined by $5,000 million since 1930 and for the first time since 1926 the United States had an adverse trade balance. There were bank failures in Rumania and Hungary, and in both countries British loans were frozen. In so uncertain and disturbed a world, the formation of the National Government was accepted initially as proof of Britain's sincere determination to mend her ways and to apply the measures of economy and deflation which she had so consistently recommended to others as a cure for financial troubles. Pressure on sterling relaxed and on 28 August, three days after the government's formation, credits of £50 million were opened in Paris and New York. But on 3 September the bankers once again warned the government of the dangers of the situation. The Bank of England had lost £35 million in gold and about £120 million in foreign exchange since the middle of July, and this included the £50 million credit granted on 23 July. There remained £130 million of reserves in gold, of which £50 million were required to pay the first credit, and £74 million of the second credit. The Bank advised that a rise in bank rate would have no effect in preventing withdrawals, as investors were no longer interested in income but only in the safety of their capital. The classical rules for operating the gold standard had ceased to apply and throughout the crisis bank rate remained at four per cent.

But the Bank still refused to consider the possibility of devaluation, and the Cabinet, which throughout accepted its advice without question, never doubted that its primary task was still to balance the Budget and save the pound. It accepted the figure of £57 million of economies agreed by the Labour Government, together with the additional ten per cent cut in unemployment relief, which brought the total up to £70 million, but was unable to find room for any further reductions. Much time was spent in overcoming departmental resistance to the reduced estimates. The Admiralty reported discontent in the Navy and declared that it was incapable of carrying out its tasks if a major war were to break out. The king was gravely displeased by the reduction of twenty per cent in royal expenditure, which would diminish the splendour of ceremonial occasions and might even entail the abolition of Gentlemen at Arms and Beefeaters; the Cabinet hurriedly reduced the cuts to ten per cent.

Parliament reassembled on 8 September, and in the debates that followed many of the false assumptions on which the government was based were dispelled. MacDonald had privately received many messages of sympathy and encouragement from Labour supporters (including Sir Stafford Cripps), but faced with the Labour rank and file and with trade unionists, few Labour members could bring themselves to admit publicly that they saw no alternative to saving the pound at the cost of the social services. In the debates MacDonald ceased to be the greatly admired and venerated leader with whom his Cabinet colleagues had parted on a relatively minor matter of about £12 million. The feelings of respect, loyalty and gratitude for his years of service vanished, and he became, as he remained to the Labour Party for the rest of his life, the traitor, turncoat and renegade who had betrayed the working class at the command of the bankers.

In the passion, bitterness and acrimony of debate it became clear, especially to the foreigner investor, that the National Government was not what it had at first seemed to be; that is to say, a genuine all-party coalition symbolizing a united national will to carry through the measures required to save the pound. It appeared rather as the product of a precariously balanced parliamentary arrangement, exposed to the fierce opposition of the great mass of the Labour Party and exposed to the risk of a General Election in which its victory was highly uncertain.

This was not what MacDonald had intended, nor was it what had been demanded in New York as the condition of a loan. The doubts and anxieties of foreign investors were already renewed and intensified by the uncertainty of the political situation in Britain when their wavering confidence was dealt a shattering blow by an event which seemed to justify their worst fears about the condition of Britain.

On 14 September, naval ratings of the Atlantic Fleet, on shore leave at Invergordon, attended a meeting of protest against the cuts in naval pay. The following day they prevented the fleet from putting to sea for its autumn exercises, which were cancelled, and the ships of the fleet dispersed to their home ports while the men's complaints were being investigated. An astonished world learned that the British Navy had mutinied.

Reports of the 'mutiny' were greatly exaggerated. Genuine discontent at the cuts had been increased by a failure of communication between the Admiralty and the fleet, and while their complaints were being investigated the ratings returned to their normal duties; pending the inquiry the cuts were restored and disciplinary action against offenders was confined to a minimum.

But abroad the 'mutiny' assumed a significance out of all proportion to its real significance, and was magnified into an event of world-shaking importance. The pound sterling and the British Navy had been two essential pillars of the world order created by Britain in the nineteenth century, and which had still survived, though severely battered and mauled, into the twentieth. Now both appeared to be threatened at the same time, leaving a yawning gap where once there had been solid and secure foundations. Moreover, for foreigners who had survived the cataclysms of the First World War, the mutiny had sinister associations; disorders in the fleet had preceded the fall of both the Romanov and the Hohenzollern empires. Naval mutinies and revolution had gone hand in hand; in English history the navy had played a more vital role than in that of any other empire; if the Royal Navy could not be depended upon, what was there left of England? Even more, what was left of the pound sterling?

Today, such fears seem hysterical and exaggerated, and they emphasize to what an extent, in the summer and autumn of 1931, psychological factors had come to dominate all others, and indeed this is the best evidence of how acute the crisis was. And in a sense foreigners were right in the importance they attached to the events at Invergordon and their relationship to the economic crisis. The pound and the Royal Navy really had been essential supports of the old order and the weakness of both was a sign that it could no longer function as it had done before. Foreigners perhaps would have had better reason for alarm than the 'mutiny' at Invergordon if they had known of the Admiralty's declaration that the Royal Navy, as a result of economies and naval limitation, could no longer fulfil its historic tasks.

The effect of the mutiny on opinion abroad was all the greater because other events in September reflected and added to the general sense of insecurity and apprehension. When the Berlin stock exchange, after being closed for two months, reopened on 3 September, there was an immediate fall in values of 25 per cent; there was a further collapse on 14 September, the day of Invergordon, and perhaps even more significant was the default by the Bank für Textilindustrie on a loan of £1 million; this was the first case of a German default on a long-term loan, and it was evident that the slight recovery of confidence which had followed the negotiation of the standstill agreement was not likely to be sustained.

Germany's weakness was immediately translated into heavy selling on the Amsterdam stock exchange, where investors had been particularly hard hit by the German financial crisis, and also by the catastrophic fall in commodity prices in the Dutch East Indies. Between 14 and 15 August, Unilever fell by 17 per cent, Dutch Ford by 20 per cent, Amsterdam Bank by 20 per cent, Netherlands Trading Society by 28 per cent. The heaviest loss of all was recorded by Kreuger and Toll, which fell by 40 per cent. This was attributed to the operations of an international bear group which, with Russian support, was speculating heavily against Kreuger and Toll.

Stock exchange losses abroad led to renewed withdrawals of foreign balances in London and throughout the week of Invergordon the pound had to be supported by the Treasury. On 16 September, British Government stocks were heavily sold. On Thursday, 17 September, the Deputy-Governor of the Bank of England informed the government that owing to the increased rate of withdrawals the latest credits from New York and Paris were almost exhausted. Harvey gave five reasons for the heavy pressure in London: the general insecurity of conditions abroad; the large deficit, estimated at between £50 million and £100 million, in the balance of trade; the repercussions of Invergordon; an internal, as well as a foreign, flight from the pound; and the uncertainty of the political situation in Britain, which inspired fears of a general election. Yet, even at this late moment, the Bank did not raise the question of suspending the gold standard, and the Treasury was consulting the financial authorities in New York and in Paris with a view to raising further large credits for the defence of the pound.

The replies to the Treasury's inquiries were sympathetic but not encouraging, and according to Snowden offered no prospect of 'assistance on the scale that was by that time obviously necessary'. On Friday, 18 September, it was at last necessary to face the decision which up to that moment had seemed unthinkable and which the National Government had been formed to prevent. On that day, there was a heavy decline on both the New York and the Continental stock exchanges. Withdrawals reduced the Treasury credits by a further £18 million, and the Prime Minister in consultation with the Bank decided that, unless conditions improved on the following day, the gold standard must be suspended.

The next day put an end to any hopes that remained. Withdrawals amounted to £20 million, and Harvey wrote to the Prime Minister that the last remaining credits were exhausted and the

THE FALL OF STERLING

Bank had no further resources with which to meet the continuing drain from New York, Paris, and Amsterdam. The letter ended with an urgent request for the suspension of the gold standard and the government, having throughout the crisis followed the Bank's advice that the pound must be defended at all costs, saw no alternative to continuing to follow its advice when it changed its mind. At last the game was really up.

That night a telegram was sent by Harvey and Peacock at the Bank to Montague Norman, now a day out at sea from Quebec on his return voyage to England. It ran: 'Old Lady goes off on Monday.' Its meaning was either so obscure or so unbelievable to Norman that he concluded it must refer to his mother's holiday plans, and he landed at Liverpool on Monday, 21 September, to learn from the evening papers at the dockside the incredible news which meant the defeat of everything for which he had laboured since the end of the war.

The Treasury announcement of the government's decision to suspend the gold standard had been issued the previous evening and relieved the Bank of England immediately of its obligation, under Section I of the Gold Standard Act of 1925, to sell gold at a fixed price. The announcement stated that since the middle of July more than £200 million had been withdrawn from the London market, and that these claims had been met partly from the Bank of England's reserves, partly from the credits of £50 million secured by the Bank in Paris and New York, and partly from the £80 million of French and American credits secured by the government. In the last few days, however, the rate of withdrawals had so accelerated and international money markets had become so 'demoralized' that the government had no alternative but 'to protect the financial position of this country by the only means at our disposal'. At the same time, bank rate was raised from 4½ per cent to 6 per cent, the London stock exchange was closed for two days, and British residents were prohibited from dealing in foreign exchange except for normal trading purposes, and travel or other personal expenses.

On Monday, 21 September, a Bill was hurriedly passed through Parliament suspending the gold standard. 'They never told us we could do that,' said Tom Johnston, a member of the former Labour Government. His comment was a perfectly fair one. At no point,

[189]

up to the very last, had any of the government's financial advisers suggested that it might be possible to go off gold without certain disaster, or ceased to warn against the catastrophic results that would follow. Nor, when at length the government was forced off gold by *force majeure*, was it suggested that in fact the government had gained a new liberty of action which might make it easier rather than harder to solve its financial problems.

'The fall of the pound sterling,' wrote Professor Toynbee, about the events of 21 September 1931, 'was the greatest single event, up to that date, in the progressive collapse of the structure of world finance which had been taking place since May; and the shock administered by the news was proportionately violent.' Stock exchanges were closed throughout the world, dealings in foreign exchange were either prohibited or placed under severe control, and all the financial institutions of the world were struck with a momentary paralysis.

The fall of the pound, indeed, might be taken as the turning point in the crisis of capitalism provoked by the depression, and it was perhaps appropriate that it should have had its origin in Britain, the country which had done most to promote and develop the capitalist system as it had existed up to that date. The essence of the system had been the international exchange of goods and services on the freest possible basis, and Britain had played the primary role in promoting this system because of her need for cheap food to feed her industrial population and for the raw materials required by her industries. The system had developed certain characteristic features which were all of British creation and these had acquired an almost religious significance for those who operated it; they were the *lares* and *penates* of the capitalist world, exercising as powerful an influence on the mind of the capitalist as on his pocket. Free trade was not only an economic but a moral principle, because it was ultimately dependent on the maintenance of peace and goodwill among nations. The Royal Navy was not merely an instrument of British foreign policy, as, for instance, the German Navy was the instrument of German foreign policy; it was also, or until recently had been, a guarantee that, whatever happened on land, the seas should be free to the ships of all nations. The pound sterling was not only a national currency, but an international currency, indeed *the* international currency which provided the means of exchange for a large proportion of the world's trade, and the operations of millions of individual traders throughout the world were dependent on its stability and reliability as a standard of value.

The Great War of 1914–18, and the growth of nationalism of which it was both an effect and a cause, had given a fatal shock to this system, and indeed Britain's own involvement in it was a contradiction of what had hitherto been her traditional policies. It left behind a Britain which had lost her industrial, naval and financial supremacy and could no longer afford, out of her own resources, to act as the guarantor of the system as a whole. Moreover, the war had raised political and commercial barriers between nations which dislocated the working of the system and had left behind a burden of inter-governmental debts too heavy for its financial structure to carry. The gold standard had been painfully restored, at great cost to some countries, including Britain; but its rules were more often broken than observed, in particular by the two countries, the United States and France, in whose vaults the larger part of the world's monetary gold was effectively sterilized.

Many efforts had been made to find alternatives which would compensate for the dominating part which Britain had previously played in the working of the system: in the League of Nations, in an elaborate network of treaties by which nations mutually guaranteed each other against the instincts of aggression which all of them shared, in naval limitation and attempts to reduce the burden of armaments, in central bank cooperation to apply an international credit policy, in the creation of a special institution, the Bank of International Settlements, to ease the problem of inter-governmental debts. Britain herself had tried to reassume her former role as an international lender by drawing on the unused resources of other countries, particularly France and the United States; indeed, the weakness of sterling was largely a reflection of her efforts to finance Germany and Central Europe through the depression.

All these efforts failed in their underlying purpose of trying to restore confidence and faith in the system as a 'going concern' and of providing centres of resistance to the forces which were pulling it apart. For some years, during the boom of 1924 to 1928, it appeared that they might succeed but the depression itself was the best proof of their failure. No calamity of such intensity and duration had ever struck the system before; it was still possible to believe, like Brüning or Hoover, that one day it would stop of its own accord if only they could survive so long, but at the end of 1931 there was still little or no evidence that the end was yet in sight. The prudent view was that things would get worse before they got better, and in the meantime the only safe course was to find what shelter one could from the storm.

The prudent view was, in this case, the right one, though its consequences were something very different from that restoration of confidence for which statesmen had hoped. The kind of shelters in which men sought refuge from the storm were the best evidence of how far the system had lost its international character. Though nations might still pay lip service to, or even sincerely believe in, the ideal of free trade, in practice what they put their trust in henceforward were the restrictions and constraints of economic nationalism: in tariffs, exchange control, quotas, import prohibitions, trade agreements, anything indeed which might help to protect their own share of a steadily diminishing total of world trade or promote their own self-sufficiency. Such arrangements had existed even in the most flourishing periods of the system and indeed classical economic theory allowed for cases in which they might be justified. But they had been regarded as transitional and exceptional; now they became the rule and in doing so profoundly changed the nature of the capitalist system as a whole.

If internationalism had been its characteristic feature in its earlier phase of development, economic nationalism became its distinguishing mark in the period which followed Britain's abandonment of the gold standard, and nothing illustrated the change more strikingly than the adoption of a protective tariff by Britain herself, for whom free trade had for a century been the essential condition of her prosperity. The change was all the more significant because economics embodied only one of the aspects in which the growing force of nationalism revealed itself; in the new phase of capitalist development economics became subordinated to politics to a degree which had never been known and in some cases became the instrument of nakedly aggressive forces.

For those to whom the virtues of capitalism had outbalanced its vices, the change which took place after 1931 seemed wholly

[192]

deplorable and they continued to hope, against the evidence, for some relaxation of political and economic tensions which would allow it to recover its international character. To others, for whom the depression was sufficient proof that the classical model of capitalism had broken down, the nationalist economics of the thirties were welcome because they allowed nations a greater degree of control over their own economic development, insulated them against the impersonal forces of a free economic market, and gave the opportunity for increased direction and planning of their domestic economies. Planning indeed became a keyword of the new era, largely because men saw in it the means both of finding a way out of the depression and of preventing its recurrence.

Both views embodied their own kind of hope that the depression could be overcome and that capitalism could be made viable. Neither foresaw that the forces of nationalism, in which political and economic motives reinforced each other, had acquired a ferocity and violence which could no longer be contained within the existing system. In the summer of 1931, while the attention of the western world was absorbed by the financial crisis, an incident in the Far East, hardly noticed at the time, gave warning of even graver developments. On 17 August the Japanese War Office announced that a Japanese staff officer, Captain Nakamura, with three companions, had been arrested and murdered by local Chinese forces in Manchuria and that the Japanese Foreign Office had demanded an apology, an indemnity and the punishment of those responsible. The incident seemed of little importance compared with the events which were shaking the financial structure of the world. Yet in fact it had even more sinister implications. It was an announcement that in Asia also the effects of the depression had become intolerable and that Japan, its leading industrial nation, had forsaken the attempt to solve her economic problems by peaceful means and had chosen instead the path of territorial conquest. In a different, yet equally significant way from Britain's abandonment of the gold standard, this decision also foreshadowed the end of the post-war attempt to restore the capitalist system in its pre-war image.

Yet, paradoxically, the fall of sterling did not entail for Britain the catastrophic consequences which had been foreseen by those who, to the last moment, had clung to gold. 'We have all had a dreadful time,' wrote Harvey pathetically to Norman, at the same time expressing the hope that Norman would continue to rest his nerves and stay away from the Bank. The pound itself, on the day after devaluation, fell to $4·28, on the following day to $4·10½ and on 24 September to $3·85. By the end of November it fell to $3·25, or roughly 70 per cent of its former parity. It continued to fluctuate around this point for the next two years, at its highest, in April 1932, showing a discount of 23 per cent against its former gold parity and at its lowest, in September 1933, a discount of 35 per cent. If at its former parity the pound was overvalued by about 10–15 per cent, it could now be said to be undervalued by about 20 per cent, and the Bank of England, and the country with it, was relieved of the long and unsuccessful struggle to maintain sterling at an artificially high gold parity.

The relative stability of sterling, after the departure from the gold standard, was due largely to the relief from political uncertainties provided by the general election held in October 1931, which dispelled all doubts about the National Government's majority in Parliament. Against the expectations of all those who believed that the Labour Party might gain by the unpopularity of the economy measures, its representation in Parliament was reduced from 265 to a mere 52 in one of the most crushing defeats ever suffered by a British political party, and the National Government was returned with the overwhelming majority of 502.

The victory of the National Government registered the British electorate's reaction to the shocks it had suffered during the summer. It was, in the main, the same reaction which revealed itself elsewhere under the strain of the crisis; that is to say, a sense that the only port in a storm was provided by the old and tried precepts of orthodox financial practice, by a balanced budget, strict economy, reduced government expenditure. The fact that such measures had been tried and failed elsewhere, and were even thought by some people to be responsible for prolonging and intensifying the depression, had little effect on the British people; such arguments assumed a level of economic sophistication which was rare even among the better educated. Like the May committee, the British people knew instinctively that Britain had sinned against the principles of sound finance and must now pay the penalty.

Yet if in one sense the election reflected a reversion to the past, in another it set Britain free to choose new paths out of the depression; for it heralded the abandonment of that rigid adherence to the principle of free trade which, as personified in Snowden, had so inhibited the Labour Government in its attempts to master the depression. The victory of the National Government opened the way to the adoption of protectionist policies which were a decisive breach with the past, and showed that Britain was no more immune than other countries to the economic nationalism which was beginning to give a new look to capitalism. It was one of the curiosities of the situation that the triumphant conservative forces created conditions which made possible a greater degree of intervention in economic life than ever before.

For the victory was only nominally one for the principle of national, that is to say, all-party government, which the American bankers had stipulated as the essential condition for a new loan. Of the government's total of 554 supporters, 471 were Conservatives, and Britain entered into a period of Conservative government which lasted for ten disastrous years, the years, as Winston Churchill later described them, 'which the locust hath eaten'. The overwhelming victory of the National Government was attributed by many to the influence of women, who voted for the first time in the 1931 election and registered at the polls their overwhelming preference for security and stability.

The election and its results once again emphasized the paradoxical nature of the British crisis. The National Government was formed primarily to restore foreign confidence as a means to saving the pound. It failed in both objects, and only succeeded in restoring confidence, both at home and abroad, after sterling had been devalued. The Labour Party's electoral campaign, which was overwhelmingly defeated, was based on the claim that the financial crisis was an artificial one, a 'banker's ramp', and this was strictly true, in the sense that its immediate cause was the refusal of bankers in New York and Paris to grant a loan except on political conditions. But the claim lost much of its force because the object of the ramp was to force Britain into doing something, that is to say, to save the pound, which all parties, including the Labour Party, agreed to be unavoidably necessary. It seems equally true that, when this proved in fact to be impossible, the devaluation of the pound would have been carried out under far more unfavourable circumstances if it had taken place under a Labour and not a National Government.

But if the consequences of devaluation were not, as the government's financial advisers predicted, immediately catastrophic to Britain, neither did Britain gain the advantages which might be expected to follow. Exports did not rise in response to reduced sterling costs but continued to fall; in October 1931 they stood at £32,833,000 and a year later at £30,440,000. Nor did British internal prices rise in proportion to the fall in the value of sterling, but in fact showed a remarkable stability. The index of wholesale prices which stood at 99 in September 1931 rose to 106 in December but by September 1933 had fallen again to 103.

Nor did Britain derive any of the other advantages, such as a relaxation of credit, which might be expected to follow from a managed currency, such as sterling had become. This is not perhaps surprising, however, for the conception of a managed currency was so novel and alarming to established ways of financial thinking that in practice no one knew what to do with it, and the instinct of the Bank and the Treasury, having gone off gold, was to behave as nearly as possible as if they were still on it, and the bank rate, which had remained unchanged throughout the sterling crisis, was immediately put up once it was over. The government and its advisers, throughout the years which Mr Chamberlain later described as those of *Bleak House*, remained after as before devaluation convinced that the only way out of the depression was through economy and deflation and sternly refused to take advantage of the increased freedom of action which it bestowed upon them.

Such an attitude earned the severe condemnation of critics who, like Keynes, believed that the first duty of monetary policy is to stimulate the growth of a nation's economy, particularly in a period of acute deflation. But it is possible that such a criticism ignored psychological factors which, in the strained and hysterical atmosphere of 1931, had become of greater importance than any others. The bank rate had remained unchanged throughout the crisis simply because normal rules no longer applied in view of the universal and overwhelming desire for liquidity at all costs. The suspension of the gold standard had plunged Britain and every other capitalist country into what was an unknown and frightening world of fluctuating and unstable currencies which had nightmare associations with the political and economic upheavals of the immediate post-war period, still only recently past. In such a world, no one could go to bed at night knowing what his money would be worth in the morning, and no one could calculate what the effect of any particular policy might be; a relaxation of credit was as likely to provoke panic as to stimulate enterprise.

In the summer of 1931, the Bank, the Treasury and the government believed that what was above all necessary was to restore confidence, and that the way to do it was to appeal to the virtues of 'sound finance'. There is no way of showing that, at that moment, they were wrong; they were facing what had become a psychological rather than a strictly economic crisis and economics does not always make good psychology. Since 1931 economics has made great theoretical advances, but even today it is far from being an exact science, most of all because it is based on psychological assumptions which often, and especially at moments of crisis like 1931, have little relation to the people to whom they are meant to apply. In 1931 the British electorate, especially its women, out of bewilderment, fear and ignorance, gave an overwhelming vote of confidence to policies which in all probability were prejudicial to the economic interests of the great majority of them; it would still be impossible to say with confidence that they were wrong to do so.

If, after the devaluation of sterling, the British people found that little seemed to have changed, for better or for worse, in their condition; if they saw few signs of the catastrophic consequences which they were warned would follow; and if, as a result, they were inclined to take a somewhat cynical view of the wisdom of their political and financial leaders; all this is not to say that such consequences did not take place or that the warnings were without foundation. Where they were wrong was in the assumption that the consequences would fall most directly, heavily, and immediately on Britain herself. The assumption was a natural one because of the established belief that British interests, more than those of any other people, were identified with those of an international economic order which, already gravely disturbed, was even further disturbed by the fall of sterling.

The case was in fact rather the reverse. In the post-war world, Britain had made heavy sacrifices to try and preserve, or to restore, that international order and had undertaken many obligations as an international lender, as a repository of foreign balances, as the guarantor of the principal international currency, which had strained her resources to the utmost. The devaluation of sterling, the relief from her dependence on other financial centres, especially New York and Paris, freed Britain from many obligations she could no longer support, and gave her the opportunity, even if she did not take it, of cultivating her own garden, or rather, her own industry, with some measure of protection against the risks and uncertainties of what had become a demoralized world market.

Not that she did not suffer direct losses as a result of devaluation. The real value of the sterling debts owed her from abroad, which were still very large, was correspondingly diminished, while some countries took direct retaliatory action against British exports. In Germany, the Ruhr coal industry was relieved of all state and federal taxes in order to meet the competition of cheaper British coal, while other countries offered direct subsidies as a bonus to exporters.

But the immediate effect of devaluation was to relieve the strain on Britain and divert the crisis away from her to other countries, in particular to the United States and also, for the first time, to France. Just as it had first fallen on Germany and thence migrated to Britain, so it now passed to the United States, which it now attacked with unexampled, and almost intolerable, intensity. Like all the countries which did not follow Britain on the path of devaluation, she now suffered a catastrophic process of deflation, and in the eighteen months after the fall of sterling the American wholesale price index fell from 71 to 60, or nearly 18 per cent. The United States was not alone; France and Germany and most of the countries of continental Europe still clung formally to the gold standard, and the whole of the trade of Central Europe had come virtually to a complete standstill. The exceptions in Europe were the Scandinavian countries; Denmark's foreign trade was so closely tied to the British market that the krone was immediately devalued in conformity with sterling and Denmark's example was followed by Sweden and Norway; Bolivia, Colombia, Argentina and Egypt also abandoned the gold standard.

The effect of the devaluation of sterling indeed was to introduce an unparalleled degree of confusion into the world's monetary system. By April 1932, of the world's principal countries twenty-two remained on the gold standard; these included the United States, France, the Netherlands and Italy, but also Mexico and Persia whose adherence to it was purely nominal. In fifteen countries, including Germany and Canada, the gold standard was still legally in force but in practice was ineffective. Twenty countries had abandoned the gold standard; six countries still clung to the silver standard, and these included China and Manchuria, where the currency was completely chaotic, and Tibet which in practice observed no standard at all.

This was the currency nightmare against which the gold standard, even in the modified and weakened form in which it had operated since the war, had provided a defence, and the confusion was all the greater because of the conflicting motives and purposes which directed different countries' monetary policies. Some, like the United States and France, which together owned nearly 60 per cent of the world's stock of monetary gold, remained on the gold standard while sterilizing the reserves which made it possible for them to do so.* Others, like Germany, did so, not because they were financially strong, but because they were so weak that to have abandoned the gold standard would have destroyed confidence altogether; Germany in particular was only able to preserve the gold standard by erecting so elaborate and formidable a system of exchange control that the mark in effect ceased to be a unit of international exchange. It could be said that the world's monetary system, in so far as it remained a single system at all, had ceased to fulfil its function of providing a means of exchange between nations and now added one more impediment to the free movement of goods between them; so much so, indeed, that in some cases they were driven to the primitive method of direct barter.

Paradoxically, also, the abandonment by Britain, and those countries which followed her example, increased rather than

* France and the United States possessed gold reserves largely in excess of the amounts required to back their countries and had refused to undertake a credit expansion which would have stimulated an export of gold. Thus a large part of the world stock of monetary gold was in effect removed from circulation.

diminished the demand for gold. Since the war it had become the practice of central banks to hold a large proportion of their reserves in foreign exchange as well as in gold; the devaluation of sterling, and the currency chaos which followed, drove them to hold as much of their reserves as possible in the form of gold. The wave of distrust of all foreign currencies struck particularly hard at the United States, which between 21 September and 21 October lost $329 million of gold, mostly to France and Europe. Throughout the world there was a rush for liquidity at all costs, and private hoarding of gold reached immense proportions. This contraction of the monetary supply dealt a further blow to world trade; an additional difficulty was that in a world of increasingly strict exchange control, traders were in many cases unable to protect themselves against the risks of currency fluctuations by dealings in futures. No such situation of universal confusion, uncertainty, fear and panic had ever previously existed in the international markets of the world. 'The abandonment of the gold standard by Great Britain,' wrote Professor Robbins, 'was the end, for the time being, of the international monetary system. Henceforward the course of the depression in different centres varied with the fortunes of the local monetary system, the disunity itself giving rise to new complications and disturbances.'

The effects of the financial crisis of 1931 were all the more over-whelming because they were superimposed on a system which was already gravely weakened by the economic depression. In some countries the strain proved too much to bear, and from the end of 1931 onwards the economic crisis became transformed into a political crisis and perhaps also into something which went even deeper; a profound psychological crisis which drove some nations into paths of violence and aggression which marked yet another stage in the collapse of the existing world order.

In no country was this process more clearly revealed than in Japan, the most advanced industrial country of Asia. Since the end of the war, and particularly the Washington Conference of 1921–2, Japan had for ten years turned away from the aggressive expansionist policy she had hitherto followed; in 1922 she withdrew her troops both from Russia's Maritime Province in China and from the Chinese province of Shantung. She had tried to find in industrial expansion, in the growth of her foreign trade, and in political cooperation, the answer to her population problem, which had grown more pressing every year; in the five years up to 1930 the average annual increase in her population had amounted to nearly a million.

The coming of the depression appeared to demonstrate the hopelessness of such an attempt; and in particular the passing of the American Hawley-Smoot Tariff; in 1929 convinced Japanese public opinion that American policy would not tolerate the legitimate expansion of Japanese trade. In the three years from 1929 to 1931 Japanese foreign trade fell by nearly a half, imports falling from 2,169 million yen to 1,206 million, and exports from 2,100 million yen to 1,116 million. The murder of Captain Nakamura (if Captain Nakamura ever existed) was a warning that Japan had passed from trade to conquest. The announcement of the murder passed almost unnoticed in the West, and seemed of little importance compared with the fall of sterling; but it was quickly followed, on 18 September, by the opening of Japanese military operations north of Mukden in the South Manchurian Railway Zone, and by the Japanese occupation of Mukden.

The Manchurian 'incident' not only signalled the opening of full-scale military hostilities between Japan and China; it was also a direct blow to the system of collective security which had been slowly and painfully built up after the war, and it was a blow from which the system never recovered. Thus by the end of 1931 it was not merely the financial foundations of capitalism which had been shaken; its political foundations also had begun to disintegrate.

One incident in particular illustrated how far Japan had departed from the principles of collective security, embodied in the League of Nations, to which so many hopes had been attached since the war. In August 1931 China was suffering from the appalling catastrophe of the Yangtse floods, which were estimated to have caused eighty million deaths. In response to China's appeals for assistance men and women throughout the world, including the Japanese themselves, contributed generously, and in October the Council of the League of Nations despatched Sir John Hope-Simpson to China as Director of the Chinese National Flood Relief Commission; at the beginning of February 1932 he stood and watched helplessly while Japanese fighter planes bombed the refugee camps which he had established as part of his mission. There could be no better example of the kind of savagery and ferocity with which nations were beginning to respond to the problems with which they were faced at the end of 1931.

CHAPTER TWELVE

The Death of Hope

The successive financial crises of 1931 left the capitalist world in a curiously ambivalent state. The experience had been of a kind which it had never known before and at moments it had seemed as if the system had been shaken to its foundations. The year that followed was, by contrast, in the economic field one of lethargy and apathy, as if the system had been so enfeebled by the strains which had been inflicted on it that it had lost the power of recovery.

On the other hand, as economic conditions continued to deteriorate, they reached a point at which for many people it seemed that they could be endured no longer, particularly because their established leaders seemed powerless to amend them and could hold out no promise of improvement. During 1931 the four largest hospitals in New York, the richest city in the richest country in the world, recorded ninety-five cases of starvation, of which twenty proved to be fatal. In Detroit, eleven thousand families were driven off relief in the city's attempt to achieve a balanced municipal budget. In the South, people were reduced to the condition of beasts of the field. 'We have been eating wild greens since January this year,' wrote a farmer from Kentucky; 'such as Polk salad, violet tops, wild onions. Forget-me-not wild lettuce and such weeds as cows eat, as cows won't eat a poisoned weed . . . I can't clear a dollar a month, that is why I am here. That is why hundreds are here, they can't ship their families home. But I am glad we can find a few wild greens to eat.'

Such conditions reflected an economic collapse such as the world had never seen before and the impotence of governments to relieve it. In both these respects, during 1932, matters grew worse and not better. Of all the countries in the world, only in Australia could there be detected the first signs of recovery.

That is not to say that, during the year, no efforts were made on a national or an international scale to solve the problems which were held to be responsible for the continued decline of the world's industry, agriculture and trade. At the Lausanne Conference in June and July a determined attempt was made to solve the problem of reparations, with the clear implication, in the minds of the participants, that it should also lead to a solution of the interconnected problem of inter-governmental debts; but though the conference was successful, in the sense that it finally put an end to reparations, this hardly did more than officially recognize the fact that, whatever the conference decided, it was not possible, either politically or economically, for Germany to pay reparations any longer. Nor did the agreement reached conceal the profound divisions that existed between the participants in the conference and between them and the United States.

To a far greater extent than to the Lausanne Conference, the hopes of the world for some alleviation of its troubles were directed to the World Disarmament Conference which, after years of arduous preparation, opened at Geneva on 2 February; the most important international conference, it was thought, since Versailles, attended by fifty-nine countries and 'the chosen representatives of seventeen hundred million people', yet destined to prove almost entirely barren of results. It was a sinister omen of failure that the opening of the conference had to be postponed for an hour, from 3.30 to 4.30 p.m., in order to allow a meeting of the Council of the League of Nations to consider the emergency created by the landing of two Japanese divisions at Shanghai.

Again at Stresa, in September, an attempt was made to assist, by international agreement, the agrarian states of Central and Eastern Europe by removing obstacles to international trade, by granting them import quotas and customs preferences and by concerted action to raise agricultural prices; but though the conference was able to reach agreement in principle, its proposals were so hedged about by reservations that by the end of 1932 no progress had been made in putting them into action.

What all those efforts at international cooperation had in common was their notable lack of practical success. Nothing, it appeared, could be achieved in practice to halt the progressive breaking up of the capitalist world as a unitary system. International action, in trade as in politics, was constantly thwarted by the disruptive forces within the system; and this was all the more striking when, as in the case of the Disarmament Conference, the objects aimed at had the overwhelming support of world opinion. Indeed, world opinion was rapidly becoming exposed as an illusion; what increasingly mattered were the goals set themselves by particular nations and in the case of some of the most powerful these were increasingly determined by the narrowest and most aggressive form of self-interest.

The difficulty of achieving effective international action was all the greater because of internal political instability. The political and economic chaos which reigned in China was even worse confounded by Japanese aggression, while Japan herself had entered a period in which any government was at the mercy of the assassin. Both France and Germany, in 1932, held general elections, with changes of government which also involved important changes of policy, while Germany, in addition, had two presidential elections which provoked the most violent political passions, and the United States one. Mr Hoover, indeed, was of the opinion that the failure of business and industry in the United States to show any signs of recovery was due to the doubts, fears and uncertainties created by the possibility of a Democratic victory. It was particularly ironic and tragic that while in France the elections gave power to the left, which was prepared for concessions to Germany, in Germany they marked the triumph of the National Socialists, to whom any concessions were unwelcome unless accompanied by unqualified admission of the justice of all German demands, however extreme.

Lastly, in the circumstances of 1932 there was a fatal weakness at the heart of all attempts to solve the world's political and economic problems (which had in fact become almost indistinguishable) by international cooperation. All, whether they concerned war debts, or disarmament, or tariffs, or exchange control, or prices, involved long, complicated and difficult negotiations whose success depended on a measure of goodwill and mutual confidence which was most frequently absent; and even when agreement was reached, it was normally on proposals which were essentially long-term in their effects, and required time and patience before they could begin to work. But by 1932 in many countries time and patience were wearing out; so far as the direct victims of the depression were concerned, what was required was direct action to alleviate their immediate needs, or the promise that such action was at hand. Neither the action, nor the promise of it, was within the scope of any form of international institution then in existence.

In the conditions of 1932 it was natural and perhaps inevitable that people should have turned away from international cooperation to the only institution then existing, the national state, which was both strong enough, within its own boundaries and sometimes outside them, and self-confident enough, to promise recovery. Until then, indeed, the state itself had been only half aware of its own power to plan and direct the economic life of its own people; 1932 marked the beginning of a dawning awareness, and acceptance, of the fact that the state, if it so wished, could take the direction of economic life into its own hands, and might thereby provide a better life for its own citizens, even if, maybe, at the cost of others. A large, perhaps the decisive, part in this voluntary restraint on the part of the state had derived from the ruling orthodoxy that state interference in economic life should be reduced to a minimum.

To some, the idea that the state should take an active and positive part in directing economic activity was a heresy that had died with the mercantile system and a large part of traditional economic theory had been devoted to exposing its errors and fallacies. To others it was welcome because, in a situation which was rapidly becoming intolerable to millions of people, it offered at least some way of escape and hope, even if only a temporary one; it was possible, for instance, to continue to believe, like Keynes, in the long-term virtues of free trade, and at the same time to advocate a moderate tariff as an emergency measure in an exceptional situation. After all, if the world economic order had collapsed to a point at which it could no longer provide for the primitive needs of millions of human beings, and if international cooperation was powerless to restore it, it might be time for the state to look after its own interests and citizens. To yet others, the idea of state direction and planning of economic affairs was welcome on grounds in which economics played little part, as an assertion of the supremacy of the state, and of politics, which is the life of the state, in all spheres of national existence; and to these the evident disintegration of the economic system was yet another proof that economics was far too important a matter to be left to bankers, industrialists and businessmen. Certainly one of the most important effects of the depression was in the long run the extent to which it lent added strength and force to this view.

For the depression, besides undermining the material conditions of men's existence, also, for many people, destroyed the moral assumptions on which it had hitherto been believed to rest; by 1932, such people included men of the most disparate opinions who would have been shocked and surprised to find that they shared the same beliefs. When a United States Congressman declared in the House of Representatives that a man had a right to steal rather than starve, it meant that even the firmest believers in capitalism had begun to doubt its moral basis. What else was he doing except to repeat Bertold Brecht's succinct summary, in the *Dreigroschenoper*, of Marxist ethics:

Erst kommt das Fressen, dann kommt die Moral
(Grub first, Morality later)?

The doctrine that the state has the right, even the duty, to look after its own, at whatever cost to others, represents the same morality on a different level; it was the morality of *homo homini lupus* on an international scale, and it was a doctrine which the depression, after two long winters and the prospect of a third, was making increasingly persuasive and attractive.

In the winter of 1932 there occurred two events which seemed to illustrate with peculiar clarity how much the depression had achieved in exposing the illusions, both good and bad, from which men had suffered. They both happened in Paris, and by a peculiar coincidence they both happened on the same day; indeed, they were so close in time and space that the one had some effect on the other, though otherwise they were entirely unconnected, except as events in a single historical process.

The day was 12 March, an ice-cold clear day in Paris, on which the body of Aristide Briand was carried to its burial place. He had been prime minister of France eleven times, the architect, with Austen Chamberlain and Stresemann, of the Treaty of Locarno, the joint sponsor of the Briand–Kellogg pact outlawing war as an instrument of policy, and a winner of the Nobel Peace prize. A

[207]

German visitor to Paris, the cosmopolitan Harry Graf Kessler, known as the 'Red Count' because of his left-wing sympathies, described the scene in his diary: the crowds lining the route, no military display except for a few mounted *Gardes Républicaines*, the huge mountain of flowers on the funeral carriage, the foreign ministers and diplomats following it, but most striking of all the seemingly endless processions of pacifist organizations, war veterans, youth groups, chanting rhythmically as they marched: *La Paix, La Paix!* and *Dés-ar-mons! Dés-ar-mons!* while the spectators applauded and repeated their slogans. They were appealing not only to the memory of Briand; they were appealing to the World Disarmament Conferences then in session at Geneva and already engaged in the almost theological subtleties and distinctions which would soon reduce it to a state of suspended animation.

Briand was not a heroic figure, but in many ways a typical French petty bourgeois. However, he represented, as no one else of such outstanding political gifts had done since the death of Stresemann, the profound longing for peace that inspired millions of men and women throughout the world and indeed had inundated the Disarmament Conference with innumerable petitions and appeals when it had opened only a month before. He represented a dream that had come nearer to becoming a reality in his lifetime than ever before or since; but it was also a dream that died with the depression.

The passing of Briand's funeral cortège had seriously held up the deliberations of an anxious body of men sitting in a hotel room in Paris. They were awaiting a messenger from the world's greatest financier, Ivar Kreuger, who had fled to Paris to avoid the pressing inquiries that were being made into his affairs. The messenger had been delayed because he could not get across the funeral route before the procession of mourners had passed; when he arrived, it was with the news that Kreuger had shot himself.

The information was suppressed until the stock exchanges of the world had closed, because there was not one in which it would not have affected share prices disastrously. The shares of his main company, Kreuger and Toll, were among the most widely quoted and popular in the world, even though they had fallen from about $21 to $9 a share during the last year. Besides, Kreuger had dominated the financial world for many years like a Colossus; he was a figure not only in the world of banks and stock markets but in the counsels of governments, with whom he bargained as an equal and on occasions had been the only person who would or could come to their aid. He was credited with being the outstanding financial genius of his time, a consistent expansionist even after the onset of the depression, a bull when everyone else was a bear, with ideas which reputable authorities believed to hold the key to world economic recovery; 'a man,' said the *Economist*, 'of great constructive intelligence and wide vision, who planned broadly, yet on a basis which seemed to be protected by carefully devised safeguards.'

Kreuger was above all a man whose word was his bond, so much so indeed that no one ever dreamed of questioning it; his word proved to be as worthless as his bonds were. The vast and labyrinthine financial structure headed by his main company, Kreuger and Toll, had been built upon a worldwide network of match monopolies, concessions and holdings, but it extended also to pulp, timber, gold and iron mines, banks, investments (real and imaginary), telephones and engineering; by the end, it had come to rest on nothing more than $142 million of counterfeit Italian government bonds and the fact that Kreuger's accounts, and the structure of his companies, were a secret which no one except Kreuger understood.

The truth is that no one tried, or cared, to understand them. With his American associates, the respected banking house of Lee, Higginson & Co., in 1923 Kreuger founded IMCO (International Match Corporation), which until its bankruptcy in 1932 sold $148 million of shares to the American investing public. In 1925, IMCO and Swedish Match transferred $25,421,875 to GARANTO, Kreuger's Polish match monopoly, and this in turn was paid out to Kreuger personally. Lee, Higginson, who were active in promoting Kreuger's shares, were closely concerned in these transactions and were represented on the board of all his main companies; but they never troubled to attend board meetings or asked for any further information about his frequently mystifying and obscure transactions, or the impenetrably complicated relationship between his own personal accounts and those of his companies, than Kreuger chose to give them.

The announcement of Kreuger's suicide was accompanied by the tributes appropriate to one who was regarded as both a Titan and a saint of finance. 'Least of all does personal suspicion light on him,' said *The Times*; 'a very Puritan of Finance,' said the *New Statesman*. His defalcations were not known until later; indeed it took many years, and the labours of a whole army of accountants, before his affairs were completely investigated. But when the extent of his failure was made known, it was rumoured that the favoured few of the financial world had been informed in time to get out of Kreuger and Toll, and IMCO, before they totally collapsed.

The same rumours circulated in the case of another colossal swindler, Samuel Insull, whose affairs were already under investigation at the time of Kreuger's suicide. His colossal public utilities corporation, a masterpiece of the art of 'leverage' carried to its extreme, displayed the same almost unintelligible ramification of holding companies as Kreuger and Toll; when finally indicted for fraud he fled to Greece to escape extradition and there tearfully complained that he did not see why he should be blamed because he had only done what everyone else was doing. Perhaps indeed 'swindler' is the wrong word to apply to Insull; what he suffered from in matters of finance was a kind of hypertrophy of the imagination, based on a belief that profits can be plucked out of the air by the simple process of multiplying them on paper.

Briand on the one hand, Kreuger or Insull on the other, each represented dreams and hopes that were proved false by the depression, though in the one case they were noble and idealistic ones, in the other greedy and materialistic. Briand's dreams of peace could not withstand the increasingly nationalist policies to which states were driven by the depression; they became irrelevant when Japan looked for a solution to her economic difficulties in the invasion of China. Kreuger and Insull's insubstantial fabric of dizzily pyramiding companies was the product of the dream of easy and indiscriminate wealth which the depression had finally killed.

This withering away of hopes, however false, gave an additional bitterness to the depression at the beginning of its third year. Millions of men and women now had nothing more to expect of the future than another winter on the dole or the breadline, or in the army of the destitute who queued for the privilege of collecting scraps from the refuse of restaurants and catering establishments. With this death of hope there grew a feeling in many that a condition which could be endured if only temporary was intolerable as a permanent way of life. The astonishing patience and fortitude with which, for the most part, the unemployed and dispossessed had accepted their fate as something unavoidable began to turn sour, and a sense of anger and indignation against those in power, who seemed powerless to help them, took their place. Men began to feel that things could not go on much longer as they were, and faced by the apparent helplessness of their leaders began to look elsewhere for the means to end their troubles.

Such feelings were increased because, to the victims of the depression, the helplessness or passivity of those in authority on occasions appeared to take the form of coldhearted indifference to the suffering that was involved. Men noted that, despite the depression, the very rich remained very rich; paper fortunes may have vanished overnight, but the concentrations of great wealth remained for the most part untouched and in the same hands, and on the whole it was the small man who had gone to the wall. Indeed, the well established might profit at his expense. When three banks in Toledo failed in 1931, the Toledo Trust Company was reported to be jubilant at the many new accounts and the surprising amount of deposits it received; when the Bank of Pittsburgh closed, the two Mellon houses in Pittsburgh remained open all day to handle the torrent of new accounts. About a quarter of all the banks in the United States failed during the first three years of the depression; in 1932 the American Bankers' Association announced to their satisfaction that closures had left the large banks in a stronger position 'as measured in terms of average capital, resources, available volume of business and qualities of management'.

The rich showed a capacity for defending their own which was in sharp contrast to the meekness and patience which they preached to the poor. Their stubborn refusal in the United States to tolerate any form of federal unemployment relief may have sprung quite sincerely from a conviction that the evils of the 'dole' would undermine the American spirit of rugged individualism and personal initiative. 'Of all diseases known to pathology,' declared Senator Gore of Oklahoma, 'the passion for a pension such as this is the most debilitating. This is a civil pension. This is the dole. The disease is infectious. The disease is contagious. In the beginning the disease is acute. It soon becomes chronic, and at last, so far as the individual is concerned, the disease becomes incurable, and so far as the community is concerned the disease becomes endemic, becomes ineradicable . . . It is the paresis of the soul and it defies all cure, defies all remedy.'

But opposition to federal relief also reflected the knowledge that it would have to be paid for out of federal taxation, which fell most heavily on the rich themselves, and which they showed a matchless ingenuity in both resisting and evading. Throughout the years of the depression, from 1929 to 1932, J.P.Morgan paid no federal tax and in 1931 and 1932 all of his partners were in the same happy position. Colonel Robert McCormick, the millionaire proprietor of the *Chicago Tribune*, valued his personal property in Chicago at $25,250, and paid tax of $1,518. Some rich men, for purposes of taxation, appeared to have no property at all.

No doubt all rich men were not, in Roosevelt's phrase, 'malefactors of great wealth', but a sufficient number of them were to make the words carry conviction to those who had nothing and it corresponded to a mood of heightened and sharpened antagonism between the rich and the poor. When, in the summer of 1932, a reduction of ten per cent was made in the salaries and pay of federal employees, President Hoover sent a secret message to Congress asking that the armed forces should be exempted, as it might lower their morale at a moment when their services might be required in support of the civil power in suppressing disorder. In the two greatest industrial countries in the world, by 1932, millions of people had ceased to believe in the established order and, the established order having failed them so completely, were looking for both new men and new measures which might offer them salvation. Propaganda posters in Germany portrayed masses of starving, haggard and despairing men looking up to Hitler as *Unser Letzte Hoffnung* – Our Last Hope; and he himself claimed the unemployed as the strongest support of his movement. In the United States, they were looking to the Governor of New York as the man with the will to save them from their destitution. '1932,' Professor Schlesinger has written, 'was providing a last chance for politics'; and both these men, in their different ways, represented a political answer to the crisis; economics was a subsidiary matter. But the question was whether either of them could contain the rising tide of bitterness, anger, disillusion and despair within the existing framework of the economic system, and by 1932 it began to seem doubtful whether they could.

In a world of deepening and darkening crisis one of the few, and feeble, signs of reassurance was the relative stability of Britain after the crisis of devaluation. On 30 October 1931 the Bank of England repaid £20 million of the joint Franco-American loan, and the balance of £20 million was repaid three months later. The Treasury loan of £40 million, borrowed in a last desperate effort to defend the gold standard, was repaid at the end of February 1932. Sterling recovered from a discount of 30 per cent against its gold parity in February 1932 to one of less than 20 per cent in April. The bank rate fell from 5 per cent in February to 4 per cent on 9 March and to 3½ per cent a week later.

These were signs of Britain's fundamental financial strength, which was still great, but they did not contribute to any revival of British trade and industry; they were part of a process, which was going on all over the world, by which nations mobilized and repatriated their overseas resources and reduced their foreign commitments. In a world in which all currencies, even the dollar, were under suspicion, there had been a revival of confidence in Britain as a safe place to keep one's money after the National Government's sweeping victory in October 1931; and she was helped also by large movements of gold from India, where it was tempted out of her vast private hoards by the appreciation of the rupee against sterling.

For Britain, none of the catastrophic effects ensued which had been predicted as a result of the devaluation of sterling; indeed, her position, like that of other countries which followed her in going off gold, improved relatively to those which did not, but this gave small grounds for optimism in view of the steady and continuous decline in world trade and industry. If, after the financial hurricane which had struck the capitalist world in 1931, there now followed a period of relative calm, it was the calm of exhaustion, as when men contemplate the wreckage left behind after a storm. Nothing, it seemed, could halt the continued fall in world prices, the rise in unemployment, the withering away of world trade; the system could still react effectively to sudden emergencies, like the German banking crisis of 1931, but was helpless, it appeared, against the long-term tendencies of which they were the result. During the first four months of 1931, the total value of world trade had fallen to 42 per cent of what it had been in the same period of 1929; during the year as a whole, world imports fell from the $2,613 million of 1929 to $1,651 million and world exports from $2,358 million to a mere $980 million. In June 1932, the United States for the first time in its history showed an adverse balance of trade, and its exports were lower than in any month since 1914 and the lowest in June since 1904.

World production continued to fall. In the United States, in July 1932, the steel industry was working at less than 12 per cent of capacity; in Germany, production was little more than half of what it had been in 1928. All the remaining gold standard countries, including the United States, France, Poland, Switzerland, and especially Belgium and Holland, suffered a period of severe deflation which contributed further to the enfeeblement of world trade and industry.

Moreover, trade and commerce in 1932 took a course which was a complete reversal of what had hitherto been regarded as normal. International lending virtually ceased and the flow of capital from creditor to debtor countries turned in the opposite direction, as the creditors mobilized their overseas resources in order to defend their own positions. The debtors replied by imposing exchange controls and restrictions, and throughout the world large sums of money were immobilized by standstill agreements, and the normal processes of international exchanges were brought to a halt.

The strain upon the debtor countries, indeed, had become in-intolerable as a result of the catastrophic fall in gold prices, representing a large increase in the real value of their debts, and in the proportion of their resources required to service and repay them. The average fall in gold prices in the countries which still adhered to the gold standard was about 30 per cent since December 1929 or 30–35 per cent on the average for the whole year. But the fall in commodity prices was even higher; on the world market they had fallen by 50–60 per cent, and this affected debtor countries with particular severity, as they were to a large extent dependent on the export of primary commodities. A striking example was Hungary, which was particularly dependent on the export of wheat, the price of which had fallen by 75 per cent since 1925. For the debtor countries in general, the volume of exports required to produce a given amount in terms of gold had increased by over 120 per cent, which is a measure of how greatly the real burden of their debts had grown. For most of them indeed the strain proved too great, and in country after country a moratorium was declared on the repayment of their foreign loans, both as to capital and to interest.

The attempt to discharge the burden of debt led to an acute intensification of competition in the world's export markets, as debtors attempted to secure an increasing share of a dwindling volume of world trade, and importing countries, in self-defence, raised higher and higher barriers against the flood of exports seeking an outlet. The world drive for exports increased still further the difficulties with which Germany, as one of the world's greatest debtor countries, had to contend. By intense efforts she had converted an adverse balance of trade of £40 million in 1929 to a favourable balance of £80 million in 1930 and of £140 million in 1931, but by 1932 it had fallen again to £53 million. She had suffered particularly by Britain's conversion to a moderate form of protection. Up to 1931, over 89 per cent of German exports to Britain had been free of duty; by the end of 1932, over 85 per cent were subject to duties ranging from 10 per cent to over 20 per cent. In reply, Germany imposed discriminating measures against imports of British coal.

From the point of view of international trade, the universal tariff war that raged in 1932 was disastrous; but it was also symptomatic of an even deeper reaction against the ideas and hopes of international cooperation which had flourished in the twenties. Trade had ceased to be an activity binding nations together, by which, through the mechanism of international lending, the more advanced came to the aid of the less well developed countries. It had become a weapon with which, to their mutual disadvantage, nations attempted to defend themselves and attack each other, and the spirit in which it was employed could, as in the case of Japan, turn to even worse purposes if and when occasion demanded. Yet the idea of international cooperation still lingered on, however feebly, and among the other preoccupations of statesmen in 1932 were the preparations for the opening of the World Economic Conference in 1933.

CHAPTER THIRTEEN

Revolt in
America

Nowhere did the depression strike harder than in the world's two most advanced industrial countries, the United States and Germany, and the shock was all the greater both by contrast with the prosperity that had gone before and the potentialities of wealth which were still inherent in the economic system. Indeed, by 1932 the shock was so great that it had begun to seem doubtful to many people in those two countries whether the capitalist structure of society could maintain itself much longer.

One symptom of this general sense of confusion and alarm was a world-wide desire for liquidity. In so precarious a world, in which no one could foresee the future, men wished to realize all available assets, particularly if they were held abroad, and in many cases this desire was strengthened by the need to compensate for sterling losses.

In the United States the immediate effect of the devaluation of sterling was heavy pressure upon her stocks of gold as foreigners rushed to repatriate their holdings, and in the three months which followed Britain's abandonment of the gold standard the United States reserves of gold were reduced by $715 million. The result was to promote credit restriction and severe deflation, followed by a renewed crop of bank failures which stimulated attempts at assistance both by private institutions and by the administration.

The first attempt at assistance, and at relieving the credit shortage, was the creation in October 1931 of the National Credit Corporation, with the object of helping the weaker banks. It was intended that the corporation should dispose of a fund of $500 million, to be provided by private industry and finance, but in fact no more than $10 million was subscribed. In the end the capital

Rudolf Hilferding,
German Finance
Minister 1928–9.

The British Cabinet,
31 August 1931.
(*left*) Philip Snowden,
Chancellor of the
Exchequer, talking to
Stanley Baldwin.

Hermann Brüning,
German Chancellor
1930–2, arriving at the
Ministry of the Interior,
Paris, in July 1931.

Ivar Kreuger 1880–
1932, International
Financier and swindler.

had to be provided by the United States Treasury and was handed over to a new institution, the Reconstruction Finance Corporation. Among the recipients of its bounty was Charles Gates Dawes of Chicago, who obtained an $80 million loan by threatening that otherwise he would close his Chicago bank. Indeed, the Reconstruction Finance Corporation was largely administered in the interests of large-scale industry and finance and not, as was intended, of smaller and weaker institutions. The Missouri Pacific bank borrowed several millions from the Reconstruction Finance Corporation, used it to repay a Morgan loan, and promptly went into bankruptcy.

A further effort to expand credit was made at the beginning of 1932, with the passage of the Glass-Steager bill which authorized the substitution of 'eligible paper', that is to say, first-class securities, for gold in the statutory reserves which provided backing for the currency; at the same time the Federal Reserve System entered into large-scale purchases of government securities on the open market. It would, however, have conflicted with the administration's economic principles if the large pool of credit thus created had been administered by a federal agency and it was entrusted to 'the most powerful coalition of financial leadership since the days of the Liberty Loan Committee', consisting of the representatives of twelve of the most powerful industrial and financial corporations in the country. They included, among others, Owen D. Young, of General Electric, Walter S. Giffard of American Telephone and Telegraph, Charles E. Mitchell of the National City Bank, Alfred P. Sloan, Jnr, of General Motors, and Albert H. Wiggin, of the Chase National Bank.

These measures to stimulate business activity did indeed have some success, and the first five months of 1932 were marked by a slight, though temporary, recovery, which encouraged Mr Hoover, once again, to believe that the depression had been overcome. June, however, was marked by a renewed outbreak of banking failures, particularly in Chicago.

The long-term situation, indeed, remained sombre and menacing, with falling production matched by a continued increase in unemployment. From 8,000,000 in 1931 it rose to over 12,000,000 in 1932, which meant that one out of four workers in the United States was out of a job. Even this figure, however, was almost

[217]

certainly an underestimate, as it took no account of rural unemployment nor did it include the huge army of migrants, homeless, jobless, and those separated from their families, estimated at over two million, who in 1932 were aimlessly roaming across the United States.

There were in fact no figures which could accurately measure the true extent of unemployment, much less the degree of human suffering involved; but the administration itself made very little effort to improve on this situation. In the summer of 1931, Mr Hoover decided, perhaps because the next presidential election was not much more than a year away, that the administration could not dissociate itself entirely from the condition of the unemployed, even if its principles forbade any positive action to alleviate it. As so often before and after, Mr Hoover's decision took the form of appointing a committee, in this case the President's Organization on Unemployment Relief, under the chairmanship of Walter S. Giffard. Beside him stood Owen D. Young and other leading figures of the industrial and financial world. Yet despite the wealth of executive talent at his disposal, the committee proved far less effective in dispensing aid to the unemployed than the Reconstruction Finance Corporation was to be in assisting needy bankers; it was not so much a medium for action as a substitute for it, largely no doubt because, by definition, it had no access to federal funds.

The committee promised the United States 'the thrill of a great spiritual experience' and that 'the fear of cold and hunger will be banished from the hearts of thousands'. Yet when Giffard was questioned on the committee's activities, in February 1932, by the Lafollette sub-committee of the Senate, he confessed that it had 'no definite information' on the needs of the unemployed, or on how many unemployed were in need of assistance; that he did not know how many unemployed there were in the cities of New York, Pennsylvania, or Illinois (by others conservatively estimated at $3\frac{1}{2}$ million); that he did not know what the need of relief was in the rural areas of the United States. Asked by Senator Costigan 'how many people in the United States at this hour are on the verge of starvation', Giffard replied, 'I have no such information.'

So bleak a confession of ignorance argued an indifference bordering on callousness, not merely in Giffard and his colleagues, but in the President himself, and this was something that would not be forgiven or forgotten. As so often, Mr Hoover appeared to believe that, positive action being prohibited, words and phrases were all that could be offered to the victims of the depression, but by 1932 they had begun to ring hollow. Yet Mr Hoover was not a callous man, and in his own lifetime no one had proved more effective in the relief of human suffering.

It was only his own countrymen that he could not, or would not, help. This attitude, a kind of apathy and languor in the face of the problems of the depression, was the symptom of a strange, almost psychopathic, paralysis of the will in so essentially practical a man as Mr Hoover. It was not the result of hardheartedness; it was the product of a system of ideas, held with the absolute conviction of dogma, which rendered Mr Hoover incapable of action: of the belief that Federal intervention in business was an evil that must be restricted to a minimum, that the self-interest of businessmen was the only reliable guide in economic affairs, that the depression was the inevitable result of immutable economic laws which would one day, equally inevitably, provide their own cure for it. Such beliefs immobilized Mr Hoover as effectively as if he had been physically bound hand and foot, and perhaps it was a sense of his own helplessness, of being martyred to a stonyhearted creed which for him had the force of a religion, which deepened the shadows which gathered around the White House, until its sombre atmosphere became intolerable both to inmates and visitors. And for Mr Hoover himself it had the tragic result of transforming one of the most respected and admired of Americans into the most hated man in the United States.

This hatred was only one aspect of the increasing violence and bitterness with which, during 1932, men responded to the conditions imposed on them by the depression, and this response was not confined only to the unemployed, who indeed for the most part continued, to the dismay of radical elements, to display an extraordinary capacity for enduring the fate which had been thrust upon them. It applied equally to those who were in employment but found themselves increasingly exposed to wage cuts, short time and deteriorating conditions of work; to farmers, who on incomes that had been reduced by a half found it impossible to sustain the burden of mortgages and bank loans contracted before the precipitous fall in farm prices; even to war veterans; accustomed to regard

[219]

themselves as the most loyal and patriotic of Americans, but for whom patriotism was no longer enough.

With the deflation which, in the United States as in all countries that continued to adhere to the gold standard, followed the devaluation of sterling, American industry was given an added stimulus to reduce costs, and in particular labour costs; the attempt to maintain wage rates, which had been remarkably successful in the early years of the depression, and helped to temper its effects, could not be sustained, and this brought an added bitterness into industrial relations, particularly in the coal industry, where the depression accentuated and intensified factors which already condemned it to decline. The spring and summer of 1932 witnessed a long series of strikes, in some cases leading to outbreaks of violence which threatened the entire structure of public order, in Illinois, in Johnson County, Arkansas, in Hocking Valley, Ohio, at the Dixie Bee mine, Indiana, and in West Virginia.

The coal-mining area of Bloody Williamson and its adjacent counties in Southern Illinois, the scene of many outbreaks of violence in the past, justified its name by a strike which began in April 1932 and continued into 1933. It contained the richest coalfield in the United States; the Orient mine near Benton was the largest in the world, and was both highly mechanized and highly efficient. Only a few years earlier the miners had been among the aristocrats of labour. But since 1927 the prosperity of the coal-field had declined, according to the mine owners as the direct result of high wages which had made it uncompetitive, and the economy of the whole area was near to collapse. At Benton, with a population of ten thousand, a member of the Board of United Charities stated that at least two thousand children had not tasted milk for a year. Out of forty commercial banks in Franklin and Williamson counties, all except two had closed. Four hundred families in and near Benton were living on charity, which provided each family with an income of $1·30 a week. Other towns were even worse off. At Coello there was neither work, money nor relief of any kind, and only two men, who found occasional work in a neighbouring town, had any employment or income.

On 1 April 1932, 150,000 men went on strike in the South Illinois coal-field. It was an act of desperation as much as of policy, as in the condition of the mining industry, the strike could have no prospect of success. When John L. Lewis, as president of the United Mineworkers of America, negotiated a new contract, accepting a cut in wages, with the mine owners, it was twice rejected by an overwhelming majority of the miners; and when Lewis nevertheless declared the contract in force, only 3,000 men returned to work.

The miners' strike in Illinois was directed as much against Lewis and the UMWA as against the mine owners, and both Lewis and the mine owners united in trying to drive the miners back to work. Intimidation did not stop short of violence, and even murder. Strike leaders mysteriously disappeared. One was shot down on his own doorstep by hired gunmen. Franklin County was declared a 'closed territory' by the authorities and no one might enter it without their permission.

On 18 August, 10,000 miners camped outside Taylorsville, the capital of Christian County, where 1,500 men had returned to work in the Peabody mines, but dispersed when faced by a show of military strength by the authorities. Four days later, 25,000 miners marched on Franklin County, where picket lines at the Orient mine had been attacked by 1,000 specially sworn-in deputies, armed with clubs, revolvers and machine-guns. At the county line, the marchers were met by a force of deputies who opened fire with machine-guns and shot-guns and drove the marchers off, refusing them permission to return and collect their dead and wounded.

The strike had become a revolt; throughout the summer civil disorder mounted, until finally the governor of Illinois, under pressure from the Peabody interests, ordered the National Guard into Taylorsville where they established a military regime and terrorized both the miners and the townspeople.

The strike in Illinois dragged on into 1933. It was an expression of a mood of desperation that was becoming general throughout the United States and, though it never had any chance of success, it had been sufficient, during the summer of 1933, to reduce Southern Illinois to a state of open civil war.

The strike in Illinois was only one manifestation, though among the most violent and protracted, of the crisis which had struck the United States. Throughout the country men were increasingly turning away from the established order, which having held out

[221]

promises of infinite wealth had so totally failed them in their need, and were trying to find their own way out of the destitution which threatened to become a permanent way of life. Out of the sterile ground of the depression new organizations and new movements sprang up, designed to give men an alternative to the despair which was all the existing system had to offer them.

Most of them were short-lived; some were utopian attempts to escape from the fundamental conditions of modern industrial organization; some, though they did not succeed in achieving their immediate objective, left a permanent mark on national economic policy. In Seattle, the Unemployed Citizens' League, which for a short time enjoyed considerable success, rested on the hope that its members, having become redundant to the existing economic system, might create an alternative system of their own, outside the cash nexus, and depending on the direct barter between each other of whatever goods and services they could produce by their own efforts. The same hope inspired the Mid-West Exchange, at Yellow Springs, Ohio, and similar organizations in over thirty states, based on 'the idea', according to the Labour Review, 'of a resumption of the interrupted flow of goods and services by means of barter'. But in none of them did the original idea survive in its original simplicity. By the end of 1933, most of them had developed their own form of scrip which served as an internal means of exchange and had an established value in terms of the national currency. The Unemployed Citizens' League, founded by the unemployed to serve their own needs, quickly became an important political movement in Seattle, elected its own reform candidate for mayor, and fell under the direction of a committee consisting of a contractor, a road haulier, a physician, a banker and a lawyer.

Of much greater importance than such movements were the attempts of the farmers to regain, both by direct action and by political pressure, what they considered to be their rightful place in the economic system. Farmers in the United States, like farmers all over the world, had been among the worst victims of the depression; their case was in many ways worse than that of the industrial worker because they were to a large extent ignored by official statistics of employment or unemployment and did not even share in the meagre provision of relief that was available in the cities. Between 1929 and 1931, total farm incomes had fallen from nearly $12 million to about $7 million; it has been estimated that the fall in net incomes, after deduction of tax and the service of mortgages and loans, was even greater and was of the order of 75 per cent. Farmers, in relation to industry, were in the same position as the debtor countries of the world towards their creditors; the fall in prices, which was particularly severe in the case of agricultural commodities, had increased to a point at which it was impossible to discharge the burden of debt incurred during more prosperous times as a means to increasing agricultural efficiency and productivity; and increased efficiency and productivity had themselves helped to drive prices lower and increase the burden of debt, measured in real terms, even further.

On the other hand, the farmers, unlike the urban unemployed, represented a large, and in the long run a stable and essential interest in the economy of the United States. They could appeal to a long tradition of hostility to the largely Eastern, financial and industrial interests which had dominated the United States since the Civil War, of inflationary monetary doctrines as against the prevailing orthodoxy of deflation, of bi-metallism as against the prevailing worship of gold. The banks, finance companies, orthodox economic theory, the single monetary standard, had long been the farmers' natural enemies and the depression sharpened this antagonism to the point at which the farmer was ready to revolt.

This tradition, with its memories of populist agitation and disaffection, helps to explain why the farmers, unlike other groups which had suffered by the depression, found able and energetic leaders to press their claims for a radical revision of their status in society: Ed O'Neal, of Alabama, president of the Farm Bureau, John A. Simpson of the Farmers' Union of Oklahoma, and Mike Reno, an ex-president of the Iowa Farmers' Union. Reno especially advocated that the farmers, in default of legislation to raise farm prices, should take direct action by refusing to deliver their goods to the cities at prices which did not cover the cost of production.

In the spring of 1932 Reno founded the Farmers' Holiday Association, in ironic imitation of the 'holidays' taken by banks when forced to close their doors. The association both provoked direct action itself and found many imitators who acted independently. During the summer of 1932 there were farmers' strikes in Iowa, South Dakota, Nebraska and Missouri, where farmers armed with sticks, clubs and pitchforks blocked the roads with logs and agricultural machinery to prevent the delivery of farm products to the towns. The strikes spread into North Dakota, Michigan, Indiana, Ohio, New York and Tennessee, and though in general local feeling was sympathetic to the farmers, on occasions the strikes led to violence. Mike Reno proclaimed that 'you could no more stop this movement than you could stop the revolution of 1776'. In some states, farmers picketing the roads were forcibly disarmed and arrested; at County Bluffs they were attacked with tear-gas bombs. At Clinton, Cherokee, Sioux City, Des Moines, the arrested men were released when crowds of angry farmers threatened to storm the gaols.

The Farmers' Holiday, though a revolt, was in no sense a revolutionary movement. Attempts were made, as in the case of industrial strikes, to turn it into one; the Communist Party attached itself to the movement and sent one of its ablest organizers, Ella Reeve Bloore, to the Dakotas to work among the wheat farmers. But the farmers were not interested in reconstructing society or creating a new one; they were interested in restoring an economic order which had assured them of a livelihood before it had broken down and, given the economic situation, what was remarkable about communist and radical agitation was not its success but its failure.

At no point did the Farmers' Holiday, or any other manifestations of revolt during the spring and summer of 1932, threaten the basic social and economic structure of the United States. They were demonstrations, largely spontaneous, by angry and desperate men against the paralysis of will displayed by government in the face of the destitution of millions of Americans; but it was becoming a question of how much longer such feelings could be contained if the depression continued. So much so, that even some of the most conservative began to feel that, without some change, another winter of depression was more than the system could bear. 'We cannot endure another winter of hardship such as we are now passing through,' declared the governor of the State of Washington, a diehard Republican and an inveterate enemy of organized labour. 'I am fearful of what may happen unless Congress comes to our aid.' To some observers it seemed that, since organized labour, the unemployed, and the farmers could not force Congress into action,

REVOLT IN AMERICA

the only choice left to the United States after another winter of
discontent would be some form of American fascism.

Indeed, during 1932, the most remarkable demonstration of
popular discontent came not from radical forces but from men who
regarded themselves, and were regarded by others, as the most
loyal and patriotic of Americans; the veterans of the First
World War.

In May a group of ex-service men in Portland, Oregon, came to
the conclusion that their only remaining asset was the 'adjustment
compensation certificate', the bonus for war-time service which was
due for payment in 1945. Since their present need was greater than
any future one could possibly be, they decided to go to Washington
to demand from Congress the immediate payment of the bonus,
and as their leader in this enterprise chose an ex-World War
sergeant named Walter H. Waters, a married man with a wife and
two daughters who had not worked for eighteen months.

From Oregon they made their way to East St Louis, Illinois,
where they tried to commandeer a freight car belonging to the
Baltimore and Ohio Railway and were forcibly dispersed by units
of the Illinois National Guard and sent out of the state in trucks.
But the 'Battle of the Baltimore and Ohio' had made them front-
page news and inspired other veterans in different areas of the
United States to follow their example. For the most part they were
drawn from the thousands of homeless migrants scattered throughout the country, to whom Washington was as good a place as any
other to which to direct their wanderings. They were helped on
their way by charitable agencies who were glad to get them off
their hands and by local grocers and merchants who felt that
immediate payment of the bonus would be good for business.

By the time the BEF, or Bonus Expeditionary Force, as the Portland veterans had christened themselves, had reached Washington,
their numbers had increased to over a thousand. In the following
weeks they were joined by other contingents converging on the
capital, until the Bonus Army had swollen to 25,000 men. They
made camp on the mud flats across the Anacostia River, and Waters
tried to give his besieging force as military a character as possible.
He was a strict disciplinarian, forbade drinking and was opposed to
any form of radicalism, and he used all his influence to ensure that
the Bonus Army should take every opportunity to demonstrate its

[225]

patriotism and devotion to the flag and should at no time constitute a threat to law and order. Yet in the capital, in Congress, in the White House, its presence across the river was felt as a vague menace, and this feeling grew throughout the summer, as the army waited for Congress to decide on its claim to immediate payment of the bonus.

If the menace did not become anything more, it was largely because of Waters's insistence on discipline and because of the humane and sympathetic attitude adopted by the superintendent of the Washington Metropolitan Police, Pelham D. Glassford, himself a World War veteran who had once been the youngest brigadier-general in the AEF in France. Glassford took the army under his protection, helped it to feed and house itself, prevented police interference, and on one occasion paid a thousand dollars out of his own pocket to supply it with food.

On 15 June, the House of Representatives passed a bill authorizing the immediate payment of the bonus, and two days later, while the army gathered on Capitol Hill, the bill came before the Senate. When Waters was told that the bill had been rejected, he gave out the bad news, called on his troops to sing 'America', and then the army formed ranks and marched back to camp.

The bill was dead, and with it the army's hopes and the purpose which had brought it to Washington. Many of the veterans began to leave, but many, estimated at 15,000 or more, remained; after all, Washington was as much, or more, of a home to them as anywhere else, and the BEF offered them a kind of comradeship, a sense of belonging, that was not available to them elsewhere. The camp at Anacostia, which had been given the name of Hard-Luck-on-the-River, began to assume the air of a permanent settlement; many of the veterans had been joined by wives and children, they built shacks for themselves or lived in army tents procured for them by General Glassford, organized their lives on military lines, dug latrines, inevitably christened 'Hoover villas'. Throughout the summer they waited, hardly knowing what they were waiting for, amid the heat of Washington, the miasma of the mud flats, the growing stench of garbage and sewage. Hygiene was inadequate, food poor and insufficient; sickness and disease began to spread among the Bonus Army and its wives and children.

In such conditions, as in any army, tempers became frayed and

[226]

morale began to break down; Waters tried to combat the disintegration of the BEF by introducing stiffer discipline and increasing his own authority. He dreamed of converting the army into the spearhead of a revolutionary movement, compounded of nationalism and socialism, which would lead a general uprising of the unemployed; looking abroad for models, he thought of calling them the Khaki Shirts, with himself as their Hitler or Mussolini. His position was challenged by the communists, who rushed to goad the BEF into action, and denounced and jeered at the passivity of its leaders, but they remained a tiny minority and shared with Hoover and the bankers the impartial detestation of the BEF.

The White House ignored the existence of the Bonus Army. The administration regarded it as a purely local, not a national, matter, which concerned only the Federal District commissioners. Mr Hoover refused to receive a delegation from the army, or to make the remotest gesture of sympathy with their condition, which was after all typical of millions of American families that summer. His cold aloofness earned him a reproof from Walter Lippman; 'Mr Hoover,' he wrote, 'does not shrink from holding conferences and issuing statements. How can he justify the fact that he never took the trouble to confer with the bonus marchers?' His only action was to secure the passage of a bill approving loans to veterans who wished to return home, the cost to be deducted from their bonus when it was eventually paid. Yet the White House did not omit to take precautions for its own safety; the security guards were strengthened and troops secretly assembled in preparation for an emergency. In the meanwhile the army newspaper, the *BEF News*, became increasingly critical and contemptuous of its inactivity and castigated the veterans as dumb oxen who waited passively while their families starved, 'yellow cowards', with 'the guts of a louse'.

At length, an 'emergency' occurred which gave the federal authorities a reason, or a pretext, for intervention. The continued presence of the destitute army at Anacostia was becoming an embarrassment, an irritation and a reproach, and it is not possible to say whether the administration found or manufactured a pretext for getting rid of it. On 28 July the Federal District police were ordered to evict a group of veterans who had occupied some abandoned buildings on Pennsylvania Avenue. Some communists among the veterans resisted the entry of the police and in the disturbance which followed the police opened fire and two veterans were shot dead and others wounded.

When Glassford ordered the shooting to cease, the disturbance immediately came to an end and there is no evidence that the main body of the veterans had any intention of offering resistance. The District Commissioners, however, now judged that federal intervention was called for; a request to the White House for the assistance of federal troops was immediately granted.

In the late afternoon a mixed force consisting of four troops of cavalry with drawn sabres, six tanks, and a column of infantry with fixed bayonets and tear-gas bombs in their belts moved on the Bonus Army camp at Hard-Luck-on-the-River. At its head, on a white horse, rode General Douglas MacArthur, Chief of Staff of the United States Army, accompanied by his aide, Colonel Dwight D. Eisenhower. That day was the first, and last, occasion on which Colonel Eisenhower saw shots fired in anger until the invasion of Europe twelve years later, but it was a poor preparation for the fighting Germans. The Bonus Army and its dependants were given an hour to evacuate the camp; then the troops moved in, throwing tear-gas bombs among those veterans who still lingered on and setting fire to their shacks and huts. A seven-year-old boy who had returned to recover a toy was bayoneted in the leg by a soldier; Major George S. Patton, Jnr, personally accomplished the destruction of a shack which happened to belong to a veteran who, during the war, had been decorated for saving the major's life.

The Bonus Army, declared General MacArthur, was 'the essence of revolution', and about to seize control of the government. There is no more evidence for the statement than there is for many of the general's later military bulletins. And in retreat the Bonus Army showed no greater powers of resistance or aggressiveness than it did at Anacostia. The roads out of Washington into Virginia were barred by regular soldiers and those into Maryland by state troopers. Malcolm Cowley, who watched the flight of the Bonus Army, has described how the veterans and their families wandered in dazed confusion from street to street or sat in ragged groups, 'the men exhausted, the women with wet handkerchiefs laid on their smarting eyes, the children waking from sleep to cough and whimper from the tear-gas in their lungs. The flames behind them were climbing into the night sky.'

[228]

REVOLT IN AMERICA

At length, at four in the morning, the ragged army was permitted to enter Maryland, on condition that it left immediately for another state. Many of the veterans pressed on to Johnstown in Pennsylvania, where the mayor was reported to have offered them the hospitality of the city. But they met with little of the sympathy and assistance they had encountered on their initial march on Washington. The administration, having tolerated their presence for so long, was now determined to expose them as dangerous radicals, the dregs of the population, for the most part with criminal records and in many cases not veterans at all, and was about to indict them on these and similar charges. Only a short time ago they had been, to themselves and to many who had sympathized with them, heroes; now they had become outcasts, or, in the words of the *Johnstown Tribune*, alarmed by the mayor's humane initiative, 'thieves, plug-uglies, degenerates'.

At Jennerstown the trucks which carried the Bonus Army out of Maryland into Pennsylvania were directed westward by the state police away from Johnstown and into Ohio. Some veterans, however, abandoned the convoy and struggled on, in a long straggling line, along the northern road to Johnstown, and made camp for the night at Ideal Park. Malcolm Cowley was still following the flight of the Bonus Army. A haggard face appeared at the window of his car, 'eyes bloodshot, skin pasty white under three days' beard', and suddenly announced: 'Hoover must die.' Another face appeared: 'You know what this means? This means revolution.'

It did not mean revolution. The flight of the Bonus Army before General MacArthur's infantry, cavalry and tanks was sufficient evidence of that. Yet it did mean that, under the influence of the depression, a profound change had taken place in the relations between the government of the United States and the American people. 'If any revolution results from the flight of the Bonus Army,' wrote Cowley afterwards, 'it will come from another source, from the government itself. The army in time of peace, at the national capital, has been used against unarmed citizens – and this, with all that it threatens for the future, is a revolution in itself.'

Yet this also was a false analysis; or, in so far as it was correct, it was in a sense which Cowley had not intended. Despite the suffering, and the social and economic dislocation caused by the depression, despite the desperation of its victims, the apparent

[229]

callousness or indifference of government, the violence of the reaction of the men of property against any threat to their interests, the American people were not yet ready for revolution. It was not revolution they were looking for but hope, and the overwhelming majority of them still fundamentally believed that their greatest hope lay in the powers of the federal government, if only it were willing to use them.

It was precisely because Mr Hoover, in his rigid adherence to social and economic dogma, stubbornly refused to avail himself of the powers, actual and potential, entrusted to him by the constitution, that millions of men and women had come to believe, like Cowley's haggard apparition, that 'Hoover must die', and that the president, and with him the Republican Party, had become objects of hatred, obloquy and contempt.

For the same reason, during the summer of 1932 the hopes of the American people were increasingly directed towards the alternative offered them by the constitution and by the forthcoming presidential election – if only they could wait so long. Those hopes were represented by the Democratic Party, and most of all one single figure in it, the governor of New York, Franklin Delano Roosevelt.

Governor Roosevelt was no revolutionary, and he had no carefully considered policy or programme for overcoming the depression; and indeed on some subjects, as for instance the necessity and virtue of balanced budgets, his theoretical views were as inflexible as Mr Hoover's. But fundamentally Mr Roosevelt was everything that Mr Hoover was not, more especially in his buoyant and ebullient temperament as opposed to the sour sense of failure that cast such a gloom over the White House; he was the Happy Warrior as against the Knight of the Sorrowful Countenance. In practice, he had an aristocratic contempt for theory and for all forms of abstractions, including the prevailing economic orthodoxies. His contempt for ideas was so great that he was quite willing to sacrifice even his own if he found that they did not work. Some said that the contempt was so great that it extended beyond ideas to principles, and pointed to the care he took to maintain good relations with the notoriously corrupt Democratic Party organization in New York; to these he was no better than a Tammany politician with good manners and social graces. 'He is no crusader,' wrote Walter Lippman. 'He is no tribune of the people. He is no enemy of entrenched privilege. He is a pleasant man who, without important qualifications for the office, would very much like to be president.'

Yet Roosevelt had one belief which corresponded closely with the unspoken, confused, frustrated instincts of millions of despairing men and women in the United States in the summer of 1932. It was a belief in the immense reserves of power entrusted by the constitution of the United States to its democratically elected representatives and in their right and duty to use that power to the full in an emergency, such as existed at that moment; and he had the optimist's belief that that power was so great that there was no problem it could not solve. As governor of New York, he had advocated, and applied, positive action in such fields as the public control of power facilities, soil conservation and afforestation, and, more especially, unemployment relief; in June 1931, at the annual Governors' Conference, he had taken the opportunity to declare that the state must undertake 'the better planning of our social and economic life' in such matters as sickness and unemployment, insurance, taxation, tariffs, land utilization and population redistribution. 'State and national planning is an essential to the future prosperity, happiness and the very existence of the American people.'

Roosevelt was re-elected as governor of New York in 1930 by the unprecedented majority of nearly three-quarters of a million votes, and from then on had conducted a meticulously organized campaign to secure the Democratic nomination in 1932. He was opposed by the conservative wing of the Democratic Party, and in particular by John J. Raskob, the millionaire chairman of both the Democratic National Committee and the Chrysler Corporation, but Roosevelt's careful preparations had made him the only candidate with a nation-wide organization and appeal, and the struggle for the nomination became a desperate effort by the conservatives to prevent Roosevelt securing the required two-thirds majority in the convention.

The convention opened in Chicago on 27 June, with Roosevelt assured of a bare majority, but some 200 votes short of a two-thirds vote. But on the fifth ballot, with the issue still uncertain, California switched its votes to Roosevelt and assured him of the nomination; on the Saturday of that week Roosevelt took the unprecedented step of flying to Chicago to accept the nomination in person. His instinct was a right one because the situation was itself an unprecedented one; the American people was being offered its last chance to overcome the depression by democratic means. In his acceptance speech Roosevelt told the convention that the Democrats who looked to the past and not to the future were out of step with the party. He promised relief to all groups who had suffered by the depression: retrenchment and economy in Washington; repeal of prohibition; public works; a reduced working week; agricultural planning; reafforestation; legislation on securities. But specific promises were less important than the man who made them and the spirit in which they were made. What was needed, Roosevelt said, was a government of liberal thought and planned action, which would give the American people what they wanted most of all: work and security. 'I pledge myself,' said Roosevelt, in a phrase which gave its name to his peacetime administration and to a whole decade of American history, 'to a new deal for the American people.' It was what they wanted, and needed, most of all to hear.

CHAPTER FOURTEEN

The Fall of Brüning

Roosevelt's promise of a New Deal for America represented a hope, and a belief, that the United States could find its way out of the depression by means consistent with the established political and constitutional system. It implied that the resources of that system were not yet exhausted, and that if properly exploited they were sufficient to overcome the crisis engendered by the depression; it was not the means to action which were lacking but the will to use them and millions of Americans had come to see in Roosevelt the embodiment of that will, the Happy Warrior who was willing to take up arms against the sea of troubles by which they were surrounded. In a sense he was the greatest moral and psychological asset that the capitalist system in America still possessed.

The fact that such a man should emerge as a possible saviour of his country was in itself sufficient evidence that the overwhelming mass of the American people had not yet lost faith in the established social and economic order. Despite the sufferings of the depression, the outbreaks of violence and civil disorder, of strikes and the reaction which they provoked from the men of property, a revolutionary solution to the crisis had attractions only for relatively small groups of radicals and intellectuals who were never able to provide effective leadership for the vast, unorganized body of discontent bred by the depression. And perhaps in this more than in anything it is possible to see why America was able to surmount the depression without any fundamental reconstruction of her characteristic institutions.

Across the Atlantic, however, in Germany, the crisis had a different ending. There, by 1932, the resources of the liberal parliamentary and democratic regime of Weimar were already exhausted, and there was no party, or any possible combination of parties, which could offer the German people effective government within the terms of the Weimar constitution.

The nature of the regime established and maintained by Dr Brüning was in itself proof of this. Its only claim to legitimacy, within the terms of the constitution, rested on the exercise, as the basis of day-to-day government, of presidential powers which had been intended to be temporary and exceptional, and on the inability of the Reichstag to produce a majority which would exercise its constitutional right to annul the decrees issued by the President under his emergency powers. In Germany the exception had become the rule; and while Dr Brüning's regime maintained a formal pretence of legality, in reality it merely registered the fact that the constitution had already broken down.

Nor was this simply a matter of political and parliamentary procedure. The pretence of legality which covered Dr Brüning's use of the President's emergency powers corresponded to a situation in which the rule of law had broken down, not merely in terms of parliamentary government, but as it applied to the daily life of the ordinary citizen. By 1932 the streets of German cities had become the scene of endemic civil war, in which private army battled with private army, political murder had become a commonplace, and riot, bloodshed and assault had become nightly occurrences. Christopher Isherwood has described the scene in Berlin as the winter of 1931 dragged on, 'like a long train which stops at every dingy little station'.

Berlin was in a state of civil war. Hate exploded suddenly, without warning, out of nowhere; at street-corners, in restaurants, cinemas, dance-halls, swimming baths; at midnight, after breakfast, in the middle of the afternoon. Knives were whipped out, blows were dealt with spiked rings, beer mugs, chair-legs or leaden clubs; bullets slashed the advertisements on the poster-columns, rebounded from the iron roofs of latrines. In the middle of the street a young man would be attacked, stripped, thrashed, and left bleeding on the pavement; in fifteen seconds it was all over and the assailants had disappeared ... The papers were full of photographs of rival martyrs, Nazi, Reichsbanner amd Communist. My pupils looked at them and shook their heads, apologising to me for the state of Germany. 'Dear, dear!' they said, 'it's terrible. It can't go on.'

This is not merely a writer's vision of a society in the throes of disintegration. It is amply verified by police statistics. In 1932, between June and July alone, there were 461 political riots in the federal state of Prussia, in which 82 people were killed and over 400 wounded. On 10 July, 18 people were killed in civil disorders; on 17 July a Nazi parade which marched through the streets of Hamburg-Altona was ambushed by snipers on the rooftops and 19 people were killed and 85 wounded. Political murder reached a peculiarly horrible climax at Potempa, near Beuthen, in Upper Silesia, when five of Hitler's storm-troopers beat and kicked a communist miner to death, and severely injured his brother, before their mother's eyes.

The sequel was as characteristic of the state of moral and social disintegration into which Germany had fallen as the murder itself. When the murderers were brought to trial and sentenced to death on 22 August the court was packed with Nazis led by Edmund Heines, himself a convicted murderer, who openly threatened the judge with the vengeance of the National Socialists when they came to power.

The crime, and the death sentence, placed Hitler in a difficult position. To sympathize with the murderers would be to throw doubt on the respect for legality which he assiduously claimed as the basis of his policy; to abandon them would be to shake the confidence and morale of the storm-troopers, already restive under the restraint imposed upon them. Hitler did not hesitate; he immediately despatched a telegram to the murderers assuring them of his 'limitless loyalty' and followed it with a proclamation in the *Völkischer Beobachter* denouncing the 'bloodthirsty objectivity' of the sentence passed on them. Hitler's declaration was in fact sufficient to deter the authorities; the sentence was commuted to life imprisonment and the murderers later released after Hitler became Chancellor.

The Potempa murder, and Hitler's reaction to it, no doubt shocked a section of German public opinion; it did nothing to check the growth of the National Socialist movement. Indeed, under the strain of the depression, political life in Germany had been reduced to so naked and brutal a struggle for power that for many Germans moral considerations no longer had any weight.

The struggle was conducted in a kind of vacuum created by the breakdown of the Weimar system, which continued to survive in theory but in practice had ceased to function; the only question was who would succeed to the inheritance. During 1932 a number of dubious and improbable claimants appeared, occupied the lime-light for a moment, then disappeared into the shadows, while around them circled even more sinister figures, who crept out of the interstices of German society like bugs from crumbling masonry and together they conducted a macabre and eerie dance of death around the decaying body of the Republic. The claimants pressed their cause by every means which came to hand, by violence, by propaganda, by lies, by shady political manœuvres, by intrigue and treachery; even personal charm, as exercised by an ambitious and empty-headed ex-cavalry officer on a senile presi-dent, became an important political factor; nothing was neglected. But behind these transitory figures there loomed the gigantic and terrible shadow of Hitler, a greater master than any of the blacker arts of politics, a djinn sprung up from the lower depths of society, filled with all the hatred, resentments and desire for vengeance of a twice-ruined lower middle class; during 1932 all that was left to be decided was how long, if at all, he could be excluded from power.

The first victim of the progressive deterioration in the political and economic situation of Germany was Brüning; though it might be said that an old man's treachery and ingratitude played as large a part in his fall as the fact that by March 1932 unemployment had risen to 6,036,000, an increase of $1\frac{1}{4}$ million since the same month of 1931, and that Brüning had no other remedy for the problems it presented than further and even more severe measures of deflation.

In October 1931 Brüning had formed his second Cabinet, in which he was both Chancellor and Foreign Minister, and the indispensable General Groener became Minister of the Interior as well as Minister of Defence. Groener's dual appointment was due largely to the skilful persuasion of his 'political cardinal', General von Schleicher, who saw in it the means by which the Ministry of the Interior could be brought under the control of the Reichswehr; Brüning defended it before the Reichstag on the ground that the critical state of the nation required the concentration of all the means of maintaining internal order in a single hand.

The reconstruction of the government had been brought about by the resignation of the Foreign Minister, Dr Curtins, as a result of the abandonment of the ill-fated project of an Austro-German Customs Union. As Foreign Minister himself, Brüning looked forward hopefully, and with considerable confidence, to achieving two major diplomatic successes: the recognition by the Disarmament Conference of Germany's claim to equality of rights, and the permanent settlement, by international agreement, of the reparations problem by the Lausanne Conference. In November 1931 he asked the Bank of International Settlements to summon its special advisory committee to consider Germany's obligations under the Young Plan, and was gratified by the committee's conclusion that the suspension of all inter-governmental debts, including reparations, was the surest means of achieving economic stability and a genuine peace. He was encouraged also by the sympathetic response which his efforts to secure a postponement of Germany's obligations had met with abroad, particularly in Britain. Brüning indeed believed that he had two assets which would enable him to ride out the depression and confound his internal enemies: the first was the confidence of President Hindenburg, which he believed he possessed entirely; the second was the trust and respect he enjoyed abroad, on which he counted to bring him the diplomatic success which would compensate for the continued sacrifices which he demanded from the German people. In both matters he gravely miscalculated.

The economic crisis continued to grow. In December, unemployment passed the five million mark, and Brüning responded with an emergency decree 'for the protection of the German economy and finances and the insuring of domestic peace'. The most comprehensive and severe of all Brüning's emergency decrees, it represented a hitherto unprecedented degree of intervention by the state in economic life, and imposed larger measures of control than any capitalist state had ever experienced. It was an attempt to meet the crisis by reducing prices and costs throughout the economy and to relieve the burden of the depression by protecting real purchasing power, and in the attempt to do so imposed heavy sacrifices on every class in the community. Wages and salaries were reduced to the level of 1927. A National Price Commissioner, Herr Goerdeler, the Mayor of Leipzig (later executed for his part in the plot of July 1945 to assassinate Hitler) was appointed, with the task of reducing prices to the level of July 1931. Rents were cut by ten per cent and fixed interest rates reduced. The decree did nothing either to prevent the growth of unemployment, nor to hinder the decline of German industrial activity, which by the end of 1931 had become acute. Most large industrial firms had to pass their dividends for the year, and there were some spectacular failures, including that of the famous machine-tool firm of Borsig, which had played a large part in the rise of German industry in the nineteenth century, and of Germany's largest brewing concern, Schultheiss-Patzenhofer, amid circumstances of great scandal, because of its efforts to avert bankruptcy by large-scale speculation in its own shares.

Indeed, German industry, like large sections of the German working class, was beginning to look outside the confines of the established order for a way out of its difficulties; there was desperation, a willingness to adopt extreme remedies, at the top as well as at the bottom of society. It was a decisive and historic moment both for German industry and for the National Socialist movement when on 7 January, through the introduction of the Ruhr steel magnate, Fritz Thyssen, Hitler addressed the Industrial Club in Düsseldorf and after a two-and-a-half-hour speech, one of the most effective he ever made, was given a rapturous ovation by the assembled industrialists. The essence of Hitler's address was that the time had come when economics must give way to politics, and that Germany could only overcome her difficulties by the exercise of a single and united political will determined, at any cost, to smash the obstacles, foreign and domestic, which stood in the way of her recovery. This thesis, combined with a defence of private property and of the application of the leadership principle in industry, came sufficiently close to the feelings of the industrialists to win Hitler their enthusiastic support.

The Düsseldorf meeting was part of the process by which Hitler, despite the violence of his public utterances, succeeded, with extraordinary skill and persuasiveness, in making himself acceptable to those who occupied the real citadels of power in Germany, in making himself respectable and *salonfähig*, in convincing them that he was no dangerous revolutionary but a defender of Germany's historic long-term interests; the appeal became irresistible when united with what only he had to offer: a national mass movement capable of providing the basis for a stable government.

Hitler's acceptance by the conservative forces had already been given a spectacular demonstration in October 1931 at Harzburg, when Hitler appeared on a common platform with Hugenberg, von Seekt, Schacht, and several Hohenzollern princes at a mass meeting in which Nationalists and National Socialists, Stahlhelm and storm-troopers, paraded together. That acceptance was even more important to him than conquering the streets, and throughout 1932, with tireless patience, he conducted a long series of meetings and conversations, some open, some secret, with the industrialists, with Reichswehr generals, with nationalist politicians, with Brüning, with the President himself, in the effort to achieve power by legal means. His success in disguising his true nature can be judged by the fact that the aristocratic Franz von Papen could describe Hitler, the demagogue, ex-lance-corporal and Austrian immigrant as 'a German gentleman', while Groener wrote of him as 'a decent modest chap full of good intentions. His air is that of a diligent, self-made man ... determined to wipe out revolutionary ideas.'

It is difficult to believe that anyone could genuinely hold such a view of Hitler; yet his powers of deception and dissimulation were so great that many others similarly misjudged him long after his true character had repeatedly revealed itself. Yet at no time in his career, perhaps, was he required to display his gifts as a politician to a fuller extent than in 1932; the year was for him, as for Germany, the year of decision, in which five major electoral contests had to be fought in five months, while behind the events played out on the public stage there proceeded a protracted and sinister game of tortuous intrigue and counter-intrigue, of gambits offered, accepted, refused, of alliances made only to be broken, of treachery and betrayal. Through all this Hitler moved with a kind of uncanny precision of judgement, or, as he himself once said, 'like a sleep-walker' who never puts a foot wrong, and all the more remarkably because, at all stages of the game, its result centred upon him and upon the huge mass movement which, in hardly more than two years, he had conjured up out of nothing. Others, Brüning, von Papen, Schleicher, might at different moments flatter themselves that they were in command, that they negotiated with Hitler only to make use of him, allied themselves with him only to disarm him. Hitler was not averse to them thinking so, if it suited his purposes; but the truth was that he had become indispensable. None of them could do without him; he could do without any of them, and was determined to do so in the long run. In the meantime the situation called for a combination of violence and restraint, of patience and frenzied agitation, of calculated excesses and studied moderation, which strained even his powers to the utmost and left him on occasions a totally exhausted man.

Brüning was the first to attempt a bargain with him. His own personal position and his policy depended entirely on the confidence of the President; but at the beginning of 1932 Hindenburg's four-year term of office was shortly to expire. Brüning's first thought was that, to avoid an election which would provoke the most violent political passions, yet with highly uncertain results, Hindenburg's term of office should be continued, as President Ebert's had been, by a constitutional amendment, which would require a two-thirds majority in the Reichstag; for this the support of the National Socialists was essential.

On 7 January Brüning, together with Groener and Schleicher, met Hitler, who was accompanied by the Chief of Staff of the storm-troops, Captain Röhm, to discuss the proposed amendment. In principle, Hitler did not appear opposed to it; but only on condition that the Reichstag should be dissolved and that new elections should be held. The condition was unacceptable to Brüning, both because a Reichstag election had all the same dangers and disadvantages as a presidential election and because a dissolution at that moment would have lost him the support of the Social Democrats, which was even more necessary to him than Hitler's.

Neither Hindenburg nor Hitler were eager to face an election, Hindenburg because he would be dependent on the votes of Social Democrats and Catholics, both of whom he, as a general, a Junker, and a Protestant, equally detested; Hitler, because he feared a defeat which would be damaging to the prestige both of himself and of the National Socialists. Neither, however, was able to resist the pressure upon them. On 6 February Hindenburg declared his willingness to stand as a non-party candidate; on 26 February, at an immense mass-meeting in the Berlin Sportspalast, Goebbels announced, amid frenzied enthusiasm, that Hitler would be the National Socialist candidate and the next President of the Reich.

In the elections which followed, Hindenburg secured 18,650,000 votes, only four per cent below the absolute majority required for re-election on the first ballot; Hitler, 11,400,000; the Communist candidate, Thälmann, 5,000,000 and the Nationalist, Düsterberg, 2,500,000. At the second election which became necessary, held on 10 April, Hindenburg received an absolute majority of 19,395,000 votes, Hitler 13,410,000, Thälmann, 4,000,000, while Düsterberg withdrew.

Formally, the election was a defeat for Hitler; in reality it was a triumph. The Weimar parties had secured his defeat only by uniting behind a candidate who detested Weimar and was the living embodiment of everything to which it was opposed, and he had made it clear that their support was unwelcome to him. The most striking feature of the election was the immense increase in the National Socialist vote which had more than doubled since the last Reichstag elections in 1930, and even between the first and second ballots had continued to increase, by more than 2,000,000 votes. But it was not only the size of the vote which was significant. Even before the result was known, the campaign itself was a revelation of the youthful energy and dynamism of the National Socialist movement. Brilliantly directed by Goebbels who exploited all the most modern means of mass communication in a kind of inspired frenzy of activity, it was a sustained effort of propaganda such as the world had never seen before, and for many Germans was a proof that something new had arrived in the grey and twilit world of democratic politics.

Goebbels had had doubts about the wisdom of Hitler's candidature, especially as the party treasury was exhausted and there were no funds available for the campaign. But Hitler's contacts with the industrialists brought their reward and money flowed in, which allowed Göbbels to mount a campaign of unexampled intensity. Mass demonstrations, parades, torchlight processions, posters, the press, the radio were all harnessed to the service of National Socialism; the Harkenkreuz was everywhere; even the sky was pressed into service, and the aeroplane allowed Hitler to speak and to show himself to the German people in every city and town of the Reich; his voice and presence were ubiquitous.

Such methods announced the opening of a new political era; beside the National Socialists the older parties looked staid and conventional and it was only a last upsurge of devotion and loyalty to the ideals of Weimar which gave Hindenburg the victory he had done so little to deserve. Brüning himself campaigned tirelessly for him, and established a claim on his gratitude which was never acknowledged. Indeed, to Hindenburg it was an affront to owe anything to the efforts of democrats, socialists and Catholics and he continued to nurse a resentment against being placed in what he felt was a false position.

The growth of the Nazi Party, as revealed by the presidential election, was confirmed by the result of the third electoral contest of the year: the elections to the Prussian Landtag, or state parliament. It was hardly less important than a general election, for Prussia was by far the largest of the German federal states, controlling two-thirds of the national territory and forty million out of its total population of sixty million. And in one respect it was, under existing conditions in Germany, of vital significance, for the Prussian police force was the largest and most efficient in Germany, and in the hands of a Social Democrat Minister of the Interior, Karl Severing, had been used resolutely to restrain the excesses of the National Socialists. To capture the Prussian police was a vital objective of the revolutionaries of the right.

The elections were held on 24 April, at the same time as state elections in Bavaria, Anhalt, Württemberg and Hamburg. Hitler had declared that they would give the National Socialists' answer to the Reich government, which ten days earlier had dissolved the party's para-military organizations, the SA and the SS, as private armies which threatened the security of the state. The ban was the result of a threat by the state governments to take independent action against them, if the Reich government did not, as they had become convinced, and had much evidence to prove, that plans were in existence for an armed uprising by the SA and the SS. Plans had been discovered in the Brown House, the Nazi headquarters in Munich, for a *coup d'état* if Hitler won a majority in the presidential elections; in Eastern Germany the storm-troops had been ordered to refuse to come to the defence of the frontier in the event of a Polish attack. The ban had been opposed by General Schleicher, who cherished hopes of bringing the SA under control of the Reichswehr in an emergency and, even more, of bringing Hitler into the government. It was supported by Groener, his superior at the Ministry of Defence, and their disagreement led Schleicher to the fatal decision that Groener was no longer a suitable instrument in his devious intrigues to reconstruct the Reich government, and that he must be disposed of.

The Prussian elections made the National Socialists the largest party in the Landtag, with 162 seats instead of their previous 9. The Social Democrats lost 43 seats, the Centre 4, and together they ceased to command the majority in the Landtag which had ruled Prussia since the foundation of the Weimar Republic. On the other hand, despite their great gains, and even with the support of the Nationalists, the National Socialists could not themselves form a government with a parliamentary majority. The position in the Landtag reproduced the position in the Reichstag, that is to say, a deadlock in which it had become impossible to govern either with or without the National Socialists and this faithfully reflected the situation in the country as a whole. The vanity of General Schleicher suggested to him that only he could end the deadlock. The first step was to dispose of Groener and Brüning.

It was not in General von Schleicher's nature to approach any goal by a direct route. Though a soldier, he had nothing of a soldier's loyalty or simplicity; suppleness and finesse were his chosen weapons. His strongest motive was ambition; his greatest talent was for treachery; his greatest weakness, vanity; his greatest pleasure, intrigue. He would have made an admirable adviser to some Renaissance prince, if only he had had a sense of political reality; but the elaborate and tangled web of deceit which he wove ended in his deceiving himself, and in particular about the greatest political reality of all: the nature and character of Adolf Hitler. General von Schleicher thought that he could manage Hitler.

Groener was easier game. From his office in the Bendlerstrasse, von Schleicher whispered that the army had lost confidence in Groener, secured the ear of the President for his insinuations, let Hitler know that he was opposed to the ban on the SA and SS. On 15 April the President wrote to Groener protesting that the ban was not impartial and should be extended to other political armies, in particular the Social Democrat Reichsbanner; he based his protest on a memorandum which had mysteriously come his way from Groener's own ministry. In the Reichstag, Groener was violently attacked by Goering, and when he tried to defend himself in an effective speech he was howled down by a storm of National

Socialist abuse. Schleicher was now ready for the kill. Immediately after his speech, Schleicher, together with the commander-in-chief of the Reichswehr, von Hammerstein-Equord, coldly informed the man who had regarded him as a son, and had trusted him absolutely, that he had forfeited the army's confidence. On 13 May, after scenes of uproar in the Reichstag which had to be suppressed by the police, Groener resigned as Minister of Defence; he still remained Minister of the Interior, but he had lost the control of the Reichswehr which had been the basis of his political authority. He had been one of the few German generals who had played an honourable part in the political life of the Republic, and in this lay the cause of his downfall.

After Groener, Brüning. At this crisis in his career, the Chancellor, firm in his trust in the President, was still confident that he could weather the storm and was strangely unaware of the dangers which surrounded him. Indeed, despite Germany's acute economic difficulties, he even looked forward to the future with a cautious optimism. He had been greatly encouraged by the sympathetic response of the British Prime Minister, Ramsay MacDonald, and the American Secretary of State, Stimson, to his demand for the recognition of Germany's claim to equality of rights at Geneva, and was hopeful of a final solution of the reparations problem; moreover, he believed that Germany, having plumbed the depths of the depression, might now look forward to some alleviation, however slow and gradual, of the economic situation. He believed that the worst of the crisis was over, and in his speech to the Reichstag on 12 May, in which he loyally but vainly tried to defend Groener, he impressed these hopes on his audience and tried to temper the violence of the National Socialist opposition; 'there is particular need for calm when one is within one hundred metres of the goal.'

Even as he was speaking the plot was on foot which was to cause his fall. For Schleicher, both Groener and Brüning were obstacles to his grand design for a government which would have the support of, and would include, the National Socialists; he dreamed of a great *coup* by which he would become the architect of a government of the right which, with Hitler's help, would also have the support of the masses.

Hindenburg spent Whitsun at his estate at Neudeck. There he was exposed to, and shared, his Junker neighbours' violent hostility to the plans of Brüning's Minister of Agriculture to take over insolvent estates in Eastern Germany and distribute them for settlement and colonization by unemployed families. In the eyes of Hindenburg's friends, and his own, such proposals were 'agrarian bolshevism'. The old gentleman at Neudeck listened to their tirades with sympathy; he had made the prejudices and interests of their class his own and conceived it part of his duty as President to advance them. His military sympathies were also engaged by their arguments that popular resentment against this disruption of the traditional way of life on the *latifunchia* of Eastern Germany would weaken resistance to Polish threats against Germany's eastern frontiers.

Schleicher was also at hand to incite Hindenburg's resentment against Brüning. He had refused Brüning's offer of the Ministry of Defence in succession to Groener in terms which had given great offence to the Chancellor and provoked him to predict, rightly, that Schleicher's intrigues would one day lead to his own ruin. On a visit to Neudeck, he found a sympathetic audience for his insinuations against Brüning, and on the President's return to Berlin he summoned Brüning and curtly informed him that he would sign no more emergency decrees, that future legislation must have the approval of the Reichstag, that there must be an end to 'agrarian bolshevism' and that in future the government must have a predominantly conservative and nationalist character.

Hindenburg's refusal to sign any further emergency decrees destroyed at one blow the entire foundation of Brüning's 'presidential' regime. He immediately summoned his Cabinet and informed them of the President's statement; on the following day he presented the Cabinet's joint resignation to Hindenburg. It was received in a manner which suggested that Hindenburg himself felt guilty about his betrayal of the man who for two years, under circumstances of unprecedented difficulty, had served him so loyally and devotedly. Five minutes were given to Brüning in which to tender his resignation; then, punctually at twelve o'clock, the President left to attend a ritual occasion which lay close to his heart, the changing of the guard at the presidential palace.

The fall of Brüning, 'within one hundred metres from the goal', was the prelude to the final act in the tragedy of the Weimar

Republic. Yet the immediate sequel to its fall was less tragedy than farce. There was now no politician of national eminence left, except Hitler, who was capable of forming a government with any prospect of survival. A successor had to be found among the highways and byways, and certainly no more unsuitable one could have been found than the man whom Schleicher now presented to the astonished German nation as its new Chancellor: the Baron Franz von Papen.

The new Chancellor's only previous claim to distinction had been won as a gentleman jockey on the racecourse, and certainly there was something of the steeplechaser in the lighthearted bravado with which he faced the hazards of politics. A Catholic Westphalian aristocrat, married to the daughter of a Ruhr industrialist, with a certain specious personal charm and speaking excellent French, his political life had hitherto been played out in the Prussian Landtag, where he had made himself obnoxious to his own party, the Centre, by his violent opposition to the Prussian government, of which the Centre was one of the main supports. From this obscurity, with no political talents or virtues except ambition and a boundless duplicity, he was now suddenly elevated to be Chancellor of the Reich. It was as if Britain, at a moment of national emergency, had taken a prime minister from the Household Cavalry, or France one from the Jockey Club.

The selection of his Cabinet was as remarkable as the appointment of its chief executives. Papen himself called it 'a government of gentlemen' and this was so far true in that its members came from the very best regiments. The press named it 'the government of Barons'. None of its members had hitherto played any prominent part, or achieved any distinction, in political life, and seven of the ten of them were members of the nobility known for their reactionary views. It was the kind of Cabinet Evelyn Waugh might have formed if given the choice. 'A little clique of feudal monarchists, come to power by backstairs means,' said the Social Democrat paper, *Vorwärts*. It was a sign of how far the crisis had devoured the political talent available to Germany that it was now upon such men that her future depended.

A heavy political price had to be paid for Papen's elevation. It stripped the last pretence of legality from the presidential regime inaugurated by Brüning, whose parliamentary position depended upon the respect and trust which Brüning himself inspired and the toleration extended by the Social Democrats and the Centre towards his government. The new Cabinet could not expect this toleration to continue, more especially because Papen's own party, the Centre, was incensed by the brutal manner of Brüning's dismissal. All that the government had to depend on in the way of parliamentary or popular support was the rump of the Nationalists and a vague promise of Hitler's, which itself had to be bought at the price of two concessions; the lifting of the ban on the SA and the SS, and the dissolution of the Reichstag, followed by new elections.

The first was put into force in the middle of July: 'a provocation to murder,' said Thälmann, the Communist leader, and this prediction was immediately verified by the most violent political disorders the Reich had yet known. The Hamburg riot of 17 July in particular was taken by Papen as a pretext to remove the government of Prussia on the ground that it could not, or would not, maintain public order. On 20 July, an emergency decree removed the Prussian ministers from office and appointed Papen Reich Commissioner for Prussia, and to this decree, which was a fundamental breach of the federal constitution of the Reich, the Prussian government submitted without resistance.

The removal of the Prussian government marked a decisive stage in the collapse of Weimar. It demonstrated that the democratic and republican forces in Germany, even when they had power as well as legality on their side, no longer had the will to resist the arbitrary use of force by the right. Their refusal to do so, even with control of the police in their hands, is explained by the knowledge that behind the Papen government, and Schleicher, now Minister of Defence, stood the Reichswehr, and that resistance to the Reichswehr inevitably meant civil war.

With this victory behind him Papen faced the elections which had been fixed for 31 July. To the National Socialists they represented one more opportunity of coming to power by achieving an absolute majority of votes, and once again, for the fourth time in six months, the Nazi propaganda machine went into action. In the second half of July Hitler spoke in over fifty German cities and displayed an unparalleled power of provoking an almost hysterical response from the masses; when his plane was delayed *en route* to

Stralsund, a crowd of thousands waited in drenching rain for 2½ hours to hear him and at the end of his speech sang *Deutschland über Alles* as the dawn broke. The German people were exposed to every form of blandishment, persuasion and threat, and an organized assault upon their feelings of hope, despair, resentment, self-preservation and revenge, and once again the sheer display of energy, will and determination had their effect on millions who no longer expected anything of the existing system.

The results repeated and confirmed those of the presidential and the Prussian elections. The National Socialists had again made enormous gains, had won nearly 14 million votes and, with 230 seats, had more than doubled their representation in the Reichstag. They had become by far the largest single party in the Reichstag, and no form of parliamentary government was possible without their active or passive support. Moreover, the elections revealed for the first time an absolute majority against the Weimar Republic; the Communists, with 5¼ million votes, and the National Socialists together commanded nearly 20 million votes and more than half the seats in the Reichstag. It was not a majority that could be adapted to forming any kind of government, but it was sufficient to prevent any other combination of parties from governing effectively.

Yet though the National Socialists might rejoice at their gains, the results also gave them cause for anxiety. With 37·3 per cent of the votes they were still far short of the absolute majority for which they had hoped and which they required if they were to govern independently; moreover, there were signs that the enormous growth of the National Socialist party was losing its impetus or even coming to a halt. Between the Reichstag elections of 1930 and the second presidential election of 1932 the National Socialist vote had more than doubled. Between the presidential election and the Reichstag election it increased by only one per cent. Certainly the results gave Hitler no reason for thinking that he could achieve power alone by democratic means, unless he was to condemn himself to more long years of waiting, agitation and propaganda. And for this his party, with its voting strength of 14 million, a membership of over a million and a private army of over 400,000, was not prepared. The storm-troopers were restive under the restraints imposed on them by Hitler and were preparing to take action,

Clement Monet, Governor of the Bank of France.

(*above*) General Wilhelm Groener, German Minister of Defence 1928–32 and Minister of the Interior 1931–2.

(*left*) Hans Luther (*right*), President of the Reichsbank 1930–3, with George L. Harrison, Governor of the New York Federal Reserve Bank in Berlin, November 1930.

General Kurt von
Schleicher, German
Chancellor 1932,
with Franz von Papen,
German Chancellor
1932, at Berlin races,
September 1932.

Karl Melchior,
German Banker,
partner in M. M.
Warburg & Co.,
Hamburg.

while the violence of street fighting and political clashes between them and their opponents was increasing daily. On the night of the election itself there occurred at Königsberg 'the Night of the Long Knives', when the National Socialists took a fearful vengeance on their opponents. 'The SA is in readiness for an alarm and is standing to,' wrote Goebbels in his diary.

The election left Hitler with the choice of whether to continue the policy of constitutional legality which he had strictly imposed on himself or to commit the National Socialist movement to an armed uprising. There is no reason to think that he ever doubted what the choice would be. Perhaps indeed the decision was a less difficult one than it seemed, despite the pressure Hitler was under from his extremist followers. An armed uprising would provoke the intervention of the force which Hitler feared and respected most, the Reichswehr, and the prospect of civil war and, almost certainly, the suppression of the National Socialist movement. Legality gave him the opportunity of exploiting a situation in which the only obstacle left between him and power was a camerilla of barons for whom he had nothing but contempt. Yet it remained a question how long even he could continue to keep his followers under control.

CHAPTER FIFTEEN

Roosevelt and Hitler

When, on 30 May, Dr Brüning arrived at the presidential palace to submit his government's resignation, his appointment had been fixed for 10.30 a.m. At nine o'clock, however, the American ambassador, Frederick Sackett, telephoned to ask for, indeed to insist on, an immediate appointment in order to deliver an important message. Through an American intermediary in Paris he had been informed that the new French Prime Minister, M. Herriot, was prepared to accept the German proposals put forward at Geneva for equality of rights in respect to armaments. The proposals had already been sympathetically received by Britain and the United States, but M. Herriot's conservative predecessor had been notably cool and detached in his response, and his attitude, born of a profound mistrust of German intentions, had been a serious setback to Brüning's plans.

Sackett's message was a confirmation of Brüning's belief that, as he had told the Reichstag, he was at length within sight of his goal; and even now, after his chilling reception by the President the previous evening, it seemed possible that it might restore him to the President's favour; it was the reward of months of arduous effort and there was no other German politician who could have earned it. At this point he was informed that his appointment with the President had been postponed until 11.55 a.m., leaving precisely five minutes for Hindenburg to receive his resignation before the ceremony of changing the guard.

There was a terrible irony, of a kind which was repeated over and over again in the history of Franco-German relations after the First World War, in the French change of heart at precisely the moment when the only man in Germany who could have effectively responded to it was about to fall from power. It was an essential part of Brüning's policy that any concessions gained by Germany should have international consent and agreement and he hoped that they would both pacify extremist opposition at home and provide a basis for increased international stability abroad. Those who succeeded him had already discounted the value of any conceivable concessions to Germany and regarded them simply as a platform from which even more extreme demands could be launched.

The irony of the situation was all the greater because both France's new-found readiness for concessions and Germany's growing recalcitrance had, to a large extent, a common origin; that is to say, they both reflected the pressure of the economic crisis, but whereas it had driven Germany to the right, it had, for the moment, driven France to the left; the consequences of this divergence were, in the end, to prove catastrophic to both countries. M. Herriot had come to power as the result of a great electoral victory which had given the left 334 seats in the Chamber as against 259 to the right; in this new majority M. Herriot's own Radical party had 157 seats. The Socialists, with 129 seats, gave their support to M. Herriot's government, without, however, taking part in it.

France was the last major industrial country to be affected by the depression. In consequence she was, up to the middle of 1931, the strongest power, militarily, economically, and financially, in Europe, and possibly in the world. No one, however, was more conscious than the French that this position was likely to be only a temporary and transitory one; in the long run the cards were stacked against her. She had tried to use her strength during the crisis of 1931 to assert a hegemony to which she believed her history and her position entitled her. The attempt failed, and in the course of it France became an obstacle to international cooperation which helped to accelerate the crisis. Even by then, however, there were signs that France could not indefinitely continue to escape from the economic depression which had engulfed the rest of the world. Unemployment, though still small in comparison with other countries, increased from 14,000 to 72,000 between March 1931 and March 1932 and by the end of March 1933 rose to 347,000. The index of national production (100 in 1928) fell during 1931-2 from 102 to 73; activity in the building industry, a significant guide to investment as a whole, fell from 107 in the first quarter of 1931 to 88 in April 1932.

France also suffered from the severe deflation which followed the devaluation of sterling in the countries which continued to adhere to the gold standard; France was no more exempt than Belgium, Holland, Poland, Switzerland, the United States, and like them responded to the fall in prices which was followed by attempts to reduce costs, including wages. The victory of the left in the elections of May 1932 represented an attempt by the French working class and lower middle class to protect their standards of living against the effects of deteriorating economic conditions, but the Radical government of M. Herriot had no other remedies against the onset of the depression than those which had already been applied, and had failed, elsewhere. Indeed, in M. Herriot's case there were historical and psychological reasons why he should cling to strict principles of sound finance. He had been in power in 1925 and had been held responsible for the collapse of the franc in that year, and he was determined that he should not be held guilty of repeating the offence a second time. When the onset of the depression in France, the rise in unemployment, the fall in production, the decline in investment, showed itself in a reduction of the receipts from taxation and threatened to produce a Budget deficit, M. Herriot responded by applying the classical remedy of increasing taxation and reducing expenditure; the same remedy indeed which Brüning had pressed so hard, and with such little success, during his two years of power in Germany.

The attempt, in a period of deepening economic depression, to defend the franc and balance the budget, destroyed the collaboration between the Radicals and the Socialists which was the basis of the newly elected majority, and Socialist opposition to M. Herriot's financial proposals led to the fall of his government. But even more, it inaugurated a period of governmental confusion and instability in which, as in Germany after the fall of the Great Coalition, no party or combination of parties could command a stable majority. France, like other countries, was to learn the hard way one of the simplest political lessons of the depression; that, under a democratic system, it is very hard, if not impossible, except under the threat of some greater disaster, real or imaginary, to make people vote for a reduction in their standard of living.

Between the elections of 1932 and the beginning of 1935, no less than five governments were formed and overthrown in France in the attempt to achieve a balanced budget. And as in Germany, though with a delayed effect, in France the depression, and the failure to overcome it by orthodox means, led to the paralysis of democratic government, accompanied by the growth of extreme nationalist movements, the Action Française, the Solidarité Française, the Parti Franciste, the Croix du Feu, which in the riots provoked by the Stavisky scandal combined in an attempt to overthrow the Daladier government by force.

The formation of the Herriot government was the opening of a period in which France tried unavailingly to overcome the crisis which had come upon her so belatedly; the consequences of her failure were a protracted political struggle which paralysed her governmental institutions at a time when she faced the greatest danger she had ever known, the slow erosion of her political, economic and military strength, and an irreconcilable division between right and left that was never overcome. There are both general and particular reasons why the struggle should have taken different forms, and with different results, in France and in Germany, but the consequences were equally disastrous to both. The two countries which faced each other across the Maginot Line in the autumn of 1939 were each in its own way the products of the depression. The strength of the one was due to the brutal and murderous solution it had found for the problems it created; the weakness of the other to its failure to find any solution at all.

While Germany, and France, in the second half of 1932 followed paths which were, in the short and the long term, to lead to disaster, in Britain events began to take a slightly more hopeful turn, in the sense at least that there were signs that the grip of the depression was beginning to relax. In this Britain was not exceptional, because similar indications that a beginning of economic recovery was at hand were to be found in other countries which had followed her example in abandoning the gold standard.

Brüning, indeed, may well have been right in his belief that, if the worst of the depression was not yet over at the time of his fall, there was an appreciable hope that it would be soon, and that he was indeed 'within a hundred metres of his goal'. It would be impossible to name an exact date at which the turning point in the depression was reached, but there were many indications that the bottom was reached during the summer of 1932, and that by the end of the year a start had been made on the path to recovery.

In Britain there were several signs that this was so. During the year 1932 as a whole, industrial production, security values, profits, bank clearings, exports, all reached their lowest point, and unemployment its highest, of any year of the depression; exports, both in volume and value, and production were at their lowest, and unemployment at its highest, during the third quarter of the year. By the end of the year it could be said with some confidence that the nadir of the depression had been reached and passed, even if a real recovery did not begin until the following year. If one were to take as the turning point of the depression, not its lowest point but the moment at which the cycle began to turn upwards, it should probably be placed some time about March 1933.

It would be impossible to give any completely satisfactory explanation of why the turning point came as it did. Just as there is no single explanation of why the depression began, so there is no single explanation of why it ended. Despite the sophistication which economics has achieved in recent years, economics is not yet so exact a science that it can assign precise causes to precise effects. Sometimes indeed it is unable to distinguish between what is cause and what is effect; it is even more incapable of telling us what precise weight and influence we should give to economic factors in a total situation in which political and psychological factors are at least of equal if not greater importance. In the case of the beginnings of recovery in Britain we would have to take into account such factors as the promise of political stability provided by the National Government, with its enormous Conservative majority; the initial stimulus given by the devaluation of sterling, though this had largely exhausted itself by the end of 1932; the relief from foreign financial pressures afforded by the abandonment of the gold standard; the lowering of interest rates which followed Mr Chamberlain's conversion operation at the end of 1931; the encouragement given to British industry by her new tariff policy, and the adoption of Dominion preference at the Ottawa Conference of 1932. Perhaps one should also add the sense that some at least

of the obstacles to trade left behind by the war were being eliminated, as by the settlement of the reparations problem arrived at by
the Lausanne Conference.

Yet in the middle of 1932, it would have been difficult to look
forward to the prospect of recovery with any confidence. Such
hopes had been so often entertained before and as frequently disappointed. In March 1931 the *Economist* could write: 'Opinion is
gaining ground in responsible quarters that the rapid downward
slide has ceased, and that though substantial recovery be far off, we
have quite possibly touched the bottom of the great depression.'
This was, to say the least of it, premature, and the economy continued to decline, prices still fell, and capital investment reached
a still lower level; in the first half of 1931, capital issues were only
a half of what they had been in 1930. Yet by the end of the year
production had risen by ten per cent, for though unemployment
was still rising the working population was also increasing.

But if, from the point of view of the economic system as a whole,
the depression reached and passed its lowest point somewhere
between the middle and the end of 1932, and thereafter the
situation began to improve, for the victims of the depression, and
even for those whose business it was to study it and find means to
remedy it, the change came like a thief in the night, unheralded and
unremarked, and bringing no hope of immediate improvement. An
observer surveying the scene in the middle of 1932 could find very
few and very frail reasons for hope, and even these seemed precarious in the extreme when viewed against a background of
political instability, of monetary confusion, and of the growing
forces of economic nationalism which were producing new cracks
and fissures in the capitalist system as a whole. The League of
Nations *World Economic Survey*, 1931-2, summarizing the position
in the middle of 1932, concluded that the prospects of recovery
depended very largely on a positive credit policy in the United
States and its effects in stimulating credit expansion in other gold
standard countries. It noted that the Lausanne Conference had
removed one of the stumbling blocks to recovery, but that the
larger effects of the reparations settlement would be very largely
psychological and could not be accurately estimated. Nor was it
possible to predict the results, or effects, of the Imperial Conference
at Ottawa, or the proposed World Economic Conference, but the

survey drew some comfort from the recently signed customs agreement between Belgium, Luxemburg, and the Netherlands, 'the first definite and practical move towards free trade since the depression'.

On the other hand, elsewhere tariffs, exchange controls and other restrictions continued to multiply, and by strangling world trade were becoming a greater and greater obstacle to recovery. The *Survey* commented that the reaction of the world's stock exchanges to the situation was one of cautious optimism, but added: 'Relief is perhaps a better word than optimism. It is hoped that further disasters may have been averted; but the problems still awaiting solution are many and difficult.' Such highly qualified optimism is not far removed from pessimism, particularly when, as the *Survey* went on to say, the economic obstacles to recovery were increased by the political and psychological burdens that weighed upon business enterprise.

There was no greater obstacle to recovery than the continuation, in an acute form, of the crisis in the United States; to the other factors contributing to discourage business activity, there was added the uncertainty caused by the presidential election and the doubts and fears entertained by large sections of the business community about the intentions and policies of Franklin Roosevelt, the Democratic candidate. But apart from political uncertainty, the United States was suffering severely from the deflation which followed the devaluation of the pound; this was accentuated by the fall in sterling which took place at the end of 1932. From 3·39 to the dollar in October, sterling fell to 3·27 in December and did not rise again above 3·43 until after the American banking crisis of the following year.

Even without such an added strain, however, the American financial system was already under severe pressure. The devaluation of sterling and the suspension of gold payments in London had led to a reduction in the gold value of all balances that continued to be held there, and central banks which kept part of their reserves in the form of sterling found them correspondingly reduced in value at a time when they themselves were exposed to large withdrawals. The Bank of France was said to have lost a sum equal to the whole of its paid-up capital; the Bank of the Netherlands lost 30 million guilders. Others to suffer were all the smaller central banks which, largely under British influence, had been reconstructed on the assumption that to hold sterling was as good as to hold gold, and other financial institutions which had refrained from joining the general panic by withdrawing their balances from London.

There followed, throughout the world, a desperate struggle for liquidity, which was accentuated by the efforts of Britain's competitors in foreign markets to cut their losses resulting from the reduction in sterling prices. A further deflationary influence was the effect of the fall in sterling on commodity markets, in which demand from buyers whose money was held in the form of sterling formed a considerable proportion of the total demand. The fall in gold prices which followed came as a bonus to Britain, and protected her against a rise in sterling prices, but involved a heavy loss to producers and intensified the general struggle for liquidity. The gold standard countries, on the other hand, tried to protect their own markets by erecting a formidable wall of tariffs, quotas, exchange restrictions, import prohibitions, barter agreements and central trade-clearing arrangements.

An added deflationary consequence was the fluctuations and uncertainties of the exchanges which followed the fall of sterling. The value of sterling, and of the currencies which followed its example, did not fall to, and remain at, a fixed point but fluctuated over a wide range; from 3·37 to the dollar in December 1931 to 3·73 in April 1932 and down to 3·27 in December. The effect of the uncertainties created by fluctuations on this scale was all the greater because the traders were prevented from taking out any insurance against them, in the form of forward currency transactions, by the restrictions imposed on free dealing in the exchanges; this indeed was part of their purpose. And beyond all the damage done to normal trading, exchange fluctuations increased the risks of long-term capital investment to such an extent that for a time it almost totally ceased.

The effect of the combination of deflationary pressures to which the gold standard countries were exposed in 1932 was nowhere more evident than in the United States; the presidential campaign, which in Roosevelt's case opened on the day after his nomination, was conducted against a background of unrelieved gloom, almost indeed of desperation. Almost the only factor which relieved it was the personality of Roosevelt himself, his buoyant confidence and good humour, his insistence that it was not beyond the resources of human wisdom to beat the slump. Roosevelt approached the campaign in something of the spirit of a military commander taking over a defeated army, who conceives it as an essential part of his task to restore his men's morale and inspire them with his own absolute assurance of victory; only in his case that army was the American people. He took control of his own campaign to a degree to which no presidential candidate had ever previously done, cheerfully delegating to subordinates responsibilities which other men might have thought to be their own, yet directing every aspect of it in a manner which left no doubt in anyone's minds where the final decisions lay.

Most of all he succeeded in presenting an exhilarating contrast to that mood of helplessness, of indifference, of lethargy which seemed to have taken command in the White House. He quickly determined, against the advice of many of his supporters, to campaign personally in the autumn, partly indeed because he wished to dispel any doubts about his physical ability to bear the burdens of presidential office; he wanted to show himself to the American people and he wanted them to see him. And if his campaign triumphantly achieved both objects, it also gave him a deeper and closer understanding of the mood of America, of the traumatic experience which the depression had been for Americans. 'I have looked into the faces of thousands of Americans,' he told a friend on his return from his campaign trip to the West. 'They have the frightened look of lost people.' What they were thinking was, he said: 'Perhaps this fellow can help us.'

Perhaps indeed this was the only clear message that his campaign conveyed; perhaps nothing more was needed. Certainly any ordinary American would have been hard put to it to distil any coherent political programme, or any specific remedy for the depression, out of his many speeches and pronouncements. They were, at the best, confused, contradictory, the product sometimes of directly conflicting policies and attitudes. He was quite happy sometimes to have two drafts representing completely opposite points of view combined into a single speech.

The inconsistencies, the confusions, the contradictions of Mr Roosevelt's speeches did not only reflect the temper of his own mind, which never liked to commit itself completely to an absolute solution of any problem, either in theory or in practice. Nor were they merely the effect of the various intense pressures to which he was exposed from different sections of the Democratic Party, which was wide enough to embrace opinions which varied from the most extreme and reactionary conservatism to the radicalism of a Huey Long; or of the often conflicting advice he received from his own chosen circle of advisers, the brains trust of Berle, Moley, General Hugh Johnson, Felix Frankfurter, and many others less close to him, whom he had chosen precisely in order to provoke a continuous debate and discussion out of which a concrete political programme might evolve. They also reflected a deeper conflict, and an attempt to reconcile it, between differing theoretical solutions to the crisis which was threatening to destroy America, and it was typical of Roosevelt, and in the end a source of strength to him, that while remaining receptive to all of them, he never believed that there was any single intellectual explanation that would account for all the manifestations of the depression.

It was as if, during the campaign of 1932, Roosevelt was thinking aloud on behalf of the American people. For him, as for them, the depression was a kind of doom, or a destiny, far too all-embracing to be comprehended within any single theory, and, with an intellectual modesty unusual in one not otherwise inclined to modesty, he was content to choose among the various answers which offered themselves those which seemed most appropriate as a basis for political action, without bothering too much whether together they composed a consistent and coherent whole. Roosevelt was not concerned with finding a satisfactory intellectual answer to the problems presented by the depression, and this was lucky, because there was none available; he was concerned with finding a programme for positive action which would dispel from the minds and hearts of Americans the hopelessness and desperation to which they had been reduced.

Yet however eclectic he might be in choosing what suited him best, there were some views to which he was unresponsive, even though he might try to conciliate those who heed them. One of his first actions after his nomination, was to make Jim Farley, his campaign manager, national chairman of the Democratic Party, in place of John J. Raskob, and he totally rejected the pressure of the conservative wing of the Democrats to adopt a policy of government retrenchment, of reducing income tax in the higher brackets by substituting a sales tax, of restraining federal intervention in the affairs of the states or of private industry, which would in effect have been even to the right of Hoover's; indeed, there were conservative Democrats, like John W. Davies, who denounced the president for 'following the road to Socialism at a rate never before equalled in time of peace'. Even on the one point on which he was, in his public statements, as conservative as any conservative, the necessity for balancing the budget, he had reservations. When, under pressure from Barney Baruch, and his ex-partner, General Hugh Johnson, whom Roosevelt had admitted into his closest circle of advisers, he made a speech denouncing the extravagance of the Hoover administration, he also added that 'only starvation could justify a deficit', but that in such a case he would run one.

Roosevelt was also under pressure from the radical wing of the Democratic Party, and in particular from Huey Long, the Kingfish of Louisiana, whom Roosevelt described as the second most dangerous man in America. Yet the economic situation was such that Long's demands had the support of even some conservative Democrats who were alarmed by the growing radicalness of the masses and agreed that there was the danger of a violent social and political revolution unless the need for change was recognized. Fundamentally, this was an expression of Roosevelt's own instincts; no revolutionary himself, he sensed the danger of revolution unless the demand for change was satisfied within the limits of the existing order, and indeed it was this feeling which made those who did not believe in the possibility of change on such terms dismiss Roosevelt as no more than a capitalist wolf in liberal sheep's clothing. But change of some kind was unavoidable; 'Something must be done for him,' Roosevelt said, with reference to Long.

Roosevelt was by no means clear what form the change should take. For an analysis of the evident failure of the United States economy, and the measures to be taken to counteract it, he depended largely on the brains trust he had gathered around him, but even here he encountered large areas of disagreement and conflicting opinion, sometimes fundamental. There were legalists, like Felix Frankfurter, who thought that what was required was stricter regulation and control of those forces in the American economy whose excesses had led both to the extravagances of the boom and the collapse which followed it; but however strict the control, it would have left the essential structure of the economy untouched. There were others, like Raymond Moley or Adolph Berle, Jnr, whose studies of modern American business institutions had led them to believe that a far more fundamental reorganization, a restructuring as we should say today, of economic life was required if the depression was to be overcome and a repetition of it was to be prevented. Others laid the greatest emphasis on a more equitable distribution of the products of the economic system, between capital and labour, and between industry and agriculture, to cure the chronic under-consumption which had become a glaring feature of advanced capitalist society. To all these Roosevelt listened, though always with his own reservations, and from them took what suited his needs and, as he judged, the needs of the American people.

If the result was a not very satisfactory or consistent amalgam of ideas and policies, it was enough to give Roosevelt a platform and a programme which distinguished his own position and the Democratic Party's sufficiently clearly from that of Hoover and the Republicans. Roosevelt might on occasion join with others in denouncing federal extravagance or Hoover's encroachments on the rights of the states and insist as much as Hoover himself on the overriding necessity of balanced budgets. These were the stock in trade of every American politician; the difference was that many of them believed in them, while sometimes it seemed doubtful whether Roosevelt really believed in anything. But on particular questions, like federal unemployment relief, unemployment insurance, public works, control of public utilities, afforestation and land preservation, federal provision of electric power, Roosevelt showed a positive belief in the virtues of federal intervention and central planning in wide areas of social and economic life. Central planning indeed was one of the watchwords of his programme, as opposed to the classical *laissez-faire* philosophy which underlay Mr Hoover's attitudes to economic and social life.

Neither Hoover nor Roosevelt carried their beliefs to extremes which would have broken the traditional mould of American party politics. Mr Hoover's belief in *laissez-faire* went hand-in-hand with true Republican conviction of the virtues of high American tariffs; Mr Roosevelt, as a Democrat, professed devotion to the ideals of free trade, while qualifying them in practice, and his inconsistencies on this issue opened him to damaging attack by Hoover. But such confusions only slightly blurred the distinction between two fundamentally opposed political philosophies which, in relation to the problems of depression and recovery, was of profound significance. The abandonment of *laissez-faire* implied the abandonment of the entire conception of an international order based not on human decisions and plans, but on economic laws which only worked for the best when interfered with least. From this conception it followed also that the depression, whether in the United States or elsewhere, was a single phenomenon whose origin was rooted in the violent dislocation of the economic system which had followed the First World War. It followed also that the only effective steps which could be taken to cure the depression involved international cooperation and agreement, on reparations and war debts, on disarmament, on tariffs, on monetary and financial problems, to remove or reduce the obstacles which prevented the efficient working of the system.

To such a conception Mr Roosevelt was temperamentally averse and his instinctive reaction was strengthened by the intellectual conviction of his advisers that the depression, so far at least as the United States was concerned, was primarily not of international but of American origin. It arose out of specific faults in the working of the economic system in America and it lay within the power of Americans to put it right by their own efforts. Indeed, to do so was the best service they could render to the rest of the world, whose own hope of recovery depended upon the revival of the American economy; America could save not only herself but the world by her own exertions.

The belief that the depression in the United States was of independent, rather than international origin, and could therefore be overcome by her own efforts, was the American counterpart of the same trend towards national economic policy that was making itself felt throughout the world, in its most extreme form in Germany and Japan. After three years of depression, faith in international cooperation was near to exhaustion, even if nations continued to pay lip service to it; *Italia favrià da se* became the slogan of the new era that was opening, both in economics and in politics, with consequences which dominated the years preceding the Second World War.

Mr Hoover had begun by taking Roosevelt's campaign lightly. He had a certain contempt for his opponent, whom he had originally believed to be 'the easiest man to beat', and had intended to confine his own campaigning to three or four major speeches. But when the effect of Roosevelt's western tour became evident, pressure increased on him to take to the road himself; moreover, he himself had a sincere belief that Roosevelt was seducing the American people with false hopes and false promises and was genuinely apprehensive of what the consequences might be, not only for himself, but for the United States. It was typical of the grim forebodings with which he set out on his tour that he did so believing that the only remaining way to beat Roosevelt was by exciting universal fear of what would happen if he were elected.

If anything further were required to heighten the impression of optimism and energy which Roosevelt created, it was the sombre gloom which surrounded Hoover's electoral tour. It was the final act in the agony and tragedy of Hoover's presidency and he himself looked to observers like a man who had been consumed, mentally and physically, by the experience. With little support from other Republican leaders, often faced by hostile, sullen or jeering crowds, he valiantly and ably defended the record of his administration, insisting over and over again on the maintenance of the gold standard, the protective tariff, and a balanced budget, as the only sure foundation of national policy. He denounced Roosevelt as the initiator of changes which would destroy the American tradition of government, the advocate of increased federal expenditure, of currency inflation, of tariff reduction, of a swollen civil service. Roosevelt's philosophy of government, he said in November, was 'the same philosophy of government which has poisoned all Europe'. But it was not enough to make men's flesh creep with such nightmares; it was hope and not fear that America demanded. And though he summoned up all his last resources to defend his record and attack his rival, the President himself gave the impression of a man at the end of his tether, white-faced, sometimes losing the thread of his discourse, swaying with exhaustion. After one of his speeches, a Republican supporter took aside Colonel Stirling, the head of the Secret Service, and said: 'Why don't you make him quit . . . It's turning into a farce. He's tired physically and mentally.' A companion who travelled with him on his tour said it reminded him of riding on Harding's death train.

When on 8 November the returns came in, it was soon clear that Roosevelt had won, with what proved to be the landslide majority of 472 electoral votes to 59. But it was not Roosevelt that had beaten Hoover; it was the depression itself, and his own inability to find any counter to it among what he held to be the unshakeable and immutable truths of economics. He was as much the victim of the depression as any of the millions of Americans who now prepared to face its fourth winter.

The interest of the presidential election in the United States was that it provided the opportunity for a great and public debate on the causes and cure of the depression. It was proof of the fundamental strength of the American social order that the debate was conducted without violation of democratic processes and procedures, and that, despite the confusions and inconsistencies of party programmes, it presented the American people with a clear choice between alternative policies and objectives.

In Germany, at the same time, there was also a choice to be made, and indeed a far more profound and fundamental one than the American people were being asked to face. But it was made in very different circumstances. Despite the almost intolerable strain which the depression imposed on the American economic system, despite the outbreaks of violence and disorder that took place throughout 1932, despite the alienation of particular groups from the established order of society, the political system had remained fundamentally intact and still offered Americans the opportunity of settling their differences by constitutional and democratic means.

In Germany, however, where the democratic state, born of defeat, was young, weak, and fractured beyond repair by the irreconcilable division between right and left, no such opportunity was offered to the German people. The democratic state had already broken down; the only question that remained was whether the Weimar Republic could be persuaded, hypnotized, threatened or bludgeoned into voting itself out of existence, or whether other means would have to be found to put an end to it. It was a fundamental assumption of Hitler's policy that the first method provided the safest means of achieving absolute power, while preserving the forms of legality, and he clung to this belief even when it seemed to offer no further prospects of success; in the end, however, he had to abandon it, and come to power, not by the votes of the German people, but through the intrigues and conspiracies of a group of politicians and generals who enjoyed no popular support whatever.

The difficulty was that the German people itself could not bring itself to make a final choice either for or against the Republic. In the new Reichstag, elected in July 1932, in which the National Socialists held 230 seats and the Communists 89, out of a total of 609, there was formally a majority against the Republic, but it was a majority which was incapable of itself providing a basis for government. On the other hand, no government could be formed and survive in the Reichstag, without the support or the tolerance of the National Socialists, and from 10–12 August Papen once again entered into conversations with Hitler; on the 13th the President himself had an interview with him. The negotiations once again broke down owing to Hitler's refusal to accept a subordinate role in any government of which he was a member.

On 30 August the new Reichstag convened. The aged communist, Clara Zetkin, as its oldest member, presided over its opening proceedings. On 4 September Papen issued a presidential decree which reflected the feeling that the bottom of the depression had been passed and that it was now possible to take measures to stimulate the economy. Taxpayers were to receive certificates representing 40 per cent of their sales and land taxes and business licences for the year 1932–3, which would be valid as payment for federal taxes from 1934 to 1939; in the meantime they would be negotiable in the open market and be valid as security for business loans. In addition, employers were authorized to lower wages beneath the current contract rates in proportion to the numbers by which they increased their labour force. From the point of view of the Social Democrats and the trade unions, this represented a direct attack on wage rates, and prevented any possible form of collaboration with Papen.

When the Reichstag met on 12 September Papen's total isolation from all the main parliamentary parties, including the National Socialists, was nakedly revealed. A resolution rescinding the

[265]

emergency decree was passed by 512 votes to 42; amid scenes which reduced parliamentary procedure to a farce, and the chancellor himself to a *farceur*, Papen dissolved the Reichstag, and new elections, the fifth major electoral contest which Germany was to experience during 1932, and the last free elections which the Weimar Republic was to know, were fixed for 6 November. Papen remained chancellor as head of a caretaker government, the only chancellor of the German Reich who had never addressed the Reichstag.

The confusion which ruled in the political situation in these last days of Weimar was strikingly illustrated, at the beginning of November, by a transport strike in Berlin, led by the Communists and with the cooperation and support of the National Socialist transport workers' group. It was directed both against the municipally owned Berlin transport corporation, which was attempting to negotiate a reduction in wage rates, and against the Social Democratic trade unions, which refused to support the strike; for Communists and National Socialists alike, the Social Democrats represented the common enemy, the last representatives of the hated 'system' which both were determined to destroy.

The National Socialists had to pay an electoral price for their support of the strike. Their middle-class and right-wing supporters were shocked and alarmed by their unnatural alliance with the Communists; some of their more radical followers tended to join them. Contributions to party funds dwindled to a trickle, at a moment when they were exhausted by eight months of almost continuous electoral campaigns.

The elections were held while Berlin was still paralysed by the strike; their results seemed to show that the growth of the National Socialist movement had passed its peak and that at last the party was on the decline. For the first time since the beginning of the depression there was a large fall in the National Socialist vote, of over two million, and though they remained the largest party in the Reichstag, their 233 seats had been reduced to 190. The greater part of their lost votes had gone to the Communists, who gained one million, and to the Nationalists, whose vote increased by nearly a million and raised their representation in the Reichstag from 37 seats to 51.

On the morning after the elections a strangely assorted pair breakfasted together: Papen and Bernard Shaw. Papen was delighted with the results. Shaw, on the other hand, said that Germany reminded him of some immense, admirably equipped chemical laboratory, in which everything was organized to perfection. Only there were one or two small pieces of equipment he would not like to handle, as they were capable of blowing the whole place to bits. Papen was amused.

The election results, combined with the feeling that the depression had passed its worst, convinced many people, not only in Germany, that the National Socialists were no longer a danger. 'The day when they were a vital threat is gone,' wrote Harold Laski in the *Daily Herald*. 'Accidents apart, it is not unlikely that Hitler will end his career as an old man in some Bavarian village who, in the Biergarten in the evening, tells his intimates how nearly he overturned the German Reich.'

Nothing was ever less likely than that Hitler should end his days so peacefully. 'If the Party falls apart, I shall shoot myself immediately,' he said a few weeks later to Goebbels. For it was not only its enemies who judged that the party had lost its chance of ever obtaining an independent majority; within the party itself there was an atmosphere of panic and desperation, intensified in December by the results of the elections in Thüringen, which showed a fall of 40 per cent in the National Socialist vote. There were those who, like Gregor Strasser, head of the Nazi Party organization, believed that the party now had no choice except to enter a coalition as a subordinate partner.

Papen's satisfaction was not surprising. It was true, no doubt, that his parliamentary position, with the support of some 60 members out of a house of 584, was a hopeless one. But he had demonstrated his ability to inflict a serious defeat on the National Socialists, and was willing if necessary to govern without the Reichstag. He envisaged a period in which, while the National Socialist decline continued, he would govern with dictatorial powers entrusted to him by the president, whose devotion to Papen was by now unbounded. Their relationship had come to resemble a kind of love affair, in which a senile admirer watches with loving solicitude and admiration the eccentricities of his youthful *inamorato*, who on his side knows that there is nothing he can do which will prove too much for his lover's infatuation. Such factors were by now of decisive importance in the politics of the German Reich.

From these dreams Papen was awoken by the intrigues of Schleicher. Just as Papen and Schleicher together had overthrown Brüning by withdrawing the confidence of the Reichswehr and promising a government which would have National Socialist support, so now Schleicher turned the same weapons against Papen. It had never been Schleicher's intention that, with the help of the President, Papen should aspire to an independent role in politics: his part was to serve as a cover and mouthpiece for Schleicher's more subtle designs. Nor was Schleicher attracted by the idea of a form of dictatorship that rested on nothing except presidential support and the bayonets and machine-guns of the Reichswehr; so crude a plan did not appeal to so refined a political manipulator.

On 17 November Papen's government, unable to face the Reichstag, resigned, and from 19–24 November Hindenburg and Hitler entered into conversations with a view to Hitler's entry into a government headed by Papen. But once again there was no common ground between them. Hindenburg's view was that the ex-lance-corporal should bring the support of the National Socialist masses to a regime in which he, the ex-field-marshal, should assume wider powers; Hitler's, that he should be the effective head of a Cabinet to which the President would entrust the exercise of his authority.

A week later Papen, with the President's consent, assumed what were virtually dictatorial powers. But he had reckoned without Schleicher. During November he had directed his assistant, Major Ott, at the Ministry of Defence, to conduct a tactical exercise in the Bendlerstrasse devoted to studying the role of the Reichswehr in a situation in which it was called upon to act in defence of the civil power while at the same time threatened with a Polish attack on its eastern frontier; a situation which conceivably might arise under a Nazi dictatorship opposed by both the National Socialists and the Communists.

On 2 December Schleicher presented the result of Major Ott's war game to the Papen cabinet, with the conclusion that, in the situation envisaged, the Reichswehr would be unable to fulfil its tasks. This was in effect a declaration that the Reichswehr could not support the Papen government. Even Papen and Hindenburg knew that without the Reichswehr it was impossible to govern; it was indeed the only source of their power. Reluctantly, sadly, sobbing, according to Papen, Hindenburg accepted Papen's resignation; as a memorial of his affection and devotion the field-marshal presented to his favourite statesman a photograph of himself inscribed with a line from an old soldier's song: *Ich hatt' einen Kameraden* – I had a comrade.

Even Schleicher could not discover another Papen. The Republic had come to the end of its political resources, and it was now necessary for Schleicher himself, after so many years of working in the dark, to face the full publicity of power as Chancellor and Minister of Defence. His regime lasted for fifty-four days.

It seems curious today to see in this Machiavellian general the last defender of the Weimar Republic. Yet in fact he was its last hope, and to Schleicher himself it did not seem an unreasonable one. He was by nature an optimist; and besides he thought of himself as a professional in politics as compared with an amateur like Papen. Since November he had been in active contact with Leipart, the head of the trade unions, and with Gregor Strasser; he dreamed of detaching the trade unions from the Social Democrats and Strasser's radical followers from Hitler, and thus providing a popular base for a government to which he himself could bring the support of the Reichswehr.

The prospects of creating a split in the National Party, indeed, seemed favourable. The party had reached a disastrous point in its fortunes. Its financial resources were exhausted and it was faced with bankruptcy. Its debts amounted to between twelve and twenty million marks, while Hitler himself owed 400,000 marks in tax arrears. SA men were rattling money boxes in the streets, like collectors for charity. A dissolution of the Reichstag, followed by new elections, would have found it penniless.

It would also have found it seriously divided between those who demanded some immediate return for their long years of struggle and sacrifice and those who were still loyal to Hitler and his patient manœuvring for power. It required all Hitler's powers of rhetoric, leadership, and will, to keep the party together, and in particular to avoid a large scale defection under the leadership of Gregor Strasser.

Moreover, in December the regime received a political windfall in respect to armaments. It was a legacy of Brüning's long and hard struggle to secure recognition of Germany's claim to equality of treatment, but like other concessions to Germany it had come too late. There was a time when it would have implied the duty of other powers to disarm; now it implied the right of Germany to re-arm. In a radio address to the German people on 15 December Schleicher handsomely acknowledged how much Germany owed to Brüning; at the same time he outlined his government's domestic policy, which included a large programme of public works, the suspension of the wage reductions introduced by Papen, and plans for the large-scale settlement of urban workers and their families on 750,000 acres of land in East Prussia, Mecklenburg and Pomerania. It was perhaps as intelligent and hopeful a policy as had been offered to the German people for many years. It was also well designed to conciliate the parties of the centre and moderate left. Nevertheless, Schleicher's negotiations to secure the support of the Social Democrats broke down; it was the last chance offered to the Socialists of active participation in government, and they refused it.

But the sands were already running out for Schleicher. His part in the fall of Papen had not endeared him to Hindenburg; moreover, his plans for rural settlement in East Germany exposed him to precisely the same charges of 'agrarian bolshevism' that had been made against Brüning; they were all the more violent because of the ugly rumours that were circulating of large-scale misappropriation of funds, to the advantage of the large East Elbian landowners, in the administration of the *Osthilfe*. The President himself, and his family, were said to be implicated.

Papen had not lost his desire for power. In the middle of December he gave an address to the aristocratic *Herrenklub* in Berlin, advocating the inclusion of the National Socialists in the government; and once again he re-opened negotiations with Hitler. In the New Year, on 4 January, Germany was startled to learn that Papen and Hitler had met in secret at the house of the Cologne banker, Schröder. There a provisional agreement was reached, though Hitler again insisted on the leading part in any government of which he was a member. Papen however was able to assure Hindenburg that power would be shared between him and Hitler.

The fatal bargain had been struck; among other things it included arrangements by which the Nationalist Socialist party should be relieved of its financial embarrassments. They immediately seized the opportunity to revive their prestige by mounting a flamboyant and spectacular election campaign in the tiny state of Lippe-Detmold, in which they secured forty per cent of the votes. Papen was also able to reassure Hitler against the danger of new Reichstag elections, because he knew that Schleicher did not have the president's authority to dissolve the Reichstag.

By the middle of January Schleicher's doom was sealed. Following the Lippe-Detmold elections, the German Nationalist Party issued a violent attack on him, which destroyed any possibility of his securing support from the right. He was in fact almost totally isolated, and told the Hungarian ambassador that he would resign unless he was allowed to dissolve the Reichstag.

The last days of Schleicher's regime form a grotesque interlude in which the fate of Germany, and of the German people, was decided by a small group of conspirators who, lacking any widely based popular support, feverishly contrived to bring pressure to bear on Hindenburg to accept Hitler as Chancellor; it was as if a giant were being done to death by pygmies. On 25 January the Budget committee of the Reichstag, which was due to meet on 30 January, voted to set up a committee to inquire into the administration of the Osthilfe; between 18–25 January urgent conversations took place between Papen, Hitler, the president's son, Oskar von Hindenburg, and Meissner, the president's state secretary; on 26 January Papen enlisted the support of Hugenberg, the leader of the German Nationalist Party. At a meeting on the 25th, Hitler took Oskar von Hindenburg aside and talked with him alone for half an hour. There is no record of their conversation, but it is possible that Hitler threatened him with exposure of the facts regarding the Osthilfe. After they parted Oskar von Hindenburg was noticeably silent and thoughtful.

Hindenburg had already, on 23 January, refused Schleicher's request for a dissolution of the Reichstag. On 28 January, he resigned and the president immediately invited Papen, as a kind of presidential agent, to investigate the possibility of forming a new government. The following day he was able to present the president with a government with Hitler as Chancellor, himself as

Vice-Chancellor, and Hugenberg as Minister of Economics. Apart from Hitler the National Socialists had only one representative in the Cabinet, Frick, but his was the vital one of Minister of the Interior; in addition, Goering was to become Prussian Minister of the Interior, with control of the Prussian police, so that the internal security forces were firmly in National Socialist hands.

There remained to Schleicher only his control of the Reichswehr; but a substitute for him as Minister of Defence had already been found in General von Blomberg, commander of the East Prussian military area and military adviser to the German delegation at the Disarmament Conference. Summoned from Geneva, von Blomberg arrived in Berlin to be met at the station by both Major Ott, Schleicher's assistant, and Oskar von Hindenburg. One ordered him to the Bendlerstrasse; the other to the presidential palace. Blomberg obeyed the latter.

That night Berlin was alive with rumours of a *putsch* by the Reichswehr. But even in the Bendlerstrasse Schleicher's power was gone. He had been outmanœuvred, out-intrigued and he disappeared from history to meet his death from an assassin's bullet on 30 June 1934. On the following day, when the new Cabinet met Hindenburg, Blomberg was first, even before Hitler, to receive his commission as minister, and it was not until 12.30 that at length Adolf Hitler walked down the steps of the palace as Chancellor of the German Reich.

The long struggle for power, the long game of deception and counter-deception, of bluff, threats, oratory, treachery, violence and bloodshed, was over at last. That night the triumphant National Socialists took over Berlin and an air of festival filled the streets. An endless torchlight procession of SA and SS men singing the Horst Wessel song poured down the Wilhelmstrasse and across its broad avenue the two heroes of the occasion stared at each other and the celebrating crowd beneath: in the President's palace the Prussian field-marshal, bewildered, bemused, hardly knowing what he had done, yet dimly and feebly aware that the days of glory had returned; in the Reichschancery, the new dictator, already meditating vengeance on his enemies.

CHAPTER SIXTEEN

Conclusion

On 30 January, when Hitler watched his storm troopers parade in triumph through the streets of Berlin, Franklin Roosevelt celebrated his fifty-first birthday. There was still slightly more than a month to go before his inauguration as president on 4 March; during that period the United States was to undergo an acute financial crisis which, on Inauguration Day itself, closed down the entire banking system of the country.

The banking crisis, however, was only one aspect of the general crisis by which the United States was afflicted; once again, as so often before, it was the financial system which reflected most dramatically and acutely the intense pressures generated by the depression. At the turn of the year there was a minimum of 13,000,000 unemployed throughout the country, and since local arrangements for relief had broken down, and the sources of charity had dried up, large numbers of the unemployed and their families were entirely without any means of subsistence at all. On occasions, the presence of this great army of the wretched and destitute made itself felt in many ways that seemed a direct threat to the institutions of government in the United States. When the lame-duck 72nd Congress convened in Washington on 5 December, 1,200 communist hunger-marchers converged on the capital for the occasion. Herded into a detention camp along New York Avenue by the police, freezing, starving, without food or shelter, they were permitted to march to Capitol Hill under an escort of armed police, while the steps of the Capitol were guarded by a double row of policemen equipped with tear-gas and riot bombs; it was as if Congress were in a state of siege.

The confrontation might have been taken as a visible symbol of the political and intellectual bankruptcy of the American system of

[273]

government. For it appeared that its established leaders, including its president, its legislators, its industrialists and financiers had literally nothing to offer in theory or practice which could in any way mitigate the moral and material degradation in which millions of American families were condemned to live. In February, representatives of American finance and industry testified before the Senate Finance Committee to their inability to offer any positive advice on means of defeating the depression. General Atterbury, of the Pennsylvania Rail Road, thought that there was nothing to be done except to wait and watch it reach the bottom. Barney Baruch, a presiding financial genius of the Democratic Party, thought there was only one answer; everyone, including the government, ought to stop spending money, and everyone ought to pay more taxes: 'Tax – tax everybody for everything.'

This kind of advice was all the more infuriating to many Americans, already driven to the point of desperation, because they were at the same time being given a revelation of how the rich and powerful evaded their own tax liabilities and helped themselves and each other through the depression. In January the Senate Banking and Currency Committee, with the assistance of its new counsel, the patient and persistent Ferdinand Pecora, extended its investigation into banking and stock exchange practices. Under Pecora's ruthless questioning, Charles E. Mitchell of the National City Bank, one of the great promoters of the Wall Street boom, testified that in 1929 he had avoided all income tax payments by selling stock at a loss to a relative and later buying it back. He also told how the National City Bank had placed $2·4 million at the disposal of its directors in order to prevent them being sold out of the market; little of it was ever paid back. The Pecora investigation served to intensify a nation-wide crisis of confidence in the nation's acknowledged leaders. The great men of the post-war era had become objects of contempt and derision; people felt that they had been swindled, betrayed and sold down the river. 'In the past five years,' Walter Lippman wrote, 'the industrial and financial leaders of America have fallen from one of the highest positions of influence and power they have occupied in our history to one of the lowest.'

There were other reasons for the feelings of mistrust, helplessness and apprehension which filled the minds of Americans in the period between Roosevelt's election and his inauguration. That interregnum itself created a kind of governmental vacuum, in which there was nothing to be done except to wait passively for the worst to happen; general uneasiness was increased by the publication of the accounts of the Reconstruction Finance Corporation which revealed the weakness of many hitherto respected financial institutions, while the manner in which its funds had been administered increased suspicions that its main purpose was to save bankers from the consequences of their own folly, or worse.

This sense of incipient disaster had its objective counterpart in the weakness of the American banking structure as a whole. Even in good times bank failures had been common; up to 1929 they had averaged over six hundred a year. As early as 1931 Keynes had warned that the weakest point in the American economic system might be the position of the banks. But by 1933 this rickety and ramshackle financial structure had come under unprecedented and intolerable strain, particularly in rural areas, owing to the enormous accumulation of debts incurred at a time when their real value, in terms of goods, represented something like one-third of what it had become as a result of the fall in the price level. The burden of debt indeed continued to agitate the countryside throughout the winter of 1932–3, leading to direct action by the farmers to protect themselves against foreclosures and forced sales. In Iowa, one-third of the total value of all farms was pledged to banks and insurance companies; during the winter, in the farming states, in Iowa, Kansas, Nebraska, Ohio, action committees were formed to resist foreclosures, and agents of the banks and insurance companies were threatened, intimidated and sometimes forcibly run out of the district. In Kansas, a man who had attempted to foreclose was found murdered. In Washington farmers' leaders warned Congress that unless something were done quickly there would be revolution in the countryside within the year.

The loans and mortgages owed by the farmers were in fact in many cases irrecoverable without provoking what John A. Simpson of the Farmers' Union called 'the biggest and finest crop of little revolutions . . . all over this country'. Nor were agricultural loans and mortgages the only doubtful assets held by the banks; there were also stocks which appeared in their books at values which had been made entirely unrealistic by the fall in the market. Between 1929

[275]

and 1933 there had been over three thousand failures, and the public had become sharply aware that a bank, even of the highest reputation, might not be the fortress of integrity and probity it had once appeared. And to all the other reasons for uneasiness was added a conviction that sooner or later a devaluation of the currency had become inevitable. There was an increasing inclination to exchange cash for gold, stock or other real assets; during February there was a marked fall in the gold reserves, large withdrawals of deposits, and other indications of a flight from the dollar.

Uneasiness reached panic proportions when, on 14 February, the governor of Michigan closed all the banks in the state and declared an eight-day banking holiday. On the following day there was an added reason for tension and alarm when, in Miami, an unemployed bricklayer called Joe Zingara shot and killed the Mayor of Chicago, Anton Cernak, in an unsuccessful attempt to assassinate Roosevelt. Zingara's crime stemmed from no more than his stomach ulcers and his hatred for the rich and powerful, including all presidents. It was a reminder to Americans of how much their hopes depended upon one man and of how much they were at the mercy of chance.

The initial cause of the Michigan banking holiday was the impending failure of the Union Guardian Trust, one of the two bank holding companies which dominated the financial affairs of the state. When it applied for a $50 million loan to the Reconstruction Finance Corporation its appeal had the support of the administration, which never had any objection to federal aid to bankers; it was held up however by Senator James Couzens from Michigan who declared that he would denounce any loan advanced without adequate security. From the RFC the administration turned for help to Michigan's most important citizen, Henry Ford, who was asked to postpone his claim on the deposits made by him with the Union Guarantee Trust. But Ford had no more love for banks than any farmer threatened with foreclosure; also, he had no belief in rescuing bankrupt concerns from the consequences of their own mistakes, and thought that, if anyone should do so, it should be the government. He refused any assistance to the Union Guarantee Trust and threatened that, if it were to close, he would immediately withdraw the $25 million which the Ford Company had on deposit with Detroit's largest bank, the First National, which would involve the collapse of the state's entire banking system.

Persuasion, entreaty, warnings of what would happen if he failed to assist, had no effect on Ford: 'There isn't any reason why I, the largest individual taxpayer in the country, should bail the government out of its loans to banks.' The decision, he said, was entirely the government's; as for Ford, 'I think that Senator Couzens was probably right in saying "Let the crash come".' Ford's attitude left no alternative to a general closure of the banks in Michigan, and the beginning of a financial panic which engulfed the entire banking structure of the country.

The banking crisis emphasized the void which existed for the time being in the American machinery of government, with a defeated President on his way out and a president-elect not yet in; a void which was itself a contributory factor to panic. Mr Hoover had already once tried to enlist the President-elect's cooperation in the problems of the administration during its last months in office. In December the President had sought and obtained a meeting with Roosevelt to discuss the problem of the next instalment of America's war debts, which, the Hoover moratorium having expired, was due for payment on 15 December. But the meeting had only served to emphasize the gulf which divided the two men in their attitude towards the problem of the depression; it had also intensified the personal antagonism and mistrust which had grown up between them, and Roosevelt's determination not to accept responsibility for, and not to become involved in, the policies and decisions of the outgoing administration.

Both men started from the point of view, which they shared with each other, of opposition, on internal political grounds, to the cancellation of war debts; Roosevelt also suspected that the pressure of bankers and financiers in favour of cancellation was due mainly to a desire to make it easier for themselves to collect their own private overseas debts. But for Hoover the question of war debts was a crucial one, because it affected the stability of international currencies and the restoration of the international gold standard, in which he saw the greatest single hope of overcoming the depression. For Roosevelt, on the other hand, such questions were subsidiary ones. He had no faith in the theory that the cure for the depression in America lay in the international field; America could, and would, find its own way out of the depression, and he resisted all Hoover's attempts to commit him to policies which would restrict his administration's freedom of manœuvre when once in office.

Their December meeting confirmed Hoover's view that Roosevelt was incapable of understanding the wider issues of the depression; in fact, the difficulty was that Roosevelt understood their implications too well. Roosevelt, on his side, felt that Hoover was trying to lead him into a trap. This feeling was strengthened by the letter which Hoover addressed (or rather misaddressed, because in his agitation he misspelt Roosevelt's name) to him three days after the closure of the Michigan banks. The banking crisis, Hoover wrote, was not primarily economic, but 'psychological'. The major difficulty lay 'in the state of the public mind'. The depression had already been overcome by the summer of 1932, but then a renewed loss of confidence had set in because of fears and doubts created by the policies of the new administration. The best cure for the immediate panic would be a firm assurance by Roosevelt that there would be no manipulation of the currency, that the Budget would be balanced, even if necessary by new taxation, and that the government's credit would be maintained 'by the refusal to exhaust it in the issue of new securities'. In particular, Roosevelt should disavow 'such proposals as the bills to assume Federal responsibility for billions of mortgages, loans to municipalities for public works, the Tennessee improvements and Muscle Shoals'. In fact, the cause of the panic was the New Deal itself.

Hoover's letter was an astonishing example of how dogmatic belief in a given body of economic doctrine can blind an otherwise able and intelligent man to realities. For if indeed it was 'the state of the public mind' that was at fault, as Hoover asserted, it was for precisely opposite reasons from those given by Hoover. If Americans still possessed some faith in the future, it was largely centred on the personality of Roosevelt himself and the promises of change held out by the New Deal; if there was anything that could have more effectively plunged the American people even deeper into doubt and despair, it would have been the assurance that once in office Roosevelt would behave no differently from Hoover.

Roosevelt dismissed Hoover's letter as a 'cheeky' document;

Hoover thought that Roosevelt's refusal to accept its proposals the 'behaviour of a madman'. Nor was Roosevelt any more willing to accept suggestions from Wall Street than from Hoover. According to Thomas W. Lamont, who informed Roosevelt, J. P. Morgan believed that the seriousness of the situation could not be exaggerated; his own remedy was that the Reconstruction Finance Corporation should deposit money without security in every bank that needed it. Roosevelt did not see why banks, in their distress, should have such prior claims to Federal aid; it was the people, he said, who needed help.

Roosevelt indeed was coming to a conclusion which was diametrically opposed to Hoover's recommendations: the abandonment of the gold standard in favour of a managed currency, directed in accordance with the country's domestic needs. He believed that the war-time Trading with the Enemy Act of 1917, often amended but never repealed, still gave the president authority to prohibit the export of gold by proclamation and without consulting Congress. When Roosevelt arrived in Washington on 2 March, two days before Inauguration Day, amid sleet and rain, and in an atmosphere of panic and alarm, which by now infected and divided Hoover's own cabinet, he already had the drafts of two presidential proclamations prepared; one summoning a special session of Congress, and the other suspending gold exports under the Trading with the Enemy Act.

Yet Hoover could still not desist from a last effort to influence his successor; with the evidence of the ruin of his own policies around him, he could still not believe that there was any effective alternative to them, and to the last he fought like a tiger to defend them. He had dispensed with the traditional courtesy of inviting his successor to dinner on the eve of his inauguration; instead, on 3 March, Roosevelt and his family went to the White House to tea, where he found himself faced not only by Hoover but by Ogden Mills, the Secretary to the Treasury, and Eugene Meyer, head of the Federal Reserve Board. Fortunately, Raymond Moley had been warned by the White House staff, and hurried round to be at Roosevelt's side. Meyer argued for a general bank closure; Hoover continued to oppose it and urged some more limited form of intervention. Roosevelt once again refused to commit himself.

That night, at the Treasury, Hoover's own officials urged

[279]

Governor Lehmann of New York to declare a state banking holiday; they were opposed however by the New York bankers, who, unlike Hoover, believed that a new administration would inspire a recovery of confidence. Finally, at 4.30 a.m. on Inauguration Day, 4 March, Lehmann issued his proclamation, which was immediately followed by similar action in Illinois. By the time Roosevelt took the oath of office, the banking system of the United States was paralysed, and his first action as president was to declare a general bank holiday and suspend the export of gold.

With Franklin Roosevelt in the White House in Washington and Adolf Hitler in the Reichschancery in Berlin, the acute phase of great economic depression was over. Not that historical events ever have quite so neatly and dramatically defined endings, or beginnings; yet the period from the Wall Street Crash in November 1929 to the triumph of National Socialism in Germany, and of the New Deal in the United States, at the beginning of 1933, has a character sufficiently its own, and sufficiently unlike what went before and came after, as to be regarded as a distinct, even a unique, historical phenomenon. Nothing quite like it ever happened before; nothing quite like it has ever happened since. It fixed a gulf between what went before and what came after, and in the ways in which western society observed and judged its own development; in some strange way, which we certainly cannot wholly explain or understand, like some seismological disturbance it shifted the ground on which men stood. And perhaps it is pardonable to take the date of Roosevelt's inauguration, even though it occurred in the middle of one of the most acute financial crises which America has ever experienced, as the end of the Great Slump. That particular emergency was quickly over, and within thirteen days the American banking system was functioning normally again; of far greater significance in the era which was about to open was America's abandonment of the gold standard. But just as the Wall Street crash can, with qualifications, be taken as the beginning of the depression, so, with similar qualifications, Roosevelt's inauguration can be taken as its close. For in a sense the depression, though world-wide in its effects, was a peculiarly American phenomenon, to which what happened elsewhere was subsidiary. The economic defeat which America suffered during the depression was as much a proof of its crucial importance in the development of western society as a whole as the political and industrial predominance which it established in the years that followed.

The effects of the depression, of course, continued to operate long after March 1933; so great a crisis could not be surmounted in a few days, or months, or even years. In some senses, indeed, one can say that even by 1939 it had not been wholly overcome, and unemployment in particular continued to be a heavy burden on the capitalist economy as a whole. But what can be said is that by March 1933 the upward movement of that economy had begun and has continued ever since without any break which can be compared with the depression of 1929–33. But what also can be said is that economic recovery was not associated, as many hoped and expected, with an improvement in political conditions. Rather, it went along with a progressive political deterioration, and increased political tension, and indeed the immense increase in armaments which it provoked, especially in Germany, made a large contribution to economic recovery. Indeed, since the depression economic prosperity has come to depend, to an increasing extent, upon the growth of a military-industrial nexus which is one of the dominating features of the modern world. Thus those who, during the depression, believed that a stabilization of political conditions and the revival of confidence which would ensue were an essential ingredient of recovery, were twice confounded; recovery took place in spite of increased political tension and political tension was a positive contribution to recovery.

Indeed, the association of economic recovery with political deterioration during the thirties makes it tempting to believe that the crisis which the western world experienced during the depression was not so much surmounted as translated into another, political, form; and that, in this respect, the depression itself was only one incident in, and an aspect of, a continuous process of which we have not yet seen the conclusion.

It would be equally tempting, therefore, to regard the great depression exclusively from an economic point of view, in abstraction from its social and political context: on the ground that, between 1929 and 1933, the capitalist crisis revealed itself, for the time being, primarily in economic terms, to which other aspects of it were merely subsidiary. Yet it would be difficult to do so without falsifying the complicated interaction between political, economic, social and psychological factors: most of all perhaps without ignoring the extent to which purely personal factors determined the course of events. There can be little doubt, for instance, that the pressure of unemployment was a determining, probably the determining cause of the collapse of the Weimar Republic and the triumph of National Socialism; whether it would have led to such a result in the absence of so extraordinary a political evil genius as Hitler is, to say the least of it, highly problematical. On the other hand, it seems certain that the depression would not have taken the course it did in the United States if there had existed there a leader with the same gift of crystallizing and giving a revolutionary direction to the enormous body of mass discontent, desperation and frustration which the depression had engendered.

The depression was not only a crisis which profoundly affected and changed the lives of ordinary men and women throughout the world, condemning millions of them to destitution, misery and despair; it was also a crisis of ideas which even today continues to affect men's attitudes to economic, social and political problems. To take only one, if the most significant, example: no government today would, or could, contemplate permitting mass unemployment on the scale on which it existed during the depression, and ever since the social and political policies of all governments have been largely dominated by the objective of preventing its repetition; to such an extent indeed that other objectives have come to be regarded as subsidiary, and in consequence to assume proportions which make them equally difficult to solve.

No doubt such an attitude largely derives from growing humanitarian awareness of the waste of human lives involved in mass unemployment on such a scale, of the measureless humiliation and degradation it imposes, and from a common consciousness that it represents an intolerable affront to human dignity and to even minimum standards of civilized life. Such feelings are themselves a legacy of the depression, which left an entire generation – both of those who suffered directly by it, and of those who witnessed and sympathized with their suffering – with a conviction that such a state of affairs is intolerable. They were intensified by the vast literature inspired by the depression during the thirties, which by depicting and analysing the evils of mass unemployment impressed them upon the imagination even of those who were never likely to share them.

The left-wing writers of the thirties, indeed, however confused and often plainly misled in their political objectives, performed in a different field the same kind of task as the anti-militarist writers of an earlier generation; that is to say, they tried to depict the realities of mass unemployment truthfully and imaginatively as others had tried to paint the disasters of war. They were so far successful as to stimulate a general reaction of *Never Again!* and this effect has endured, even unconsciously, when many of their works have lost much of their original literary and artistic value.

But if there were powerful humanitarian, emotional and imaginative factors at work in the widespread revulsion from the evils of mass unemployment, there was also in it an equally strong element of rational calculation. The depression did not only bring the conviction that unemployment was morally offensive; it also involved, in economic terms, a loss of effective demand, a factor of widespread under-consumption, which threatened to bring the whole process of production to a halt, and had, for a short time, threatened the death of society in the western world. In Germany, if society had not been destroyed, certainly civilization had been; over large areas of the United States it had seemed at moments to sober and objective observers that capitalism could not endure much longer unless it had more to offer to the poor and deprived; France, the strongest country in Europe, had, though belatedly, been reduced to a condition of endemic civil war that continued up to and beyond the Second World War; Japan had been driven to a course of aggression that had set the whole of the Far East ablaze and destroyed the entire post-war structure of collective security. An elementary sense of self-preservation warned even conservative defenders of the established order that it had come very near to the end of its tether during the depression.

But if the depression had given a warning of disaster, it had also placed in the hands of governments the weapons by which it could be averted, and the freedom to use them; only they were double-edged weapons which in warding off one form of danger could also provoke another. The depression had administered an almost fatal shock to the foundations of western society, already gravely weakened by the First World War. It had brought into contempt and derision an entire class which had been used to preside over its most secret and esoteric economic and financial rituals, and in so doing it had largely discredited the system of accepted ideas which gave them an intellectual and rational basis. Among those ideas were the classical economic doctrines, largely inherited from the nineteenth century, which exercised a profoundly inhibiting effect upon governments in any effort to control their economic destinies. They rested on a conception, which even at its most valid had only been an abstraction from the real world, of an international world order, largely self-governing and self-regulating, in which peaceful exchanges between nations was guaranteed by free trade; the stability of currencies and the exchanges between them by the gold standard; the continuous growth of the system as a whole by a continually increasing division of labour between nations; and the economic relationship between the poor and the advanced countries by foreign lending on a scale sufficient to keep their accounts in balance.

By 1929 these classical conditions of an efficient and smoothly operating economic order were as much honoured in the breach as in the observance; by 1933 they had lost almost all relevance to the world as it actually was. Yet throughout the depression they still represented the ideal to which it was generally accepted that the economic order should approximate as closely as possible; and post-war history up to 1929 had been very largely a record of a patient, arduous, and, as it seemed for a time, remarkably successful effort to restore these conditions or, where that was plainly impossible, to create as close a substitute for them as was attainable in a highly imperfect world.

The first and most important of these objectives was the restoration of the international gold standard, and the conditions under which it could operate successfully. Formally, great progress was made towards this end; the shattered economies of the defeated central powers were very largely restored, currencies stabilized, foreign lending resumed, normal political relationships established. But the essential condition of the pre-war international gold standard, the willingness to allow internal credit conditions, interest rates, price levels, to fluctuate with the movements of gold was never restored; in particular, after 1927, nearly two-thirds of the world's stock of monetary gold was sterilized in Fort Knox and the vaults of the Banque de France.*

This was to maintain the fiction of the gold standard while refusing to accept its reality; instead of an effectively operating system, it became a hallmark of monetary respectability. The depression put an end to this curious combination of fact and fiction, of myth and reality, which the international gold standard had become, and intensified all the forces of economic nationalism which were already inhibiting its efficient operation. Under its relentless pressure nations were forced to abandon the attempt to restore the pre-war system and to seek their own salvation by creating national economies which were only kept in relation with one another by an increasingly elaborate and artificial structure of currency regulations, exchange controls, tariffs, quotas, import controls and trading agreements. Even relapse into primitive conditions of barter was not excluded.

The new system, if it could be so called, which emerged during and out of the depression had many disadvantages compared with its predecessor, and totally lacked the classical simplicity and coherence of its theoretical superstructure; it was more like a Gothic cathedral than a Greek temple. But it gave governments a new freedom to plan and control their own economies; planning indeed became the central concept in economic policy in the years that followed. This was possible because the depression, by *force majeure* in most cases, released men from certain categories of economic thought which had begun to conflict increasingly with reality. This was not achieved as a result of abstract theoretical analysis; it came rather out of desperation, and the attempt to construct some kind of working system out of the ruins left behind by the depression. But in most cases the attempt was only made when events had made no other alternative possible.

In observing the events of the depression one is often tempted to wonder at the kind of grim courage, or obstinacy, of a man like Brüning, in his effort to revive the German economy by repeated doses of deflation so savage that the patient nearly died of the cure;

* Both the United States and France refused to permit the expansion of credit which would have been justified by the strength of their gold reserves.

certainly the cure induced in him a kind of delirium in which anything, even a reversion to barbarism, seemed preferable to a continuation of the treatment. It is also tempting to wonder, as one might at someone in the grip of a delusional obsession, at President Hoover's continuing conviction that America's only way out of the depression was by the maintenance, or restoration, of the international gold standard, which had ceased to work in practice, and the rules of which the United States herself had long ceased to observe. With even greater astonishment one observes the total intellectual confusion of Ramsay MacDonald and the majority of his socialist colleagues when called upon to meet the financial crisis in Britain and their despairing acceptance of remedies for it which were in total contradiction with their sincerely held socialist convictions.

It is difficult today to remember that for those in authority, and with the responsibility for taking action, during the depression there was in the field of economics or finance no clear intellectual frame of reference by which to guide their policies than the one offered by the accepted doctrines of classical economic theory. Socialism indeed professed to offer an alternative; but it was one which implied the destruction of the capitalist system, and up to 1933 provided little practical guidance on how to preserve it. Certainly it offered little help to practical men faced with the kind of crises and emergencies repeatedly thrust upon them by the depression.

The Soviet Union indeed offered an example, revered by communists and radicals the world over, of what could be achieved by the total destruction of the capitalist system, and the substitution for it of one based on ruthlessly centralized planning. On some radicals, alienated intellectuals, and certain sections, which however never even approached a majority, of the working class, it exercised a powerful attraction, which led some individuals to a total commitment which sometimes had tragic results; it was during the depression that the seeds were sown of that total rejection of capitalism and all its works which led some intellectuals into the labyrinth of the communist underground from which they did not emerge, to the astonishment of the world, until nearly twenty years later. Yet in fact, during the depression the Soviet Union itself was passing through, for the most part unknown to its admirers, an acute economic and political crisis of its own, of a particularly gruesome kind, with consequences that were even worse than in the west; and in the Marxist-Leninist scheme of things there was embedded a principle of authoritarianism which made it, and continued to make it, unacceptable to western society as a whole as a solution to its own troubles, however acute. Indeed, one of the most striking features of the depression was the failure, or the refusal, of communism to derive any advantage out of the crisis which had shaken the capitalist world to its foundations.

It is true, of course, that within the capitalist system economic thought also developed its own critique of accepted doctrines and its own alternative proposals for an amelioration, or reconstruction, of an evidently defective economic system. Such criticisms and alternatives came both from academic economists, some of whom, as in the United States, had a direct and powerful influence on governmental policy, and, especially in the field of monetary theory, from a wide and varied range of cranks and eccentrics. In the last winter of the depression in the United States the ideas of a group at Columbia University called Technocracy, directed by Howard Scott, an engineer who had been a friend of Thorstein Veblen, suddenly commanded wide public attention, enjoyed a brief and spectacular vogue, and were as suddenly forgotten; and this was only one of the many unorthodox ideologies to which the depression gave rise. The great revolution in economic thought inaugurated by Maynard Keynes was yet to come; the *Treatise on Money* was published, though scarcely understood, in 1930, but the *General Theory of Employment, Interest and Money* did not appear till 1936 and what Professor Lekachman has called *The Age of Keynes*, in which his ideas had imposed a new orthodoxy, did not dawn until after the Second World War. During the depression itself there was no alternative school of economic thought which could in any way effectively challenge the authority of classical economic theory, and in obeying its precepts statesmen, financiers, administrators, were merely acting in accordance with what had come to be regarded as self-evident truths. To have acted otherwise, indeed, would have been to forfeit the confidence of those to whom society had entrusted control of the economic and financial system.

Indeed, even after the depression, and the lessons it had taught, the domination of men's minds by classical economic theory did not cease; and even today its assumptions still form an essential ingredient in the attitude of most ordinary men to economic problems. An example of how powerful they remained in the thirties is to be found in Lord Robbins's classical work, *The Great Depression*, in which the author formulated four essential conditions of recovery. They were:

1. A return of business confidence, which could only be secured by the stabilization of currencies and the foreign exchanges.
2. The restoration of the international gold standard.
3. The removal of barriers and impediments to international trade.
4. The elimination of all forms of inflexibility in the economic structure, including the inflexibility of wage rates maintained at an artificially high level by the trade unions.

In general there was also required 'a more or less complete reversal of contemporary tendencies to governmental regulation of business enterprise'.

It is probably sufficient to say that in fact recovery was achieved although none of these conditions were realized; and indeed there was no reversal of, but rather a progressive increase in, 'contemporary tendencies to governmental regulation of enterprise', which has continued to the present time. Yet Lord Robbins's view would have recommended itself to the overwhelming majority of those in commanding positions in government, finance and industry during the depression.

It is difficult therefore to condemn them. Their fault, if it was a fault, was that they acted in accordance with the world's accepted wisdom, and as a result nearly all of them met with political defeat, or the loss of a prestige and reputation which once seemed unassailable. The consequences of their actions were tragic; but for the most part they seem today like men who, in the bewildering sequence of events which overtook them, fought an unidentifiable enemy with defective weapons, in a fog which was an emanation from their own minds. Most of all, in their inability to understand what was happening to themselves or to their fellow men, they impress upon us, in Oxenstierna's words, 'the littleness of the wisdom with which the world is governed'; but since in this respect

[288]

the world has not changed much since then, it is not for us to pass harsh judgement on them.'

If one wished to, one might perhaps look to R. G. Hawtrey's view in *The Art of Central Banking*:

In 1930 and 1931 producers all over the world found demand dwindling relentlessly. In desperate efforts to keep going they cut prices deeper and deeper. Their frantic competition for such demand as remained may be compared with the desperate struggles of the prisoners in the Black Hole of Calcutta to save themselves from suffocation by getting near the two small windows which were the only means of ventilation.

It is said that it was only by inadvertence that Surajah Dowlah shut 146 prisoners in a cell 18 feet by 15 feet. He merely followed precedent in committing prisoners to the guard room. In their agonies the victims sought to bribe the guard to carry an appeal for mercy to Surajah Dowlah. But he was asleep and the guards dared not awake him. He was very like a central banker.

Bibliography

THE literature of the great depression is vast and I make no pretence to have read even a tithe of it. The following is simply a list of books which I have found most useful. On five in particular I have depended greatly and should like to acknowledge how heavily I am indebted to them. They are John Kenneth Galbraith's *The Great Crash*; Arthur J. Schlesinger Jnr's *The Age of Roosevelt*; Erich Eyck's *A History of the Weimar Republic*, Vol. II; Karl Erich Born's *Die Deutsche Bankenkrise 1930*; and the *Survey of International Affairs* edited by Arnold Toynbee.

ALLEN, F. L., *Only Yesterday*, New York, 1931.

ARNDT, H. W., *The Economic Lessons of the Nineteen Thirties*, London, 1944.

BARUCH, BERNARD, *The Public Years*, London, 1961.

BENNETT, EDWARD, *Germany and the Diplomacy of the Financial Crisis, 1931*, Harvard, 1962.

BORN, KARL ERICH, *Die Deutsche Bankenkrise 1931: Finanzen und Politik*, Munich, 1967.

BOYLE, ANDREW, *Montague Norman*, London, 1967.

BRAUN, OTTO, *Von Weimar zu Hitler*, New York, 1940.

BROWN, W. A., *The International Gold Standard Reinterpreted, 1914-1934*, Vols. I and II, New York, 1940.

BULLOCK, ALAN, *Hitler, A Study in Tyranny*, London, 1952.

CHANDLER, LESTER V., *Benjamin Strong, Central Banker*, Washington D.C., 1958.

CLAY, HENRY, *Lord Norman*, London, 1957.

Committee on Banking and Currency pursuant to Senate Resolution 84 Hearings, Washington, 1934.

CONDLIFFE, J. B. (ed.), *World Economic Survey 1931-2*. League of Nations, Geneva, 1932.

COWLEY, MALCOLM, *Think back on Us* (ed. Henry Dan Piper), London, 1967.

EYCK, ERICH, *A History of the Weimar Republic*, Vol. II, from the

Locarno Conference to Hitler's Seizure of Power (trans.), Cambridge, Massachusetts, 1964.

FISCHER, RUTH, *Stalin und der Deutsche Kommunism*, Frankfurt, 1948.

FISHER, IRVING, *The Money Illusion*, London, 1928.

The Stock Market Crash – and After, New York, 1930.

GOEBBELS, JOSEPH, *Von Kaiserhof zur Reichskanzlei*, Munich, 1934.

HALLGREN, MAURITZ A., *Seeds of Revolt*, New York, 1933.

HANNINTON, WAL, *Unemployed Struggles 1919–36*, London, 1936.

HANSEN, ALVIN H., *Fiscal Policy and Business Cycles*, New York, 1941.

HARROD, R. H. F., *The Life of John Maynard Keynes*, London, 1951.

HAWTREY, R. G., *The Gold Standard in Theory and Practice*, London, 1927.

Trade Depression and the Way Out, London, 1933.

The Art of Central Banking, London, 1932.

HEIDEN, KONRAD, *Der Führer: Hitler's Rise to Power*, London, 1944.

HODSON, H. V., *Slump and Recovery 1929–37*, Oxford, 1938.

KAHN, R.F., 'The Relation of Home Investment to Unemployment', *The Economic Journal*, December, 1931.

KESSLER, HARRY GRAF, *Tagebücher 1918–37*, Frankfurt, 1961.

KEYNES, JOHN MAYNARD, *A Treatise on Money*, London, 1931.

The Economic Consequences of Mr Churchill, London, 1928.

The General Theory of Employment, Interest and Money, London, 1936.

Two Memoirs, London, 1939.

(With PRIBRAM, KARL and PHELAN, E. J.), *Unemployment as a World Problem*, Chicago, 1931.

LEKACHMAN, ROBERT, *The Age of Keynes*, New York, 1966.

MAY COMMITTEE Report Cmd. 3920, HMSO, London, 1931.

MOSLEY, OSWALD (with STRACHEY, JOHN, and YOUNG, ALLEN), *Revolution by Reason*, London, 1925.

NICOLSON, HAROLD, *George V: His Life and Reign*, London, 1952.

ROBBINS, LIONEL, *The Great Depression*, London, 1934.

ROSENBERG, ARTHUR, *Geschichte der Deutschen Republik*, Karlsbad, 1935.

ROYAL INSTITUTE OF INTERNATIONAL AFFAIRS, *Unemployment: A World Problem*, London, 1935.

SCHLESINGER, JNR, ARTHUR M., *The Age of Roosevelt*, Vol. I, *The Passing of the Old Order*, London, 1957.

SCHUMPETER, J. A., *The Great Economists from Marx to Keynes*, London, 1952.

SHAPLAN, ROBERT, *Ivar Kreuger, Genius and Swindler*, London, 1961.

SIEGFRIED, ANDRE, *England's Crisis*, London, 1930.

SKIDELSKY, ROBERT, *Politicians and the Slump*, London, 1967.

'Crisis 1931', *The Times*, 2, 3 and 4 December 1968.

SPARLING, EARL, *Mystery Men of Wall Street*, New York, 1930.

STAGG, LAWRENCE, *Wall Street and Washington*, Princeton, 1929.

STAMPFER, FRIEDRICH, *Die Vierzehn Jahre der ersten deutschen Republik*, Karlsbad, 1936.

STRACHEY, JOHN, *The Coming Struggle for Power*, London, 1934.

STRESEMANN, *Vermächtnis. Der Nachlass*, Berlin, 1932.

SUAREZ, *Briand, L'Artisan de la Paix*, Paris, 1926.

TAYLOR, A. J. P., *History of England 1914-45*, Oxford, 1965.

TOYNBEE, ARNOLD (ed.), *Survey of International Affairs, 1929-39*, Royal Institute of International Affairs, London.

Index

Banks, Companies, towns and general topics such as agriculture and unemployment are indexed under their own names; bracketed initials after these indicate the country of origin as Britain (B), Germany (G) or United States of America (US). Political parties are indexed under the country of origin.

Numbers in italics refer to illustrations.

Germany – *cont.*
Reichstag; and emergency
  decrees, 68n, 72, 99, 100, 234
  1930 dissolution and elections,
    99–100
  Nazis in, 101, 102, 120, 243–4
  1931, recall demanded, 126
  1932 elections; Feb., 241–1
    July, 247–8, 265
    Nov., 266, 268
    session Aug.-Sept., 265–6
  1933, 271
Reichswehr, 101–2, 236, 239,
  242, 244, 247 249, 268–9,
  272
POLITICAL PARTIES:
G Catholic Centre Party, 72, 73,
  97–8, 101, 126, 240, 247
  in Prussia, 243, 246
G Communist Party, 69, 73, 74,
  101, 126, 268
  in *1932* elections, 241, 248, 265
  and Nat. Soc.s, 266
G Democratic Party, 68
National Socialist Party
  (NSDAP, Nazis), 44, 73,
  116, 117, 138
  at *1930* election, 101
  after, 102, 103–4, 120, 126,
    144, 150
  in *1932*, 235, 238–9, 240, 241–
    244, 249, 266
  at elections, 205
    July, 247–8, 265
    Nov., 266
  decline in power, 266–8, 269
  rise, 270–2
  propaganda, 138, 241, 247
National Socialists
  military organizations (SA and
    SS), 2, 44, 248–9, 272
  ban on, 242, 247
  propaganda, 138, 241, 247
Nationalists, 101, 117, 120, 126,
  128, 145, 239, 243, 247
  at *1932* elections, 241, 266, 271
People's Party, 101

Social Democrats, 68 73, 100,
  101, 126, 137, 240, 247, 265,
  266
  in Prussia, 243
  Reichsbanner, 243
  and Schleicher, 270
  Vollespartei, 126
Gifford, Walter S., 217, 218
Glassford, Pelham D., 226, 228
Glass-Steiger bill (US), 217
Goebbels, Dr Josef, 106, 240, 241,
  249, 267
Goerdeler, Karl (Mayor of Leipzig), 237
Gold Discount Bank (G), 135, 149
gold standard, system of, 8–9, 76,
  199
  in World War I, 2
  return to, 4, 7, 10, 11–13, 75, 80
    and n, 83–4, 191, 284–5, 288
  1931–2, 198–9
  Britain and, 75, 81, 83–4
  comes off, 124, 162, 173, 178,
    188–93
  consequences, 193–8, 253,
    254
    abroad, 198–200
    in Germany, 215
    in USA, 216
  France and, 7, 12
  Germany and, 96, 97, 105, 145,
    198, 199
  USA and, 11, 277, 279–80, 286
gold standard countries, deflation
  in, 84, 198, 214, 252, 257
gold supply and reserves, 29, 80n,
  83–4, 199n, 199–200, 285
  1932 fall in value, 214, 256–7
  see also under France *and* United
    States
Goldman, Sachs & Co. (US), 27–
  29
Goldschmidt, Jacob, 104, 126, 133–
  134, 135, 137, 138–9, 141, 148
Gore, US Senator, 211–12
Goering, Hermann, 101, 243, 272
Göttingen, trial at, 101–2

Physiological basis
of crop growth and
development

DATE			